The Life of Cicero, Volume I

Anthony Trollope

THE LIFE OF CICERO

BY ANTHONY TROLLOPE

IN TWO VOLUMES

VOL. I.

CONTENTS OF VOLUME I.

APPENDICES.

APPENDIX A.

APPENDIX B.

APPENDIX C.

APPENDIX D.

APPENDIX E.

CHAPTER I.

INTRODUCTION.

I am conscious of a certain audacity in thus attempting to give a further life of Cicero which I feel I may probably fail in justifying by any new information; and on this account the enterprise, though it has been long considered, has been postponed, so that it may be left for those who come after me to burn or publish, as they may think proper; or, should it appear during my life, I may have become callous, through age, to criticism.

The project of my work was anterior to the life by Mr. Forsyth, and was first suggested to me as I was reviewing the earlier volumes of Dean Merivale's History of the Romans under the Empire. In an article on the Dean's work, prepared for one of the magazines of the day, I inserted an apology for the character of Cicero, which was found to be too long as an episode, and was discarded by me, not without regret. From that time the subject has grown in my estimation till it has reached its present dimensions.

I may say with truth that my book has sprung from love of the man, and from a heartfelt admiration of his virtues and his conduct, as well as of his gifts. I must acknowledge that in discussing his character with men of letters, as I have been prone to do, I have found none quite to agree with me His intellect they have admitted, and his industry; but his patriotism they have doubted, his sincerity they have disputed, and his courage they have denied. It might have become me to have been silenced by their verdict; but I have rather been instigated to appeal to the public, and to ask them to agree with me against my friends. It is not only that Cicero has touched all matters of interest to men, and has given a new grace to all that he has touched; that as an orator, a rhetorician, an essayist, and a correspondent he was supreme; that as a statesman he was honest, as an advocate fearless, and as a governor pure; that he was a man whose intellectual part always dominated that of the body; that in taste he was excellent, in thought both correct and enterprising, and that in language he was perfect. All this has been already so said of him by other biographers. Plutarch, who is as familiar to us as though he had been English, and Middleton, who thoroughly loved his subject, and latterly Mr. Forsyth, who has struggled to be honest to him, might have sufficed as telling us so much as that. But there was a humanity in Cicero, a something almost of Christianity, a stepping forward out of the dead intellectualities of Roman life into moral perceptions, into natural affections, into domesticity, philanthropy, and conscious discharge of duty, which do not seem to have been as yet fully appreciated. To have loved his neighbor as himself before the teaching of Christ was much for a man to achieve; and that he did this is what I claim for Cicero, and hope to bring home to the minds of those who can find time for reading yet another added to the constantly increasing volumes about Roman times.

It has been the habit of some latter writers, who have left to Cicero his literary honors, to rob him of those which had been accorded to him as a politician. Macaulay, expressing his surprise at the fecundity of Cicero, and then passing on to the praise of the Philippics as senatorial speeches, says of him that he seems to have been at the head of the "minds of the second order. " We cannot judge of the classification without knowing how many of the great men of the world are to be included in the first rank. But Macaulay probably intended to express an opinion that Cicero was inferior because he himself had never dominated others as Marius had done, and Sylla, and Pompey, and Caesar, and Augustus. But what if Cicero was ambitious for the good of others, while these men had desired power only for themselves?

Dean Merivale says that Cicero was "discreet and decorous, " as with a similar sneer another clergyman, Sydney Smith, ridiculed a Tory prime-minister because he was true to his wife. There is nothing so open to the bitterness of a little joke as those humble virtues by which no glitter can be gained, but only the happiness of many preserved. And the Dean declares that Cicero himself was not, except once or twice, and for a "moment only, a real power in the State. " Men who usurped authority, such as those I have named, were the "real powers, " and it was in opposition to such usurpation that Cicero was always urgent. Mr. Forsyth, who, as I have said, strives to be impartial, tells us that "the chief fault of Cicero's moral character was a want of sincerity. " Absence of sincerity there was not. Deficiency of sincerity there was. Who among men has been free from such blame since history and the lives of men were first written? It will be my object to show that though less than godlike in that gift, by comparison with other men around him he was sincere, as he was also self-denying; which, if the two virtues be well examined, will indicate the same phase of character.

But of all modern writers Mr. Froude has been the hardest to Cicero. His sketch of the life of Caesar is one prolonged censure on that of Cicero. Our historian, with all that glory of language for which he is so remarkable, has covered the poor orator with obloquy. There is no period in Cicero's life so touching, I think, as that during which he was hesitating whether, in the service of the Republic, it did or did not behoove him to join Pompey before the battle of Pharsalia. At this time he wrote to his friend Atticus various letters full of agonizing doubts as to what was demanded from him by his duty to his country, by his friendship for Pompey, by loyalty to his party, and by his own dignity. As to a passage in one of those, Mr. Froude says "that Cicero had lately spoken of Caesar's continuance in life as a disgrace to the State. " "It has been seen also that he had long thought of assassination as the readiest means of ending it, "[1] says Mr. Froude. The "It has been seen" refers to a statement made a few pages earlier, in which he translates certain words written by Cicero to Atticus. "[2] "He considered it a disgrace to them that Caesar was alive. " That is his translation; and in his indignation he puts other words, as it were, into the mouth of his literary brother of two thousand years before. "Why did not somebody kill him? " The Latin words themselves are added in a note, "Cum vivere ipsum turpe sit nobis. "[3] Hot indignation has so carried the translator away that he has missed the very sense of Cicero's language. " When even to draw the breath of life at such a time is a disgrace to us! " That is what Cicero meant. Mr. Froude in a preceding passage gives us another passage from a letter to Atticus, [4] "Caesar was mortal. "[5] So much is an intended translation. Then Mr. Froude tells us how Cicero had "hailed Caesar's eventual murder with rapture; " and goes on to say, "We read the words with sorrow and yet with pity. " But Cicero had never dreamed of Caesar's murder. The words of the passage are as follows: "Hunc primum mortalem esse, deinde etiam multis modis extingui posse cogitabam. " "I bethought myself in the first place that this man was mortal, and then that there were a hundred ways in which he might be put on one side. " All the latter authorities have, I believe, supposed the "hunc" or "this man" to be Pompey. I should say that this was proved by the gist of the whole letter—one of the most interesting that was ever written, as telling the workings of a great man's mind at a peculiar crisis of his life— did I not know that former learned editors have supposed Caesar to have been meant. But whether Caesar or Pompey, there is nothing in it to do with murder. It is a question—Cicero is saying to his friend— of the stability of the Republic. When a matter so great is considered, how is a man to trouble himself as to an individual who may die any day, or cease from any accident to be of weight? Cicero was speaking of the effect of this or that step on his own part. Am I, he says, for the sake of Pompey to bring down hordes of barbarians on my own country, sacrificing the Republic for the sake of a friend who is here to-day and may be gone to-morrow? Or for the sake of an enemy, if the reader thinks that the "hunc" refers to Caesar. The argument is the same. Am I to consider an individual when the Republic is at stake? Mr. Froude tells us that he reads "the words with sorrow and yet with pity. " So would every one, I think, sympathizing with the patriot's doubts as to his leader, as to his party, and as to his country. Mr. Froude does so because he gathers from them that Cicero is premeditating the murder of Caesar!

It is natural that a man should be judged out of his own mouth. A man who speaks much, and so speaks that his words shall be listened to and read, will be so judged. But it is not too much to demand that when a man's character is at stake his own words shall be thoroughly sifted before they are used against him.

The writer of the biographical notice in the Encyclopedia Britannica on Cicero, sends down to posterity a statement that in the time of the first triumvirate, when our hero was withstanding the machinations of Caesar and Pompey against the liberties of Rome, he was open to be bought. The augurship would have bought him. "So pitiful, " says the biographer, "was the bribe to which he would have sacrificed his honor, his opinions, and the commonwealth! " With no more sententious language was the character of a great man ever offered up to public scorn. And on what evidence? We should have known nothing of the bribe and the corruption but for a few playful words in a letter from Cicero himself to Atticus. He is writing from one of his villas to his friend in Rome, and asks for the news of the day: Who are to be the new consuls? Who is to have the vacant augurship? Ah, says he, they might have caught even me with that bait; [6] as he said on another occasion that he was so much in debt as to be fit for a rebel; and again, as I shall have to explain just now, that he was like to be called in question under the Cincian law because of a present of books! This was just at the point of his life when he was declining all offers of public service—of public service for which his soul longed—because they were made to him by Caesar. It was then that the "Vigintiviratus" was refused, which Quintilian mentions to his honor. It was then that he refused to be Caesar's lieutenant. It was then that he might have been fourth with Caesar, and Pompey, and Crassus, had he not felt himself bound not to serve against the Republic. And yet the biographer does not hesitate to load him with infamy because of a playful word in a letter half jocose and half pathetic to his friend. If a man's deeds be always honest, surely he should not be accused of dishonesty on the strength of some light word spoken in the confidence of familiar intercourse. The light words are taken to be grave because they meet the modern critic's eye clothed in the majesty of a dead language; and thus it comes to pass that their very meaning is misunderstood.

My friend Mr. Collins speaks, in his charming little volume on Cicero, of "quiet evasions" of the Cincian law, [7] and tells us that we are taught by Cicero's letters not to trust Cicero's words when he was in a boasting vein. What has the one thing to do with the other? He names no quiet evasions. Mr. Collins makes a surmise, by which the character of Cicero for honesty is impugned — without evidence. The anonymous biographer altogether misinterprets Cicero. Mr. Froude charges Cicero with anticipation of murder, grounding his charge on words which he has not taken the trouble to understand. Cicero is accused on the strength of his own private letters. It is because we have not the private letters of other persons that they are not so accused. The courtesies of the world exact, I will not say demand, certain deviations from straightforward expression; and these are made most often in private conversations and in private correspondence. Cicero complies with the ways of the world; but his epistles are no longer private, and he is therefore subjected to charges of falsehood. It is because Cicero's letters, written altogether for privacy, have been found worthy to be made public that such accusations have been made. When the injustice of these critics strikes me, I almost wish that Cicero's letters had not been preserved.

As I have referred to the evidence of those who have, in these latter days, spoken against Cicero, I will endeavor to place before the reader the testimony of his character which was given by writers, chiefly of his own nation, who dealt with his name for the hundred and fifty years after his death — from the time of Augustus down to that of Adrian — a period much given to literature, in which the name of a politician and a man of literature would assuredly be much discussed. Readers will see in what language he was spoken of by those who came after him. I trust they will believe that if I knew of testimony on the other side, of records adverse to the man, I would give them. The first passage to which I will allude does not bear Cicero's name; and it may be that I am wrong in assuming honor to

Cicero from a passage in poetry, itself so famous, in which no direct allusion is made to himself. But the idea that Virgil in the following lines refers to the manner in which Cicero soothed the multitude who rose to destroy the theatre when the knights took their front seats in accordance with Otho's law, does not originate with me. I give the lines as translated by Dryden, with the original in a note. [8]

> "As when in tumults rise the ignoble crowd,
> Mad are their motions, and their tongues are loud;
> And stones and brands in rattling volleys fly,
> And all the rustic arms that fury can supply;
> If then some grave and pious man appear,
> They hush their noise, and lend a listening ear;
> He soothes with sober words their angry mood,
> And quenches their innate desire of blood."

This, if it be not intended for a portrait of Cicero on that occasion, exactly describes his position and his success. We have a fragment of Cornelius Nepos, the biographer of the Augustan age, declaring that at Cicero's death men had to doubt whether literature or the Republic had lost the most. [9] Livy declared of him only, that he would be the best writer of Latin prose who was most like to Cicero. [10] Velleius Paterculus, who wrote in the time of Tiberius, speaks of Cicero's achievements with the highest honor. "At this period, " he says, "lived Marcus Cicero, who owed everything to himself; a man of altogether a new family, as distinguished for ability as he was for the purity of his life. "[11] Valerius Maximus quotes him as an example of a forgiving character. [12] Perhaps the warmest praise ever given to him came from the pen of Pliny the elder, from whose address to the memory of Cicero I will quote only a few words, as I shall refer to it more at length when speaking of his consulship. "Hail thou, " says Pliny, "who first among men was called the father of your country. "[13] Martial, in one of his distichs, tells the traveller that if he have but a book of Cicero's writing he may fancy that he is travelling with Cicero himself. [14] Lucan, in his bombastic verse, declares how Cicero dared to speak of peace in the camp of Pharsalia. The reader may think that Cicero should have said nothing of the kind, but Lucan mentions him with all honor. [15] Not Tacitus, as I think, but some author whose essay De Oratoribus was written about the time of Tacitus, and whose work has come to us with the name of Tacitus, has told us of Cicero that he was a master of logic, of ethics, and of physical science. [16] Everybody remembers the passage in Juvenal,

"Sed Roma parentem
Roma patrem patriae Ciceronem libera dixit."

"Rome, even when she was free, declared him to be the father of his country. "[17] Even Plutarch, who generally seems to have a touch of jealousy when speaking of Cicero, declares that he verified the prediction of Plato, "That every State would be delivered from its calamities whenever power should fortunately unite with wisdom and justice in one person. "[18] The praises of Quintilian as to the man are so mixed with the admiration of the critic for the hero of letters, that I would have omitted to mention them here were it not that they will help to declare what was the general opinion as to Cicero at the time in which it was written. He has been speaking of Demosthenes, [19] and then goes on: "Nor in regard to Cicero do I see that he ever failed in the duty of a good citizen. There is in evidence of this the splendor of his consulship, the rare integrity of his provincial administration, his refusal of office under Caesar, [20] the firmness of his mind on the civil wars, giving way neither to hope nor fear, though these sorrows came heavily on him in his old age. On all these occasions he did the best he could for the Republic. " Florus, who wrote after the twelve Caesars, in the time of Trajan and of Adrian, whose rapid summary of Roman events can hardly be called a history, tells us, in a few words, how Catiline's conspiracy was crushed by the authority of Cicero and Cato in opposition to that of Caesar. [21] Then, when he has passed in a few short chapters over all the intervening history of the Roman Empire, he relates, in pathetic words, the death of Cicero. "It was the custom in Rome to put up on the rostra the heads of those who had been slain; but now the city was not able to restrain its tears when the head of Cicero was seen there, upon the spot from which the citizens had so often listened to his words. "[22] Such is the testimony given to this man by the writers who may be supposed to have known most of him as having been nearest to his time. They all wrote after him. Sallust, who was certainly his enemy, wrote of him in his lifetime, but never wrote in his dispraise. It is evident that public opinion forbade him to do so. Sallust is never warm in Cicero's praise, as were those subsequent authors whose words I have quoted, and has been made subject to reproach for envy, for having passed too lightly over Cicero's doings and words in his account of Catiline's conspiracy; but what he did say was to Cicero's credit. Men had heard of the danger, and therefore, says Sallust, [23] "They conceived the idea of intrusting the consulship to Cicero. For before that the nobles were envious, and thought that the consulship would be polluted if it were conferred on a *novus homo*, however distinguished. But when danger came, envy and pride had to give way. " He afterward declares that Cicero made a speech against Catiline most brilliant, and at the same time useful to the Republic. This was lukewarm praise, but coming from Sallust, who would have censured if he could, it is as eloquent as any eulogy. There is extant a passage attributed to Sallust full of virulent abuse of Cicero, but no one now imagines that Sallust wrote it. It is called the Declamation of Sallust against Cicero, and bears intrinsic evidence that it was written in after years. It suited some one to forge pretended invectives between Sallust and Cicero, and is chiefly noteworthy here because it gives to Dio Cassius a foundation for the hardest of hard words he said against the orator. [24]

Dio Cassius was a Greek who wrote in the reign of Alexander Severus, more than two centuries and a half after the death of Cicero, and he no doubt speaks evil enough of our hero. What was the special cause of jealousy on his part cannot probably be now known, but the nature of his hatred may be gathered from the passage in the note, which is so foul-mouthed that it can be only inserted under the veil of his own language. [25] Among other absurdities Dio Cassius says of Cicero that in his latter days he put away a gay young wife, forty years younger than himself, in order that he might enjoy without disturbance the company of another lady who was nearly as much older than himself as his wife was younger.

Now I ask, having brought forward so strong a testimony, not, I will say, as to the character of the man, but of the estimation in which he was held by those who came shortly after him in his own country; having shown, as I profess that I have shown, that his name was always treated with singular dignity and respect, not only by the lovers of the old Republic but by the minions of the Empire; having found that no charge was ever made against him either for insincerity or cowardice or dishonesty by those who dealt commonly with his name, am I not justified in saying that they who have in later days accused him should have shown their authority? Their authority they have always found in his own words. It is on his own evidence against himself that they have depended—on his own evidence, or occasionally on their own surmises. When we are told of his cowardice, because those human vacillations of his, humane as well as human, have been laid bare to us as they came quivering out of his bosom on to his fingers! He is a coward to the critics because they have written without giving themselves time to feel the true meaning of his own words. If we had only known his acts and not his words—how he stood up against the judges at the trial of Verres, with what courage he encountered the responsibility of his doings at the time of Catiline, how he joined Pompey in Macedonia from a sense of sheer duty, how he defied Antony when to defy Antony was probable death—then we should not call him a coward! It is out of his own mouth that he is condemned. Then surely his words should be understood. Queen Christina says of him, in one of her maxims, that "Cicero was the only coward that was capable of great actions. " The Queen of Sweden, whose sentences are never worth very much, has known her history well enough to have learned that Cicero's acts were noble, but has not understood the meaning of words sufficiently to extract from Cicero's own expressions their true bearing. The bravest of us all, if he is in high place, has to doubt much before he can know what true courage will demand of him; and these doubts the man of words will express, if there be given to him an *alter ego* such as Cicero had in Atticus.

In reference to the biography of Mr Forsyth I must, in justice both to him and to Cicero, quote one passage from the work: "Let those who, like De Quincey, [26] Mommsen, and others, speak disparagingly of Cicero, and are so lavish in praise of Caesar, recollect that Caesar never was troubled by a conscience. "

Here it is that we find that advance almost to Christianity of which I have spoken, and that superiority of mind being which makes Cicero the most fit to be loved of all the Romans.

It is hard for a man, even in regard to his own private purposes, to analyze the meaning of a conscience, if he put out of question all belief in a future life. Why should a man do right if it be not for a reward here or hereafter? Why should anything be right—or wrong? The Stoics tried to get over the difficulty by declaring that if a man could conquer all his personal desires he would become, by doing so, happy, and would therefore have achieved the only end at which a man can rationally aim. The school had many scholars, but probably never a believer. The normal Greek or Roman might be deterred by the law, which means fear of punishment, or by the opinion of his neighbors, which means ignominy. He might recognize the fact that comfort would combine itself with innocence, or disease and want with lust and greed. In this there was little need of a conscience—hardly, perhaps, room for it. But when ambition came, with all the opportunities that chance, audacity, and intellect would give—as it did to Sylla, to Caesar, and to Augustus—then there was nothing to restrain the men. There was to such a man no right but his power, no wrong but opposition to it. His cruelty or his clemency might be more or less, as his conviction of the utility of this or that other weapon for dominating men might be strong with him. Or there might be some variation in the flowing of the blood about his heart which might make a massacre of citizens a pleasing diversion or a painful process to him; but there was no conscience. With the man of whom we are about to speak conscience was strong. In his sometimes doubtful wanderings after political wisdom—in those mental mazes which have been called insincerity—we shall see him, if we look well into his doings, struggling to find whether, in searching for what was his duty, he should go to this side or to that. Might he best hope a return to that state of things which he thought good for his country by adhering to Caesar or to Pompey? We see the workings of his conscience, and, as we remember that Scipio's dream of his, we feel sure that he had, in truth, within him a recognition of a future life.

In discussing the character of a man, there is no course of error so fertile as the drawing of a hard and fast line. We are attracted by salient points, and, seeing them clearly, we jump to conclusions, as though there were a light-house on every point by which the nature of the coast would certainly be shown to us. And so it will, if we accept the light only for so much of the shore as it illumines. But to say that a man is insincere because he has vacillated in this or the other difficulty, that he is a coward because he has feared certain dangers, that he is dishonest because he has swerved, that he is a liar because an untrue word has been traced to him, is to suppose that you know all the coast because one jutting headland has been defined to you. He who so expresses himself on a man's character is either ignorant of human nature, or is in search of stones with which to pelt his enemy. "He has lied! He has lied! " How often in our own political contests do we hear the cry with a note of triumph! And if he have, how often has he told the truth? And if he have, how many are entitled by pure innocence in that matter to throw a stone at him? And if he have, do we not know how lies will come to the tongue of a man without thought of lying? In his stoutest efforts after the truth a man may so express himself that when afterward he is driven to compare his recent and his former words, he shall hardly be able to say even to himself that he has not lied. It is by the tenor of a man's whole life that we must judge him, whether he be a liar or no.

To expect a man to be the same at sixty as he was at thirty, is to suppose that the sun at noon shall be graced with the colors which adorn its setting. And there are men whose intellects are set on so fine a pivot that a variation in the breeze of the moment, which coarser minds shall not feel, will carry them round with a rapidity which baffles the common eye. The man who saw his duty clearly on this side in the morning shall, before the evening come, recognize it on the other; and then again, and again, and yet again the vane shall go round. It may be that an instrument shall be too fine for our daily uses. We do not want a clock to strike the minutes, or a glass to tell the momentary changes in the atmosphere. It may be found that for the work of the world, the coarse work—and no work is so coarse, though none is so important, as that which falls commonly into the hands of statesmen—instruments strong in texture, and by reason of their rudeness not liable to sudden impressions, may be the best. That it is which we mean when we declare that a scrupulous man is impractical in politics. But the same man may, at various periods of his life, and on various days at the same period, be scrupulous and unscrupulous, impractical and practical, as the circumstances of the occasion may affect him. At one moment the rale of simple honesty will prevail with him. "Fiat justitia, ruat coelum. " "Si fractus illabatur orbis Impavidum ferient ruinae. " At another he will see the necessity of a compromise for the good of the many. He will tell himself that if the best cannot be done, he must content himself with the next best. He must shake hands with the imperfect, as the best way of lifting himself up from a bad way toward a better. In obedience to his very conscience he will temporize, and, finding no other way of achieving good, will do even evil that good may come of it. "Rem si possis recte; si non, quocunque modo rem. " In judging of such a character as this, a hard and fast line will certainly lead us astray. In judging of Cicero, such a hard and fast line has too generally been used. He was a man singularly sensitive to all influences. It must be admitted that he was a vane, turning on a pivot finer than those on which statesmen have generally been made to work. He had none of the fixed purpose of Caesar, or the unflinching principle of Cato. They were men cased in brass, whose feelings nothing could hurt. They suffered from none of those inward flutterings of the heart, doubtful aspirations, human longings, sharp sympathies, dreams of something better than this world, fears of something worse, which make Cicero so like a well-bred, polished gentleman of the present day. It is because he has so little like a Roman that he is of all the Romans the most attractive.

Still there may be doubt whether, with all the intricacies of his character, his career was such as to justify a further biography at this distance of time. "What's Hecuba to him, or he to Hecuba? " asks Hamlet, when he finds himself stirred by the passion thrown into the bare recital of an old story by an itinerant player. What is Cicero to us of the nineteenth century that we should care so much for him as to read yet another book? Nevertheless, Hamlet was moved because the tale was well told. There is matter in the earnestness, the pleasantness, the patriotism, and the tragedy of the man's life to move a reader still—if the story could only be written of him as it is felt! The difficulty lies in that, and not in the nature of the story.

The period of Cicero's life was the very turning-point of civilization and government in the history of the world. At that period of time the world, as we know it, was Rome. Greece had sunk. The Macedonian Empire had been destroyed. The kingdoms of the East—whether conquered, or even when conquering, as was Parthia for awhile—were barbaric, outside the circle of cultivation, and to be brought into it only by the arms and influence of Rome. During Caesar's career Gaul was conquered; and Britain, with what was known of Germany, supposed to be partly conquered. The subjugation of Africa and Spain was all but completed. Letters, too, had been or were being introduced. Cicero's use of language was so perfect that it seems to us to have been almost necessarily the result of a long established art of Latin literature. But, in truth, he is the earliest of the prose writers of his country with whose works we are familiar. Excepting Varro, who was born but ten years before him, no earlier Latin prose writer has left more than a name to us; and the one work by which Varro is at all known, the De Re Rustica, was written after Cicero's death. Lucretius, whose language we regard as almost archaic, so unlike is it to that of Virgil or Horace, was born eight years after Cicero. In a great degree Cicero formed the Latin language—or produced that manipulation of it which has made it so graceful in prose, and so powerful a vehicle of thought. That which he took from any Latin writer he took from Terence.

And it was then, just then, that there arose in Rome that unpremeditated change in its form of government which resulted in the self-assumed dictatorship of Caesar, and the usurpation of the Empire by Augustus. The old Rome had had kings. Then the name and the power became odious—the name to all the citizens, no doubt, but the power simply to the nobility, who grudged the supremacy of one man. The kings were abolished, and an oligarchy was established under the name of a Republic, with its annual magistrates—at first its two Consuls, then its Praetors and others, and occasionally a Dictator, as some current event demanded a concentration of temporary power in a single hand for a certain purpose.

The Republic was no republic, as we understand the word; nor did it ever become so, though their was always going on a perpetual struggle to transfer the power from the nobles to the people, in which something was always being given or pretended to be given to the outside class. But so little was as yet understood of liberty that, as each plebeian made his way up into high place and became one of the magistrates of the State, he became also one of the oligarchical faction. There was a continued contest, with a certain amount of good faith on each side, on behalf of the so-called Republic—but still a contest for power. This became so continued that a foreign war was at times regarded as a blessing, because it concentrated the energies of the State, which had been split and used by the two sections—by each against the other. It is probably the case that the invasion of the Gauls in earlier days, and, later on, the second Punic war, threatening as they were in their incidents to the power of Rome, provided the Republic with that vitality which kept it so long in existence. Then came Marius, dominant on one side as a tribune of the people, and Sylla, as aristocrat on the other, and the civil wars between them, in which, as one prevailed or the other, Rome was mastered. How Marius died, and Sylla reigned for three bloody, fatal years, is outside the scope of our purpose—except in this, that Cicero saw Sylla's proscriptions, and made his first essay into public life hot with anger at the Dictator's tyranny.

It occurs to us as we read the history of Rome, beginning with the early Consuls and going to the death of Caesar and of Cicero, and the accomplished despotism of Augustus, that the Republic could not have been saved by any efforts, and was in truth not worth the saving. We are apt to think, judging from our own idea of liberty, that there was so much of tyranny, so little of real freedom in the Roman form of government, that it was not good enough to deserve our sympathies. But it had been successful. It had made a great people, and had produced a wide-spread civilization. Roman citizenship was to those outside the one thing the most worthy to be obtained. That career which led the great Romans up from the state of Quaestor to the Aedile's, Praetor's, and Consul's chair, and thence to the rich reward of provincial government, was held to be the highest then open to the ambition of man. The Kings of Greece, and of the East, and of Africa were supposed to be inferior in their very rank to a Roman Proconsul, and this greatness was carried on with a semblance of liberty, and was compatible with a belief in the majesty of the Roman citizen. When Cicero began his work, Consuls, Praetors, Aediles, and Quaestors were still chosen by the votes of the citizens. There was bribery, no doubt, and intimidation, and a resort to those dirty arts of canvassing with which we English have been so familiar; but in Cicero's time the male free inhabitants of Rome did generally carry the candidates to whom they attached themselves. The salt of their republican theory was not as yet altogether washed out from their practice.

The love of absolute liberty as it has been cultivated among modern races did not exist in the time of Cicero. The idea never seems to have reached even his bosom, human and humanitarian as were his sympathies, that a man, as man, should be free. Half the inhabitants of Rome were slaves, and the institution was so grafted in the life of the time that it never occurred to a Roman that slaves, as a body, should be manumitted. The slaves themselves, though they were not, as have been the slaves whom we have seen, of a different color and presumed inferior race, do not themselves seem to have entertained any such idea. They were instigated now and again to servile wars, but there was no rising in quest of freedom generally. Nor was it repugnant to the Roman theory of liberty that the people whom they dominated, though not subjected to slavery, should still be outside the pale of civil freedom. That boon was to be reserved for the Roman citizen, and for him only. It had become common to admit to citizenship the inhabitants of other towns and further territories. The glory was kept not altogether for Rome, but for Romans.

Thus, though the government was oligarchical, and the very essence of freedom ignored, there was a something which stood in the name of liberty, and could endear itself to a real patriot. With genuine patriotism Cicero loved his country, and beginning his public life as he did at the close of Sylla's tyranny, he was able to entertain a dream that the old state of things might be restored and the republican form of government maintained. There should still be two Consuls in Rome, whose annual election would guard the State against regal dominion. And there should, at the same time, be such a continuance of power in the hands of the better class—the "optimates, " as he called them—as would preserve the city from democracy and revolution. No man ever trusted more entirely to popular opinion than Cicero, or was more anxious for aristocratic authority. But neither in one direction nor the other did he look for personal aggrandizement, beyond that which might come to him in accordance with the law and in subjection to the old form of government.

It is because he was in truth patriotic, because his dreams of a Republic were noble dreams, because he was intent on doing good in public affairs, because he was anxious for the honor of Rome and of Romans, not because he was or was not a "real power in the State" that his memory is still worth recording. Added to this was the intellect and the wit and erudition of the man, which were at any rate supreme. And then, though we can now see that his efforts were doomed to failure by the nature of the circumstances surrounding him, he was so nearly successful, so often on the verge of success, that we are exalted by the romance of his story into the region of personal sympathy. As we are moved by the aspirations and sufferings of a hero in a tragedy, so are we stirred by the efforts, the fortune, and at last the fall of this man. There is a picturesqueness about the life of Cicero which is wanting in the stories of Marius or Sylla, of Pompey, or even of Caesar—a picturesqueness which is produced in great part by these very doubtings which have been counted against him as insincerity.

His hands were clean when the hands of all around him were defiled by greed. How infinitely Cicero must have risen above his time when he could have clean hands! A man in our days will keep himself clean from leprosy because to be a leper is to be despised by those around him. Advancing wisdom has taught us that such leprosy is bad, and public opinion coerces us. There is something too, we must suppose, in the lessons of Christianity. Or it may be that the man of our day, with all these advantages, does not keep himself clean—that so many go astray that public opinion shall almost seem to tremble in the balance. Even with us this and that abomination becomes allowable because so many do it. With the Romans, in the time of Cicero, greed, feeding itself on usury, rapine, and dishonesty, was so fully the recognized condition of life that its indulgence entailed no disgrace. But Cicero, with eyes within him which saw farther than the eyes of other men, perceived the baseness of the stain. It has been said also of him that he was not altogether free from reproach. It has been suggested that he accepted payment for his services as an advocate, any such payment being illegal. The accusation is founded on the knowledge that other advocates allowed themselves to be paid, and on the belief that Cicero could not have lived as he did without an income from that source. And then there is a story told of him that, though he did much at a certain period of his life to repress the usury, and to excite at the same time the enmity of a powerful friend, he might have done more. As we go on, the stories of these things will be told; but the very nature of the allegations against him prove how high he soared in honesty above the manners of his day. In discussing the character of the men, little is thought of the robberies of Sylla, the borrowings of Caesar, the money-lending of Brutus, or the accumulated wealth of Crassus. To plunder a province, to drive usury to the verge of personal slavery, to accept bribes for perjured judgment, to take illegal fees for services supposed to be gratuitous, was so much the custom of the noble Romans that we hardly hate his dishonest greed when displayed in its ordinary course. But because Cicero's honesty was abnormal, we are first surprised, and then, suspecting little deviations, rise up in wrath against him, because in the midst of Roman profligacy he was not altogether a Puritan in his money matters.

Cicero is known to us in three great capacities: as a statesman, an advocate, and a man of letters. As the combination of such pursuits is common in our own days, so also was it in his. Caesar added them all to the great work of his life as a soldier. But it was given to Cicero to take a part in all those political struggles, from the resignation of Sylla to the first rising of the young Octavius, which were made on behalf of the Republic, and were ended by its downfall. His political life contains the story of the conversion of Rome from republican to imperial rule; and Rome was then the world. Could there have been no Augustus, no Nero, and then no Trajan, all Europe would have been different. Cicero's efforts were put forth to prevent the coming of an Augustus or a Nero, or the need of a Trajan; and as we read of them we feel that, had success been possible, he would have succeeded.

As an advocate he was unsurpassed. From him came the feeling — whether it be right or wrong — that a lawyer, in pleading for his client, should give to that client's cause not only all his learning and all his wit, but also all his sympathy. To me it is marvellous, and interesting rather than beautiful, to see how completely Cicero can put off his own identity and assume another's in any cause, whatever it be, of which he has taken the charge. It must, however, be borne in mind that in old Rome the distinction between speeches made in political and in civil or criminal cases was not equally well marked as with us, and also that the reader having the speeches which have come down to us, whether of one nature or the other, presented to him in the same volume, is apt to confuse the public and that which may, perhaps, be called the private work of the man. In the speeches best known to us Cicero was working as a public man for public objects, and the ardor, I may say the fury, of his energy in the cause which he was advocating was due to his public aspirations. The orations which have come to us in three sets, some of them published only but never spoken—those against Verres, against Catiline, and the Philippics against Antony—were all of this nature, though the first concerned the conduct of a criminal charge against one individual. Of these I will speak in their turn; but I mention them here in order that I may, if possible, induce the reader to begin his inquiry into Cicero's character as an advocate with a just conception of the objects of the man. He wished, no doubt, to shine, as does the barrister of to-day: he wished to rise; he wished, if you will, to make his fortune, not by the taking of fees, but by extending himself into higher influence by the authority of his name. No doubt he undertook this and the other case without reference to the truth or honesty of the cause, and, when he did so, used all his energy for the bad, as he did for the good cause. There seems to be special accusation made against him on his head, as though, the very fact that he undertook his work without pay threw upon him the additional obligation of undertaking no cause that was not in itself upright. With us the advocate does this notoriously for his fee. Cicero did it as notoriously in furtherance of some political object of the moment, or in maintenance of a friendship which was politically important. I say nothing against the modern practice. This would not be the place for such an argument. Nor do I say that, by rules of absolute right and wrong, Cicero was right; but he was as right, at any rate, as the modern barrister. And in reaching the high-minded conditions under which he worked, he had only the light of his own genius to guide him. When compare the clothing of the savage race with our own, their beads and woad and straw and fibres with our own petticoats and pantaloons, we acknowledge the progress of civilization and the growth of machinery. It is not a wonderful thing to us that an African prince should not be as perfectly dressed as a young man in Piccadilly. But, when we make a comparison of morals between our own time and a period before Christ, we seem to forget that more should be expected from us than from those who lived two thousand years ago.

There are some of those pleadings, speeches made by Cicero on behalf of or against an accused party, from which we may learn more of Roman life than from any other source left to us. Much we may gather from Terence, much from Horace, something from Juvenal. There is hardly, indeed, a Latin author from which an attentive reader may not pick up some detail of Roman customs. Cicero's letters are themselves very prolific. But the pretty things of the poets are not quite facts, nor are the bitter things of the satirist; and though a man's letters to his friend may be true, such letters as come to us will have been the products of the greater minds, and will have come from a small and special class. I fear that the Newgate Calendar of the day would tell us more of the ways of living then prevailing than the letters of Lady Mary W. Montagu or of Horace Walpole. From the orations against Verres we learn how the people of a province lived under the tyranny inflicted upon them; and from those spoken in defence of Sextus Amerinus and Aulus Cluentius, we gather something of the horrors of Roman life—not in Rome, indeed, but within the limits of Roman citizenship.

It is, however, as a man of letters that Cicero will be held in the highest esteem. It has been his good-fortune to have a great part of what he wrote preserved for future ages. His works have not perished, as have those of his contemporaries, Varro and Hortensius. But this has been due to two causes, which were independent of Fortune. He himself believed in their value, and took measures for their protection; and those who lived in his own time, and in the immediately succeeding ages, entertained the same belief and took the same care. Livy said that, to write Latin well, the writer should write it like Cicero; and Quintilian, the first of Latin critics, repeated to us what Livy had asserted. [27] There is a sweetness of language about Cicero which runs into the very sound; so that passages read aright would, by their very cadences, charm the ear of listeners ignorant of the language. Eulogy never was so happy as his. Eulogy, however, is tasteless in comparison with invective. Cicero's abuse is awful. Let the reader curious in such matters turn to the diatribes against Vatinius, one of Caesar's creatures, and to that against the unfortunate Proconsul Piso; or to his attacks on Gabinius, who was Consul together with Piso in the year of Cicero's banishment. There are wonderful morsels in the philippics dealing with Antony's private character; but the words which he uses against Gabinius and Piso beat all that I know elsewhere in the science of invective. Junius could not approach him; and even Macaulay, though he has, in certain passages, been very bitter, has not allowed himself the latitude which Roman taste and Roman manners permitted to Cicero.

It may, however, be said that the need of biographical memoirs as to a man of letters is by no means in proportion to the excellence of the work that he has achieved. Alexander is known but little to us, because we know so little of the details of his life. Caesar is much to us, because we have in truth been made acquainted with him. But Shakspeare, of whose absolute doings we know almost nothing, would not be nearer or dearer had he even had a Boswell to paint his daily portrait. The man of letters is, in truth, ever writing his own biography. What there is in his mind is being declared to the world at large by himself; and if he can so write that the world at large shall care to read what is written, no other memoir will, perhaps, be necessary. For myself I have never regretted those details of Shakspeare's life which a Boswell of the time might have given us. But Cicero's personality as a man of letters seems especially to require elucidation. His letters lose their chief charm if the character of the man be not known, and the incidents of his life. His essays on rhetoric—the written lessons which he has left on the art of oratory— are a running commentary on his own career as an orator. Most of his speeches require for their understanding a knowledge of the circumstances of his life. The treatises which we know as his Philosophy—works which have been most wrongly represented by being grouped under that name—can only be read with advantage by the light of his own experience. There are two separate classes of his so-called Philosophy, in describing which the word philosophy, if it be used at all, must be made to bear two different senses. He handles in one set of treatises, not, I think, with his happiest efforts, the teaching of the old Greek schools. Such are the Tusculan Disquisitions, the Academics, and the De Finibus. From reading these, without reference to the idiosyncrasies of the writer, the student would be led to believe that Cicero himself was a philosopher after that sort. But he was, in truth, the last of men to lend his ears

"To those budge doctors of the stoic fur. "

Cicero was a man thoroughly human in all his strength and all his weakness. To sit apart from the world and be happy amid scorn, poverty, and obscurity, with a mess of cabbage and a crust, absolutely contented with abstract virtue, has probably been given to no man; but of none has it been less within the reach than of Cicero.

To him ginger was always hot in the mouth, whether it was the spice of politics, or of social delight, or of intellectual enterprise. When in his deep sorrow at the death of his daughter, when for a time the Republic was dead to him, and public and private life were equally black, he craved employment. Then he took down his Greek manuscripts and amused himself as best he might by writing this way or that. It was a matter on which his intellect could work and his energies be employed, though the theory of his life was in no way concerned in it. Such was one class of his Philosophy. The other consisted of a code of morals which he created for himself by his own convictions, formed on the world around him, and which displayed itself in essays, such as those De Officiis—on the duties of life; De Senectute, De Amicitia—on old age and friendship, and the like, which were not only intended for use, but are of use to any man or woman who will study them up to this day. There are others, treatises on law and on government and religion, which have all been lumped together, for the misguidance of school-boys, under the name of Cicero's Philosophy. But they, be they of one class or the other, require an understanding of the man's character before they can be enjoyed.

For these reasons I think that there are incidents in the life, the character, and the work of Cicero which ought to make his biography interesting. His story is fraught with energy, with success, with pathos, and with tragedy. And then it is the story of a man human as men are now. No child of Rome ever better loved his country, but no child of Rome was ever so little like a Roman. Arms and battles were to him abominable, as they are to us. But arms and battles were the delight of Romans. He was ridiculed in his own time, and has been ridiculed ever since, for the alliterating twang of the line in which he declared his feeling:

"Cedant arma togas; concedat laurea linguae. "

But the thing said was thoroughly good, and the better because the opinion was addressed to men among whom the glory of arms was still in ascendant over the achievements of intellectual enterprise. The greatest men have been those who have stepped out from the mass, and gone beyond their time—seeing things, with eyesight almost divine, which have hitherto been hidden from the crowd. Such was Columbus when he made his way across the Western Ocean; such were Galileo and Bacon; such was Pythagoras, if the ideas we have of him be at all true. Such also was Cicero. It is not given to the age in which such men live to know them. Could their age even recognize them, they would not overstep their age as they do. Looking back at him now, we can see how like a Christian was the man—so like, that in essentials we can hardly see the difference. He could love another as himself—as nearly as a man may do; and he taught such love as a doctrine. [28]

He believed in the existence of one supreme God. [29] He believed that man would rise again and live forever in some heaven. [30] I am conscious that I cannot much promote this view of Cicero's character by quoting isolated passages from his works—words which taken alone may be interpreted in one sense or another, and which should be read, each with its context, before their due meaning can be understood. But I may perhaps succeed in explaining to a reader what it is that I hope to do in the following pages, and why it is that I undertake a work which must be laborious, and for which many will think that there is no remaining need.

I would not have it thought that, because I have so spoken of Cicero's aspirations and convictions, I intend to put him forth as a faultless personage in history. He was much too human to be perfect. Those who love the cold attitude of indifference may sing of Cato as perfect. Cicero was ambitious, and often unscrupulous in his ambition. He was a loving husband and a loving father; but at the end of his life he could quarrel with his old wife irrecoverably, and could idolize his daughter, while he ruined his son by indulgence. He was very great while he spoke of his country, which he did so often; but he was almost as little when he spoke of himself—which he did as often. In money-matters he was honest—for the times in which he lived, wonderfully honest; but in words he was not always equally trustworthy. He could flatter where he did not love. I admit that it was so, though I will not admit without a protest that the word insincere should be applied to him as describing his character generally. He was so much more sincere than others that the protest is needed. If a man stand but five feet eleven inches in his shoes, shall he be called a pygmy? And yet to declare that he measures full six feet would be untrue.

Cicero was a busybody. Were there anything to do, he wished to do it, let it be what it might. "Cedant arma togae. " If anything was written on his heart, it was that. Yet he loved the idea of leading an army, and panted for a military triumph. Letters and literary life were dear to him, and yet he liked to think that he could live on equal terms with the young bloods of Rome, such as Coelius. As far as I can judge, he cared nothing for luxurious eating and drinking, and yet he wished to be reckoned among the gormands and gourmets of his times. He was so little like the "budge doctors of the stoic fur, " of whom it was his delight to write when he had nothing else to do, that he could not bear any touch of adversity with equanimity. The stoic requires to be hardened against "the slings and arrows of outrageous fortune. " It is his profession to be indifferent to the "whips and scorns of time. " No man was less hardened, or more subject to suffering from scorns and whips. There be those who think proneness to such suffering is unmanly, or that the sufferer should at any rate hide his agony. Cicero did not. Whether of his glory or of his shame, whether of his joy or of his sorrow, whether of his love or of his hatred, whether of his hopes or of his despair, he spoke openly, as he did of all things. It has not been the way of heroes, as we read of them; but it is the way with men as we live with them.

What a man he would have been for London life! How he would have enjoyed his club, picking up the news of the day from all lips, while he seemed to give it to all ears! How popular he would have been at the Carlton, and how men would have listened to him while every great or little crisis was discussed! How supreme he would have sat on the Treasury bench, or how unanswerable, how fatal, how joyous, when attacking the Government from the opposite seats! How crowded would have been his rack with invitations to dinner! How delighted would have been the middle-aged countesses of the time to hold with him mild intellectual flirtations—and the girls of the period, how proud to get his autograph, how much prouder to have touched the lips of the great orator with theirs! How the pages of the magazines would have run over with little essays from his pen! "Have you seen our Cicero's paper on agriculture? That lucky fellow, Editor—, got him to do it last month! " "Of course you have read Cicero's article on the soul. The bishops don't know which way to turn. " "So the political article in the *Quarterly* is Cicero's? " "Of course you know the art-criticism in the *Times* this year is Tully's doing? " But that would probably be a bounce. And then what letters he would write! With the penny-post instead of travelling messengers at his command, and pen instead of wax and sticks, or perhaps with an instrument-writer and a private secretary, he would have answered all questions and solved all difficulties. He would have so abounded with intellectual fertility that men would not have known whether most to admire his powers of expression or to deprecate his want of reticence.

There will necessarily be much to be said of Cicero's writings in the following pages, as it is my object to delineate the literary man as well as the politician. In doing this, there arises a difficulty as to the sequence in which his works should be taken. It will hardly suit the purpose in view to speak of them all either chronologically or separately as to their subjects. The speeches and the letters clearly require the former treatment as applying each to the very moment of time at which they were either spoken or written. His treatises, whether on rhetoric or on the Greek philosophy, or on government, or on morals, can best be taken apart as belonging in a very small degree, if at all, to the period in which they were written. I will therefore endeavor to introduce the orations and letters as the periods may suit, and to treat of his essays afterward by themselves.

A few words I must say as to the Roman names I have used in my narrative. There is a difficulty in this respect, because the practice of my boyhood has partially changed itself. Pompey used to be Pompey without a blush. Now with an erudite English writer he is generally Pompeius. The denizens of Africa—the "nigger" world— have had, I think, something to do with this. But with no erudite English writer is Terence Terentius, or Virgil Virgilius, or Horace Horatius. Were I to speak of Livius, the erudite English listener would think that I alluded to an old author long prior to our dear historian. And though we now talk of Sulla instead of Sylla, we hardly venture on Antonius instead of Antony. Considering all this, I have thought it better to cling to the sounds which have ever been familiar to myself; and as I talk of Virgil and of Horace and Ovid freely and without fear, so shall I speak also of Pompey and of Antony and of Catiline. In regard to Sulla, the change has been so complete that I must allow the old name to have re-established itself altogether.

It has been customary to notify the division of years in the period of which I am about to write by dating from two different eras, counting down from the building of Rome, A.U. C., or "anno urbis conditae, " and back from the birth of Christ, which we English mark by the letters B. C., before Christ. In dealing with Cicero, writers (both French and English) have not uncommonly added a third mode of dating, assigning his doings or sayings to the year of his age. There is again a fourth mode, common among the Romans, of indicating the special years by naming the Consuls, or one of them. "O nata mecum consule Manlio, " Horace says, when addressing his cask of wine. That was, indeed, the official mode of indicating a date, and may probably be taken as showing how strong the impression in the Roman mind was of the succession of their Consuls. In the following pages I will use generally the date B. C., which, though perhaps less simple than the A. U.C., gives to the mind of the modern reader a clearer idea of the juxtaposition of events. The reader will surely know that Christ was born in the reign of Augustus, and crucified in that of Tiberius; but he will not perhaps know, without the trouble of some calculation, how far removed from the period of Christ was the year 648 A. U.C., in which Cicero was born. To this I will add on the margin the year of Cicero's life. He was nearly sixty-four when he died. I shall, therefore, call that year his sixty-third year.

NOTES:

[1] Froude's Caesar, p. 444.

[2] Ibid., p. 428.

[3] Ad Att., lib. xiii., 28.

[4] Ad Att., lib. ix., 10.

[5] Froude, p. 365.

[6] Ad Att., lib. ii., 5: "Quo quidem uno ego ab istis capi possum. "

[7] The Cincian law, of which I shall have to speak again, forbade Roman advocates to take any payment for their services. Cicero expressly declares that he has always obeyed that law. He accused others of disobeying it, as, for instance, Hortensius. But no contemporary has accused him. Mr. Collins refers to some books which had been given to Cicero by his friend Poetus. They are mentioned in a letter to Atticus, lib. i., 20; and Cicero, joking, says that he has consulted Cincius—perhaps some descendant of him who made the law 145 years before—as to the legality of accepting the present. But we have no reason for supposing that he had ever acted as an advocate for Poetus.

[8] Virgil, Aeneid, i., 150:

> "Ac, veluti magno in populo quum saepe coorta est
> Seditio, saevitque animis ignobile vulgus;
> Jamque faces, et saxa volant; furor arma ministrat:
> Tum, pietate gravem ac meritis si forte virum quem
> Conspexere, silent, arrectisque auribus adstant;
> Iste regit dictis animos, et pectora mulcet."

[9] The author is saying that a history from Cicero would have been invaluable, and the words are "interitu ejus utrum respublica an historia magis dolcat".

[10] Quintilian tells us this, lib. ii., c. 5. The passage of Livy is not extant. The commentators suppose it to have been taken from a letter to his son.

[11] Velleius Paterculus, lib. ii., c. 34.

[12] Valerius Maximus, lib. iv., c. 2; 4.

[13] Pliny, Hist. Nat., lib. vii., xxxi., 30.

[14] Martial, lib xiv., 188.

[15] Lucan, lib. vii., 62:

> "Cunctorum voces Romani maximus auctor
> Tullius eloquii, cujus sub jure togaque
> Pacificas saevus tremuit Catilina secures,
> Pertulit iratus bellis, cum rostra forumque
> Optaret passus tam longa silentia miles
> Addidit invalidae robur facundia causae"

[16] Tacitus, De Oratoribus, xxx.

[17] Juvenal, viii., 243.

[18] Demosthenes and Cicero compared.

[19] Quintilian, xii., 1.

[20] "Repudiatus vigintiviratus. " He refused a position of official value rendered vacant by the death of one Cosconius. See Letters to Atticus, 2,19.

[21] Florus, lib. iv, 1. In a letter from Essex to Foulke Greville, the writing of which has been attributed to Bacon by Mr. Spedding, Florus is said simply to have epitomized Livy (Life, vol. ii, p. 23). In this I think that Bacon has shorn him of his honors.

[22] Florus, lib. iv., 1.

[23] Sallust, Catilinaria, xxiii.

[24] I will add the concluding passage from the pseudo declamation, in order that the reader may see the nature of the words which were put into Sallust's mouth: "Quos tyrannos appellabas, eorum nune potentiae faves; qui tibi ante optumates videbantur, eosdem nune dementes ac furiosos vocas; Vatinii caussam agis, de Sextio male existumas; Bibulum petulantissumis verbis laedis, laudas Caesarem; quern maxume odisti, ei maxume obsequeris. Aliud stans, aliud sedens, de republica sentis; his maledicis, illos odisti; levissume transfuga, neque in hac, neque illa parte fidem habes. " Hence Dio Cassius declared that Cicero had been called a turncoat. [Greek text: kai automalos onomazeto.]

[25] Dio Cassius, lib. xlvi., 18: [Greek text: pros haen kai autaen toiautas epistolas grapheis oias an grapseien anaer skoptolaes athuroglorros... kai proseti kai to stoma auton diaballein epecheiraese tosautae aselgeia kai akatharsia para panta ton bion choomenos oste maede ton suggenestuton apechesthai, alla taen te gunaika proagogeuein kai taen thugatera moicheuein.]

[26] As it happens, De Quincey specially calls Cicero a man of conscience "Cicero is one of the very few pagan statesmen who can be described as a thoroughly conscientious man, " he says. The purport of his illogical essay on Cicero is no doubt thoroughly hostile to the man. It is chiefly worth reading on account of the amusing virulence with which Middleton, the biographer, is attacked.

[27] Quintilian, lib. ii, c. 5.

[28] De Finibus, lib. v., ca. xxii. : "Nemo est igitur, qui non hanc affectionem animi probet atque laudet. "

[29] De Rep., lib.vi., ca. vii: "Nihil est enim illi principi deo, qui omnem hunc mundum regit, quod quidem in terris fiat acceptius. " Tusc. Quest., lib., ca. xxx. : "Vetat enim dominans ille in nobis deus. "

[30] De Rep., lib.vi., ca. vii. : "Certum esse in coelo definitum locum, ubi beati aevo sempiterno fruantur. "

CHAPTER II.

HIS EDUCATION.

At Arpinum, on the river Liris, a little stream which has been made to sound sweetly in our ears by Horace, [31] in a villa residence near the town, Marcus Tullius Cicero was born, 106 years before Christ, on the 3d of January, according to the calendar then in use. Pompey the Great was born in the same year. Arpinum was a State which had been admitted into Roman citizenship, lying between Rome and Capua, just within that portion of Italy which was till the other day called the Kingdom of Naples. The district from which he came is noted, also, as having given birth to Marius. Cicero was of an equestrian family, which means as much as though we were to say among ourselves that a man had been born a gentleman and nothing more. An "eques" or knight in Cicero's time became so, or might become so, by being in possession of a certain income. The title conferred no nobility. The plebeian, it will be understood, could not become patrician, though he might become noble—as Cicero did. The patrician must have been born so—must have sprung from the purple of certain fixed families. [32] Cicero was born a plebeian, of equestrian rank and became ennobled when he was ranked among the senators because of his service among the high magistrates of the Republic. As none of his family had served before him, he was "novus homo, " a new man, and therefore not noble till he had achieved nobility himself. A man was noble who could reckon a Consul, a Praetor, or an Aedile among his ancestors. Such was not the case with Cicero. As he filled all these offices, his son was noble—as were his son's sons and grandsons, if such there were.

It was common to Romans to have three names, and our Cicero had three. Marcus, which was similar in its use to the Christian name of one of us, had been that of his grandfather and father, and was handed on to his son. This, called the praenomen, was conferred on the child when a babe with a ceremony not unlike that of our baptism. There was but a limited choice of such names among the Romans, so that an initial letter will generally declare to those accustomed to the literature that intended. A. stands for Aulus, P. for Publius, M. generally for Marcus, C. for Caius, though there was a Cneus also. The nomen, Tullius, was that of the family. Of this family of Tullius to which Cicero belonged we know no details. Plutarch tells us that of his father nothing was said but in extremes, some declaring that he had been a fuller, and others that he had been descended from a prince who had governed the Volsci. We do not see why he may not have sprung from the prince, and also have been a fuller. There can, however, be no doubt that he was a gentleman, not uneducated himself, with means and the desire to give his children the best education which Rome or Greece afforded. The third name or cognomen, that of Cicero, belonged to a branch of the family of Tullius. This third name had generally its origin, as do so many of our surnames, in some specialty of place, or trade, or chance circumstance. It was said that an attestor had been called Cicero from "cicer, " a vetch, because his nose was marked with the figure of that vegetable. It is more probable that the family prospered by the growing and sale of vetches. Be that as it may, the name had been well established before the orator's time. Cicero's mother was one Helvia, of whom we are told that she was well-born and rich. Cicero himself never alludes to her—as neither, if I remember rightly, did Horace to his mother, though he speaks so frequently of his father. Helvia's younger son, Quintus, tells a story of his mother in a letter, which has been, by chance, preserved among those written by our Cicero. She was in the habit of sealing up the empty wine-jars, as well as those which were full, so that a jar emptied on the sly by a guzzling slave might be at once known. This is told in a letter to Tiro, a favorite slave belonging to Marcus, of whom we shall hear often in the course of our work. As the old lady sealed up the jars, though they contained no wine, so must Tiro write letters, though he has nothing to say in them. This kind of argument, taken from the old familiar stories of one's childhood and one's parents, could be only used to a dear and familiar friend. Such was Tiro, though still a slave, to the two brothers. Roman life admitted of such friendships, though the slave was so completely the creature of the master that his life and death were at the master's disposal.

This is nearly all that is known of Cicero's father and mother, or of his old home.

There is, however, sufficient evidence that the father paid great attention to the education of his sons—if, in the case of Marcus, any evidence were wanting where the result is so manifest by the work of his life. At a very early age, probably when he was eight—in the year which produced Julius Caasar—he was sent to Rome, and there was devoted to studies which from the first were intended to fit him for public life. Middleton says that the father lived in Rome with his son, and argues from this that he was a man of large means. But

Cicero gives no authority for this. It is more probable that he lived at the house of one Acaleo, who had married his mother's sister, and had sons with whom Cicero was educated. Stories are told of his precocious talents and performances such as we are accustomed to hear of many remarkable men—not unfrequently from their own mouths. It is said of him that he was intimate with the two great advocates of the time, Lucius Crassus and Marcus Antonius the orator, the grandfather of Cicero's future enemy, whom we know as Marc Antony. Cicero speaks of them both as though he had seen them and talked much of them in his youth. He tells us anecdotes of them; [33] how they were both accustomed to conceal their knowledge of Greek, fancying that the people in whose eyes they were anxious to shine would think more of them if they seemed to have contented themselves simply with Roman words and Roman thoughts. But the intimacy was probably that which a lad now is apt to feel that he has enjoyed with a great man, if he has seen and heard him, and perhaps been taken by the hand. He himself gives in very plain language an account of his own studies when he was seventeen, eighteen, and nineteen. He speaks of the orators of that day[34]: "When I was above all things anxious to listen to these men, the banishment of Cotta was a great sorrow to me. I was passionately intent on hearing those who were left, daily writing, reading, and making notes. Nor was I content only with practice in the art of speaking. In the following year Varius had to go, condemned by his own enactment; and at this time, in working at the civil law, I gave much of my time to Quintus Scaevola, the son of Publius, who, though he took no pupils, by explaining points to those who consulted him, gave great assistance to students. The year after, when Sulla and Pompey were Consuls, I learned what oratory really means by listening to Publius Sulpicius, who as tribune was daily making harangues. It was then that Philo, the Chief of the Academy, with other leading philosophers of Athens, had been put to flight by the war with Mithridates, and had come to Rome. To him I devoted myself entirety, stirred up by a wonderful appetite for acquiring the Greek philosophy. But in that, though the variety of the pursuit and its greatness charmed me altogether, yet it seemed to me that the very essence of judicial conclusion was altogether suppressed. In that year Sulpicius perished, and in the next, three of our greatest orators,

Quintus Catulus, Marcus Antonius, and Caius Julius, were cruelly killed. " This was the time of the civil war between Marius and Sulla. "In the same year I took lessons from Molo the Rhodian, a great pleader and master of the art. " In the next chapter he tells us that he passed his time also with Diodatus the Stoic, who afterward lived with him, and died in his house. Here we have an authentic description of the manner in which Cicero passed his time as a youth at Rome, and one we can reduce probably to absolute truth by lessening the superlatives. Nothing in it, however, is more remarkable than the confession that, while his young intellect rejoiced in the subtle argumentation of the Greek philosophers, his clear common sense quarrelled with their inability to reach any positive conclusion.

But before these days of real study had come upon him he had given himself up to juvenile poetry. He is said to have written a poem called Pontius Glaucus when he was fourteen years old. This was no doubt a translation from the Greek, as were most of the poems that he wrote, and many portions of his prose treatises. [35] Plutarch tells us that the poem was extant in his time, and declares that, "in process of time, when he had studied this art with greater application, he was looked upon as the best poet, as well as the greatest orator in Rome. "The English translators of Plutarch tell us that their author was an indifferent judge of Latin poetry, and allege as proof of this that he praised Cicero as a poet, a praise which he gave "contrary to the opinion of Juvenal. " But Juvenal has given no opinion of Cicero's poetry, having simply quoted one unfortunate line noted for its egotism, and declared that Cicero would never have had his head cut off had his philippics been of the same nature. [36] The evidence of Quintus Mucius Scaevola as to Cicero's poetry was perhaps better, as he had the means, at any rate, of reading it. He believed that the Marius, a poem written by Cicero in praise of his great fellow-townsman, would live to posterity forever. The story of the old man's prophecy comes to us, no doubt, from Cicero himself, and is put into the mouth of his brother; [37] but had it been untrue it would have been contradicted.

The Glaucus was a translation from the Greek done by a boy, probably as a boy's lesson It is not uncommon that such exercises should be treasured by parents, or perhaps by the performer himself, and not impossible that they should be made to reappear afterward as original compositions. Lord Brougham tells us in his autobiogiaphy that in his early youth he tried his hand at writing English essays, and even tales of fiction. [38] "I find one of these, " he says, "Has survived the waste-paper basket, and it may amuse my readers to see the sort of composition I was guilty of at the age of thirteen. My tale was entitled 'Memnon, or Human Wisdom, ' and is as follows. " Then we have a fair translation of Voltaire's romance, "Memnon, " or "La Sagesse Humaine. " The old lord, when he was collecting his papers for his autobiography, had altogether forgotten his Voltaire, and thought that he had composed the story! Nothing so absurd as that is told of Cicero by himself or on his behalf.

It may be as well to say here what there may be to be said as to Cicero's poetry generally. But little of it remains to us, and by that little it has been admitted that he has not achieved the name of a great poet; but what he did was too great in extent and too good in its nature to be passed over altogether without notice. It has been his fate to be rather ridiculed than read as a maker of verses, and that ridicule has come from two lines which I have already quoted. The longest piece which we have is from the Phaenomena of Aratus, which he translated from the Greek when he was eighteen years old, and which describes the heavenly bodies. It is known to us best by the extracts from it given by the author himself in his treatise, De Naturâ Deorum. It must be owned that it is not pleasant reading. But translated poetry seldom is pleasant, and could hardly be made so on such a subject by a boy of eighteen. The Marius was written two years after this, and we have a passage from it, quoted by the author in his De Divinatione, containing some fine lines. It tells the story of the battle of the eagle and the serpent. Cicero took it, no doubt (not translated it, however), from the passage in the Iliad, lib, xii, 200, which has been rendered by Pope with less than his usual fire, and by Lord Derby with no peculiar charm. Virgil has reproduced the picture with his own peculiar grace of words. His version has been translated by Dryden, but better, perhaps, by Christopher Pitt. Voltaire has translated Cicero's lines with great power, and Shelley has reproduced the same idea at much greater length in the first canto of the Revolt of Islam, taking it probably from Cicero, but, if not, from Voltaire. [39] I venture to think that, of the nine versions, Cicero's is the best, and that it is the most melodious piece of Latin poetry we have up to that date. Twenty-seven years afterward, when Lucretius was probably at work on his great poem, Cicero wrote an account of his consulship in verse. Of this we have fifty or sixty lines, in which the author describes the heavenly warnings which were given as to the affairs of his own consular year. The story is not a happy one, but the lines are harmonious. It is often worth our while to inquire how poetry has become such as it is, and how the altered and improved phases of versification have arisen. To trace our melody from Chaucer to Tennyson is matter of interest to us all. Of

Cicero as a poet we may say that he found Latin versification rough, and left it smooth and musical. Now, as we go on with the orator's life and prose works, we need not return to his poetry.

The names of many masters have been given to us as those under whom Cicero's education was carried on. Among others he is supposed, at a very early age, to have been confided to Archias. Archias was a Greek, born at Antioch, who devoted himself to letters, and, if we are to believe what Cicero says, when speaking as an advocate, excelled all his rivals of the day. Like many other educated Greeks, he made his way to Rome, and was received as one of the household of Lucullus, with whom he travelled, accompanying him even to the wars. He became a citizen of Rome— so Cicero assures us—and Cicero's tutor. What Cicero owed to him we do not know, but to Cicero Archias owed immortality. His claim to citizenship was disputed; and Cicero, pleading on his behalf, made one of those shorter speeches which are perfect in melody, in taste, and in language. There is a passage in which speaking on behalf of so excellent a professor in the art, he sings the praises of literature generally. I know no words written in praise of books more persuasive or more valuable. "Other recreations, " he says, "do not belong to all seasons nor to all ages, nor to all places. These pursuits nourish our youth and delight our old age. They adorn our prosperity and give a refuge and a solace to our troubles. They charm us at home, and they are not in our way when we are abroad. They go to bed with us. They travel about with us. They accompany us as we escape into the country. "[40] Archias probably did something for him in directing his taste, and has been rewarded thus richly. As to other lessons, we know that he was instructed in law by Scaevola, and he has told us that he listened to Crassus and Antony. At sixteen he went through the ceremony of putting off his boy's dress, the toga praetexta, and appearing in the toga virilis before the Praetor, thus assuming his right to go about a man's business. At sixteen the work of education was *not* finished—no more than it is with us when a lad at Oxford becomes "of age" at twenty-one; nor was he put beyond his father's power, the "patria potestas, " from which no age availed to liberate a son; but, nevertheless, it was a very joyful ceremony, and was duly performed by Cicero in the midst of his studies with Scaevola.

At eighteen he joined the army. That doctrine of the division of labor which now, with us, runs through and dominates all pursuits, had not as yet been made plain to the minds of men at Rome by the political economists of the day. It was well that a man should know something of many things—that he should especially, if he intended to be a leader of men, be both soldier and orator. To rise to be Consul, having first been Quaestor, Aedile, and Praetor, was the path of glory. It had been the special duty of the Consuls of Rome, since the establishment of consular government, to lead the armies of the Republic. A portion of the duty devolved upon the Praetors, as wars became more numerous; and latterly the commanders were attended by Quaestors. The Governors of the provinces, Proconsuls, or Propretors with proconsular authority, always combined military with civil authority. The art of war was, therefore, a necessary part of the education of a man intended to rise in the service of the State. Cicero, though, in his endeavor to follow his own tastes, he made a strong effort to keep himself free from such work, and to remain at Rome instead of being sent abroad as a Governor, had at last to go where fighting was in some degree necessary, and, in the saddest phase of his life, appeared in Italy with his lictors, demanding the honors of a triumph. In anticipation of such a career, no doubt under the advice of his friends, he now went out to see, if not a battle, something, at any rate, of war. It has already been said how the citizenship of Rome was conferred on some of the small Italian States around, and not on others. Hence, of course, arose jealousy, which was increased by the feeling on the part of those excluded that they were called to furnish soldiers to Rome, as well as those who were included. Then there was formed a combination of Italian cities, sworn to remedy the injury thus inflicted on them. Their purpose was to fight Rome in order that they might achieve Roman citizenship; and hence arose the first civil war which distracted the Empire. Pompeius Strabo, father of Pompey the Great, was then Consul (B. C. 89), and Cicero was sent out to see the campaign under him. Marius and Sulla, the two Romans who were destined soon to bathe Rome in blood, had not yet quarrelled, though they had been brought to hate each other—Marius by jealousy, and Sulla by rivalry. In this war they both served under the Consuls, and Cicero served with Sulla. We know nothing of his doings in that campaign. There are no tidings even of a misfortune such as that which happened to Horace when he went out to fight, and came home from the battle-field "relicta non bene parmula. "

Rome trampled on the rebellious cities, and in the end admitted them to citizenship. But probably the most important, certainly the most notorious, result of the Italian war, was the deep antagonism of Marius and Sulla. Sulla had made himself conspicuous by his fortune on the occasion, whereas Marius, who had become the great soldier of the Republic, and had been six times Consul, failed to gather fresh laurels. Rome was falling into that state of anarchy which was the cause of all the glory and all the disgrace of Cicero's life, and was open to the dominion of any soldier whose grasp might be the least scrupulous and the strongest. Marius, after a series of romantic adventures with which we must not connect ourselves here, was triumphant only just before his death, while Sulla went off with his army, pillaged Athens, plundered Asia Minor generally, and made terms with Mithridates, though he did not conquer him. With the purport, no doubt, of conquering Mithridates, but perhaps with the stronger object of getting him out of Rome, the army had been intrusted to him, with the consent of the Marian faction.

Then came those three years, when Sulla was in the East and Marius dead, of which Cicero speaks as a period of peace, in which a student was able to study in Rome. "Triennium fere fuit urbs sine armis. "[41] These must have been the years 86, 85, and 84 before Christ, when Cicero was twenty-one, twenty-two, and twenty-three years old; and it was this period, in truth, of which he speaks, and not of earlier years, when he tells us of his studies with Philo, and Molo, and Diodatus. Precocious as he was in literature, writing one poem—or translating it—when he was fourteen, and another when he was eighteen, he was by no means in a hurry to commence the work of his life. He is said also to have written a treatise on military tactics when he was nineteen; which again, no doubt, means that he had exercised himself by translating such an essay from the Greek. This, happily, does not remain. But we have four books, Rhetoricorum ad C. Herennium, and two books De Inventione, attributed to his twentieth and twenty-first years, which are published with his works, and commence the series. Of all that we have from him, they are perhaps the least worth reading; but as they are, or were, among his recognized writings, a word shall be said of them in their proper place.

The success of the education of Cicero probably became a commonplace among Latin school-masters and Latin writers. In the dialogue De Oratoribus, attributed to Tacitus, the story of it is given by Messala when he is praising the orators of the earlier age. "We know well, " says Messala, "that book of Cicero which is called Brutus, in the latter part of which he describes to us the beginning and the progress of his own eloquence, and, as it were, the bringing up on which it was founded. He tells us that he had learned civil law under Q. Mutius Scaevola; that he had exhausted the realm of philosophy—learning that of the Academy under Philo, and that of the Stoics under Diodatus; that, not content with these treatises, he had travelled through Greece and Asia, so as to embrace the whole world of art. And thus it had come about that in the works of Cicero no knowledge is wanting—neither of music, nor of grammar, nor any other liberal accomplishment. He understood the subtilty of logic, the purpose of ethics, the effects and causes of things. " Then the speaker goes on to explain what may be expected from study such as that. "Thus it is, my good friends—thus, that from the acquirement of many arts, and from a general knowledge of all things, eloquence that is truly admirable is created in its full force; for the power and capacity of an orator need not be hemmed in, as are those of other callings, by certain narrow bounds; but that man is the true orator who is able to speak on all subjects with dignity and grace, so as to persuade those who listen, and to delight them, in a manner suited to the nature of the subject in hand and the convenience of the time. "[42]

We might fancy that we were reading words from Cicero himself! Then the speaker in this imaginary conversation goes on to tell us how far matters had derogated in his time, pointing out at the same time that the evils which he deplores had shown themselves even before Cicero, but had been put down, as far as the law could put them down, by its interference. He is speaking of those schools of rhetoric in which Greek professors of the art gave lessons for money, which were evil in their nature, and not, as it appears, efficacious even for the purpose in hand. "But now, " continues Messala, "our very boys are brought into the schools of those lecturers who are called 'rhetores, ' who had sprung up before Cicero, to the displeasure of our ancestors, as is evident from the fact that when Crassus and Domitius were Censors they were ordered to shut up their school of impudence, as Cicero calls it. Our boys, as I was going to say, are taken to these lecture-rooms, in which it is hard to say whether the atmosphere of the place, or the lads they are thrown among, or the nature of the lessons taught, are the most injurious. In the place itself there is neither discipline nor respect. All who go there are equally ignorant. The boys among the boys, the lads among the lads, utter and listen to just what words they please. Their very exercises are, for the most part, useless. Two kinds are in vogue with these 'rhetores, ' called 'suasoriae' and 'controversiae, '" tending, we may perhaps say, to persuade or to refute. "Of these, the 'suasoriae, ' as being the lighter and requiring less of experience, are given to the little boys, the 'controversiae' to the bigger lads. But—oh heavens, what they are—what miserable compositions! " Then he tells us the subjects selected. Rape, incest, and other horrors are subjected to the lads for their declamation, in order that they may learn to be orators.

Messala then explains that in those latter days—his days, that is—under the rule of despotic princes, truly large subjects are not allowed to be discussed in public—confessing, however, that those large subjects, though they afford fine opportunities to orators, are not beneficial to the State at large. But it was thus, he says, that Cicero became what he was, who would not have grown into favor had he defended only P. Quintius and Archias, and had had nothing to do with Catiline, or Milo, or Verres, or Antony—showing, by-the-way, how great was the reputation of that speech, Pro Milone, with which we shall have to deal farther on.

The treatise becomes somewhat confused, a portion of it having probably been lost. From whose mouth the last words are supposed to come is not apparent. It ends with a rhapsody in favor of imperial government—suitable, indeed, to the time of Domitian, but very unlike Tacitus. While, however, it praises despotism, it declares that only by the evils which despotism had quelled could eloquence be maintained. "Our country, indeed, while it was astray in its government; while it tore itself to pieces by parties and quarrels and discord; while there was no peace in the Forum, no agreement in the Senate, no moderation on the judgment-seat, no reverence for letters, no control among the magistrates, boasted, no doubt, a stronger eloquence. "

From what we are thus told of Cicero, not what we hear from himself, we are able to form an idea of the nature of his education. With his mind fixed from his early days on the ambition of doing something noble with himself, he gave himself up to all kinds of learning. It was Macaulay, I think, who said of him that the idea of conquering the "omne scibile—the understanding of all things within the reach of human intellect—was before his eyes as it was before those of Bacon. The special preparation which was, in Cicero's time, employed for students at the bar is also described in the treatise from which I have quoted—the preparation which is supposed to have been the very opposite of that afforded by the "rhetores. " "Among ourselves, the youth who was intended to achieve eloquence in the Forum, when already trained at home and exercised in classical knowledge, was brought by his father or his friends to that orator who might then be considered to be the leading man in the city. It became his daily work to follow that man, to accompany him, to be conversant with all his speeches, whether in the courts of law or at public meetings, so that he might learn, if I might say so, to fight in the very thick of the throng. " It was thus that Cicero studied his art. A few lines farther down, the pseudo-Tacitus tells us that Crassus, in his nineteenth year, held a brief against Carbo; that Caesar did so in his twenty-first against Dolabella; and Pollio, in his twenty-second year, against Cato. [43] In this precocity Cicero did not imitate Crassus, or show an example to the Romans who followed him. He was twenty-six when he pleaded his first cause. Sulla had then succeeded in crushing the Marian faction, and the Sullan proscriptions had taken place, and were nominally over. Sulla had been declared Dictator, and had proclaimed that there should be no more selections for death. The Republic was supposed to be restored. "Recuperata republica— — tum primum nos ad causas et privatas et publicas adire cepimus, "[44] "The Republic having been restored, I then first applied myself to pleadings, both private and public. "

Of Cicero's politics at that time we are enabled to form a fair judgment. Marius had been his townsman; Sulla had been his captain. But the one thing dear to him was the Republic—what he thought to be the Republic. He was neither Manan nor Sullan The turbulence in which so much noble blood had flowed—the "crudelis interitus oratorum, " the crushing out of the old legalized form of government—was abominable to him. It was his hope, no doubt his expectation, that these old forms should be restored in all their power. There seemed to be more probability of this—there was more probability of it—on the side of Sulla than the other. On Sulla's side was Pompey, the then rising man, who, being of the same age with Cicero, had already pushed himself into prominence, who was surnamed the Great, and who "triumphed" during these very two years in which Cicero began his career; who through Cicero's whole life was his bugbear, his stumbling-block, and his mistake. But on that side were the "optimates, " the men who, if they did not lead, ought to lead the Republic; those who, if they were not respectable, ought to be so; those who, if they did not love their country, ought to love it. If there was a hope, it was with them. The old state of things—that oligarchy which has been called a Republic—had made Rome what it was; had produced power, civilization, art, and literature. It had enabled such a one as Cicero was himself to aspire to lead, though he had been humbly born, and had come to Rome from an untried provincial family. To him the Republic—as he fancied that it had been, as he fancied that it might be—was all that was good, all that was gracious, all that was beneficent. On Sulla's side lay what chance there was of returning to the old ways. When Sulla was declared Dictator, it was presumed that the Republic was restored. But not on this account should it be supposed that Cicero regarded the proscriptions of Sulla with favor, or that he was otherwise than shocked by the wholesale robberies for which the proscription paved the way. This is a matter with which it will be necessary to deal more fully when we come in our next chapter to the first speeches made by Cicero; in the very first of which, as I place them, he attacks the Sullan robberies with an audacity which, when we remember that Sulla was still in power, rescues, at any rate, in regard to this period of his life, the character of the orator from that charge of cowardice which has been imputed to him.

It is necessary here, in this chapter devoted to the education of Cicero, to allude to his two first speeches, because that education was not completed till afterward—so that they may be regarded as experiments, or trials, as it were, of his force and sufficiency. "Not content with these teachers"—teachers who had come to Rome from Greece and Asia—"he had travelled through Greece and Asia, so as to embrace the whole world of art. " These words, quoted a few pages back from the treatise attributed to Tacitus, refer to a passage in the Brutus in which Cicero makes a statement to that effect. "When I reached Athens, [45] I passed six months with Antiochus, by far the best known and most erudite of the teachers of the old Academy, and with him, as my great authority and master, I renewed that study of philosophy which I had never abandoned— which from my boyhood I had followed with always increasing success. At the same time I practised oratory laboriously with Demetrius Syrus, also at Athens, a well-known and by no means incapable master of the art of speaking. After that I wandered over all Asia, and came across the best orators there, with whom I practised, enjoying their willing assistance. " There is more of it, which need not be repeated verbatim, giving the names of those who aided him in Asia: Menippus of Stratonice—who, he says, was sweet enough to have belonged himself to Athens—with Dionysius of Magnesia, with Oeschilus of Cnidos, and with Xenocles of Adramyttium. Then at Rhodes he came across his old friend Molo, and applied himself again to the teaching of his former master. Quintilian explains to us how this was done with a purpose, so that the young orator, when he had made a first attempt with his half-fledged wings in the courts, might go back to his masters for awhile[46].

He was twenty-eight when he started on this tour. It has been suggested that he did so in fear of the resentment of Sulla, with whose favorites and with whose practices he had dealt very plainly. There is no reason for alleging this, except that Sulla was powerful, that Sulla was blood-thirsty, and that Sulla must have been offended. This kind of argument is often used. It is supposed to be natural, or at least probable, that in a certain position a man should have been a coward or a knave, ungrateful or cruel; and in the presumption thus raised the accusation is brought against him. "Fearing Sulla's resentment, " Plutarch says, "he travelled into Greece, and gave out that the recovery of his health was the motive. " There is no evidence that such was his reason for travelling; and, as Middleton says in his behalf, it is certain that he "continued for a year after this in Rome without any apprehension of danger. " It is best to take a man's own account of his own doings and their causes, unless there be ground for doubting the statement made. It is thus that Cicero himself speaks of his journey: "Now, " he says, still in his Brutus[47], "as you wish to know what I am—not simply what mark I may have on my body from my birth, or with what surroundings of childhood I was brought up—I will include some details which might perhaps seem hardly necessary. At this time I was thin and weak, my neck being long and narrow—a habit and form of body which is supposed to be adverse to long life; and those who loved me thought the more of this, because I had taken to speaking without relaxation, without recreation with all the powers of my voice, and with much muscular action.

When my friends and the doctors desired me to give up speaking, I resolved that, rather than abandon my career as an orator, I would face any danger. But when it occurred to me that by lowering my voice, by changing my method of speaking, I might avoid the danger, and at the same time learn to speak with more elegance, I accepted that as a reason for going into Asia, so that I might study how to change my mode of elocution. Thus, when I had been two years at work upon causes, and when my name was already well known in the Forum, I took my departure, and left Rome. "

During the six months that he was at Athens he renewed an early acquaintance with one who was destined to become the most faithful, and certainly the best known, of his friends. This was Titus

Pomponius, known to the world as that Atticus to whom were addressed something more than half the large body of letters which were written by Cicero, and which have remained for our use. [48] He seems to have lived much with Atticus, who was occupied with similar studies, though with altogether different results. Atticus applied himself to the practices of the Epicurean school, and did in truth become "Epicuri de grege porcus. " To enjoy life, to amass a fortune, to keep himself free from all turmoils of war or state, to make the best of the times, whether they were bad or good, without any attempt on his part to mend them—this was the philosophy of Titus Pomponius, who was called Atticus because Athens, full of art and literature, easy, unenergetic, and luxurious, was dear to him. To this philosophy, or rather to this theory of life, Cicero was altogether opposed. He studied in all the schools—among the Platonists, the Stoics, even with the Epicureans enough to know their dogmas so that he might criticise them—proclaiming himself to belong to the new Academy, or younger school of Platonists, but in truth drawing no system of morals or rule of life from any of them. To him, and also to Atticus, no doubt, these pursuits afforded an intellectual pastime. Atticus found himself able to justify to himself the bent of his disposition by the name of a philosopher, and therefore became an Epicurean. Cicero could in no way justify to himself any deviation from the energy of public life, from its utility, from its ambition, from its loves, or from its hatred; and from the Greek philosophers whom he named of this or the other school, received only some assistance in that handling of so-called philosophy which became the chief amusement of his future life. This was well understood by the Latin authors who wrote of Cicero after his own time. Quintilian, speaking of Cicero and Brutus as writers of philosophy, says of the latter, "Suffecit ponderi rerum; seias enim sentire quae dicit"[49]—"He was equal to the weight of the subject, for you feel that he believes what he writes" He leaves the inference, of course, that Cicero wrote on such matters only for the exercise of his ingenuity, as a school-boy writes.

When at Athens, Cicero was initiated into the Eleusinian mysteries— as to which Mr. Collins, in his little volume on Cicero, in the Ancient Classics for English Readers, says that they "contained under this veil whatever faith in the Invisible and Eternal rested in the mind of an enlightened pagan. " In this Mr. Collins is fully justified by what Cicero himself has said although the character thus given to these mysteries is very different from that which was attributed to them by early Christian writers. They were to those pious but somewhat prejudiced theologists mysterious and pagan, and therefore horrible. [50] But Cicero declares in his dialogue with Atticus De Legibus, written when he was fifty-five years old, in the prime of his intellect, that "of all the glories and divine gifts which your Athens has produced for the improvement of men nothing surpasses these mysteries, by which the harshness of our uncivilized life has been softened, and we have been lifted up to humanity; and as they are called 'initia, '" by which aspirants were initiated, "so we have in truth found in them the seeds of a new life. Nor have we received from them only the means of living with satisfaction, but also of dying with a better hope as to the future. "[51]

Of what took place with Cicero and Atticus at their introduction to the Eleusinian mysteries we know nothing. But it can hardly be that, with such memories running in his mind after thirty years, expressed in such language to the very friend who had then been his companion, they should not have been accepted by him as indicating the commencement of some great line of thought. The two doctrines which seem to mark most clearly the difference between the men whom we regard, the one as a pagan and the other as a Christian, are the belief in a future life and the duty of doing well by our neighbors. Here they are both indicated, the former in plain language, and the latter in that assurance of the softening of the barbarity of uncivilized life, "Quibus ex agresti immanique vita exculti ad humanitatem et mitigati sumus. "

Of the inner life of Cicero at this moment—how he ate, how he drank, with what accompaniment of slaves he lived, how he was dressed, and how lodged—we know very little; but we are told enough to be aware that he could not have travelled, as he did in Greece and Asia, without great expense. His brother Quintus was with him, so that cost, if not double, was greatly increased. Antiochus, Demetrius Syrus, Molo, Menippus, and the others did not give him their services for nothing. These were gentlemen of whom we know that they were anxious to carry their wares to the best market. And then he seems to have been welcomed wherever he went, as though travelling in some sort "en prince. " No doubt he had brought with him the best introductions which Rome could afford; but even with them a generous allowance must have been necessary, and this must have come from his father's pocket.

As we go on, a question will arise as to Cicero's income and the sources whence it came. He asserts of himself that he was never paid for his services at the bar. To receive such payment was illegal, but was usual. He claims to have kept himself exempt from whatever meanness there may have been in so receiving such fees—exempt, at any rate, from the fault of having broken the law. He has not been believed. There is no evidence to convict him of falsehood, but he has not been believed, because there have not been found palpable sources of income sufficient for an expenditure so great as that which we know to have been incident to the life he led. But we do not know what were his father's means. Seeing the nature of the education given to the lad, of the manner in which his future life was prepared for him from his earliest days, of the promise made to him from his boyhood of a career in the metropolis if he could make himself fit for it, of the advantages which costly travel afforded him, I think we have reason to suppose that the old Cicero was an opulent man, and that the house at Arpinum was no humble farm, or fuller's poor establishment.

NOTES:

[31] Hor., lib. i., Ode xxii.,

"Non rura qua; Liris quicta
Mordet aqua taciturnus amnis."

[32] Such was the presumed condition of things at Rome. By the passing of a special law a plebeian might, and occasionally did, become patrician. The patricians had so nearly died out in the time of Julius Caesar that he introduced fifty new families by the Lex Cassia.

[33] De Orat., lib. ii., ca. 1.

[34] Brutus, ca. lxxxix.

[35] It should be remembered that in Latin literature it was the recognized practice of authors to borrow wholesale from the Greek, and that no charge of plagiarism attended such borrowing. Virgil, in taking thoughts and language from Homer, was simply supposed to have shown his judgment in accommodating Greek delights to Roman ears and Roman intellects.

The idea as to literary larceny is of later date, and has grown up with personal claims for originality and with copyright. Shakspeare did not acknowledge whence he took his plots, because it was unnecessary. Now, if a writer borrow a tale from the French, it is held that he ought at least to owe the obligation, or perhaps even pay for it.

[36] Juvenal, Sat. x., 122,

> "O fortunatum natam me Consule Romam!
> Antoni gladios potuit contemnere, si sic
> Omnia dixisset."

[37] De Leg., lib. i., ca. 1.

[38] Life and Times of Henry Lord Brougham, written by himself, vol. i., p. 58.

[39] I give the nine versions to which I allude in an Appendix A, at the end of this volume, so that those curious in such matters may compare the words in which the same picture has been drawn by various hands.

[40] Pro Archia, ca. vii.

[41] Brutus, ca. xc.

[42] Tacitus, De Oratoribus, xxx.

[43] Quintilian, lib. xii., c. vi., who wrote about the same time as this essayist, tells us of these three instances of early oratory, not, however, specifying the exact age in either case. He also reminds us that Demosthenes pleaded when he was a boy, and that Augustus at the age of twelve made a public harangue in honor of his grandmother.

[44] Brutus, ca. xc.

[45] Brutus, xci.

[46] Quintilian, lib. xii., vi. : "Quum jam clarum meruisset inter patronos, qui tum erant, nomen, in Asiam navigavit, seque et aliis sine dubio eloquentiae ae sapientiae magistris, sed praecipue tamen Apollonio Moloni, quem Romae quoque audierat, Rhodi rursus formandum ae velut recognendum dedit".

[47] Brutus, xci.

[48] The total correspondence contains 817 letters, of which 52 were written to Cicero, 396 were written by Cicero to Atticus, and 369 by Cicero to his friends in general. We have no letters from Atticus to Cicero.

[49] Quintilian, lib. x., ca. 1.

[50] Clemens of Alexandria, in his exhortation to the Gentiles, is very severe upon the iniquities of these rites. "All evil be to him, " he says, "who brought them into fashion, whether it was Dardanus, or Eetion the Thracian, or Midas the Phrygian. " The old story which he repeats as to Ceres and Proserpine may have been true, but he was altogether ignorant of the changes which the common-sense of centuries had produced.

[51] De Legibus, lib. ii., c.xiv.

CHAPTER III.

THE CONDITION OF ROME.

It is far from my intention to write a history of Rome during the Ciceronian period. Were I to attempt such a work, I should have to include the doings of Sertorius in Spain, of Lucullus and Pompey in the East, Caesar's ten years in Gaul, and the civil wars from the taking of Marseilles to the final battles of Thapsus and Munda. With very many of the great events which the period includes Cicero took but slight concern—so slight that we can hardly fail to be astonished when we find how little he had to say of them—he who ran through all the offices of the State, who was the chosen guardian of certain allied cities, who has left to us so large a mass of correspondence on public subjects, and who was essentially a public man for thirty-four years. But he was a public man who concerned himself personally with Rome rather than with the Roman Empire. Home affairs, and not foreign affairs, were dear to him. To Caesar's great deeds in Gaul we should have had from him almost no allusion, had not his brother Quintus been among Caesar's officers, and his young friend Trebatius been confided by himself to Caesar's care. Of Pharsalia we only learn from him that, in utter despair of heart, he allowed himself to be carried to the war. Of the proconsular governments throughout the Roman Empire we should not learn much from Cicero, were it not that it has been shown to us by the trial of Verres how atrocious might be the conduct of a Roman Governor, and by the narratives of Cicero's own rule in Cilicìa, how excellent. The history of the time has been written for modern readers by Merivale and Mommsen, with great research and truth as to facts, but, as I think with some strong feeling. Now Mr. Froude has followed with his Caesar, which might well have been called Anti-Cicero. All these in lauding, and the two latter in deifying, the successful soldier, have, I think, dealt hardly with Cicero, attributing to his utterances more than they mean; doubting his sincerity, but seeing clearly the failure of his political efforts. With the great facts of the Roman Empire as they gradually formed themselves from the fall of Carthage, when the Empire began, [52] to the establishment of Augustus, when it was consummated, I do not pretend to deal, although by far the most momentous of them were crowded into the life of Cicero. But in order that I may, if possible, show the condition of his mind toward the Republic—that I may explain what it was that he hoped and why he hoped it—I must go back and relate in a few words what it was that Marius and Sulla had done for Rome.

Of both these men all the doings with which history is greatly concerned were comprised within the early years of Cicero's life. Marius, indeed, was nearly fifty years of age when his fellow-townsman was born, and had become a distinguished soldier, and, though born of humble parents, had pushed himself to the Consulate. His quarrel with Sulla had probably commenced, springing from jealousy as to deeds done in the Jugurthine war. But it is not matter of much moment, now that Marius had proved himself to be a good and hardy soldier, excepting in this, that, by making himself a soldier in early life, he enabled himself in his latter years to become the master of Rome.

Sulla, too, was born thirty-two years before Cicero—a patrician of the bluest blood—and having gone, as we say, into public life, and having been elected Quaestor, became a soldier by dint of office, as a man with us may become head of the Admiralty. As Quaestor he was sent to join Marius in Africa a few months before Cicero was born. Into his hands, as it happened, not into those of Marius, Jugurtha was surrendered by his father-in-law, Bocchus, who thought thus to curry favor with the Romans. Thence came those internecine feuds, in which, some twenty-five years later, all Rome was lying butchered. The cause of quarrelling between these two men, the jealousies which grew in the heart of the elder, from the renewed successes of the younger, are not much to us now; but the condition to which Rome had been brought, when two such men could scramble for the city, and each cut the throats of the relatives, friends, and presumed allies of the other, has to be inquired into by those who would understand what Rome had been, what it was, and what it was necessarily to become.

When Cicero was of an age to begin to think of these things, and had put on the "toga virilis", and girt himself with a sword to fight under the father of Pompey for the power of Rome against the Italian allies who were demanding citizenship, the quarrel was in truth rising to its bitterness. Marius and Sulla were on the same side in that war. But Marius had then not only been Consul, but had been six times Consul; and he had beaten the Teutons and the Cimbrians, by whom Romans had feared that all Italy would be occupied. What was not within the power of such a leader of soldiers? and what else but a leader of soldiers could prevail when Italy and Rome, but for such a

General, had been at the mercy of barbaric hordes, and when they had been compelled to make that General six times Consul?

Marias seems to have been no politician. He became a soldier and then a General; and because he was great as a soldier and General, the affairs of the State fell into his hands with very little effort. In the old days of Rome military power had been needed for defence, and successful defence had of course produced aggressive masterhood and increased territory. When Hannibal, while he was still lingering in Italy, had been circumvented by the appearance of Scipio in Africa and the Romans had tasted the increased magnificence of external conquest, the desire for foreign domination became stronger than that of native rule. From that time arms were in the ascendant rather than policy. Up to that time a Consul had to become a General, because it was his business to look after the welfare of the State. After that time a man became a Consul in order that he might be a General. The toga was made to give way to the sword, and the noise of the Forum to the trumpets. We, looking back now, can see that it must have been so, and we are prone to fancy that a wise man looking forward then might have read the future. In the days of Marius there was probably no man so wise. Caesar was the first to see it. Cicero would have seen it, but that the idea was so odious to him that he could not acknowledge to himself that it need be so. His life was one struggle against the coming evil—against the time in which brute force was to be made to dominate intellect and civilization. His "cedant arma togae" was a scream, an impotent scream, against all that Sulla had done or Caesar was about to do. The mischief had been effected years before his time, and had gone too far ahead to be arrested even by his tongue. Only, in considering these things, let us confess that Cicero saw what was good and what was evil, though he was mistaken in believing that the good was still within reach.

Marius in his way was a Caesar—as a soldier, undoubtedly a very efficient Caesar-having that great gift of ruling his own appetites which enables those who possess it to conquer the appetites of others. It may be doubted whether his quickness in stopping and overcoming the two great hordes from the north, the Teutons and the Cimbrians, was not equal in strategy to anything that Caesar accomplished in Gaul. It is probable that Caesar learned much of his tactics from studying the manoeuvres of Marius. But Marius was only a General. Though he became hot in Roman politics, audacious and confident, knowing how to use and how to disregard various weapons of political power as they had been handed down by tradition and law, the "vetoes" and the auguries, and the official dignities, he used them, or disregarded them, in quest only of power for himself. He was able to perceive how vain was law in such a period as that in which he lived; and that, having risen by force of arms, he must by force of arms keep his place or lose his life. With him, at least, there was no idea of Roman liberty, little probably of Roman glory, except so far as military glory and military power go together.

Sulla was a man endowed with a much keener insight into the political condition of the world around him. To make a dash for power, as a dog might do, and keep it in his clutch as a dog would, was enough for Marius. Sulla could see something of future events. He could understand that, by reducing men around him to a low level, he could make fast his own power over them, and that he could best do this by cutting off the heads of all who stood a little higher than their neighbors. He might thus produce tranquillity, and security to himself and others. Some glimmer of an idea of an Augustan rule was present to him; and with the view of producing it, he re-established many of the usages of the Republic, not reproducing the liberty but the forms of liberty. It seems to have been his idea that a Sullan party might rule the Empire by adherence to these forms. I doubt if Marius had any fixed idea of government. To get the better of his enemies, and then to grind them into powder under his feet, to seize rank and power and riches, and then to enjoy them, to sate his lust with blood and money and women, at last even with wine, and to feed his revenge by remembering the hard things which he was made to endure during the period of his overthrow— this seems to have been enough for Marius. [53] With Sulla there was understanding that the Empire must be ruled, and that the old ways would be best if they could be made compatible, with the newly-concentrated power.

The immediate effect upon Rome, either from one or from the other, was nearly the same. In the year 87 B. C. Marius occupied himself in slaughtering the Sullan party—during which, however, Sulla escaped from Rome to the army of which he was selected as General, and proceeded to Athens and the East with the object of conquering Mithridates; for, during these personal contests, the command of this expedition had been the chief bone of contention among them. Marius, who was by age unfitted, desired to obtain it in order that Sulla might not have it. In the next year, 86 B. C., Marius died, being then Consul for the seventh time. Sulla was away in the East, and did not return till 83 B. C. In the interval was that period of peace, fit for study, of which Cicero afterward spoke. "Triennium fere fuit urbs sine armis. "[54] Cicero was then twenty-two or twenty-three years old, and must well have understood, from his remembrance of the Marian massacres, what it was to have the city embroiled by arms. It was not that men were fighting, but that they were simply being killed at the pleasure of the slaughterer. Then Sulla came back, 83 B. C., when Cicero was twenty-four; and if Marius had scourged the city with rods, he scourged it with scorpions. It was the city, in truth, that was scourged, and not simply the hostile faction. Sulla began by proscribing 520 citizens declaring that he had included in his list all that he remembered, and that those forgotten should be added on another day. The numbers were gradually raised to 4,7OO! Nor did this merely mean that those named should be caught and killed by some miscalled officers of justice. [55] All the public was armed against the wretched, and any who should protect them were also doomed to death. This, however, might have been comparatively inefficacious to inflict the amount of punishment intended by Sulla. Men generally do not specially desire to imbrue their hands in the blood of other men. Unless strong hatred be at work, the ordinary man, even the ordinary Roman, will hardly rise up and slaughter another for the sake of the employment. But if lucre be added to blood, then blood can be made to flow copiously. This was what Sulla did. Not only was the victim's life proscribed, but his property was proscribed also; and the man who busied himself in carrying out the great butcher's business assiduously, ardently, and unintermittingly, was rewarded by the property so obtained. Two talents[56] was to be the fee for mere assassination; but the man who knew how to carry on well the work of an informer could earn many talents. It was thus that fortunes were made in the last days of Sulla. It was not only those 520 who were named for killing. They were but the firstlings of the flock—the few victims selected before the real workmen understood how valuable a trade proscription and confiscation might be made. Plutarch tells us how a quiet gentleman walking, as was his custom, in the Forum, one who took no part in politics, saw his own name one day on the list. He had an Alban villa, and at once knew that his villa had been his ruin. He had hardly read the list, and had made his exclamation, before he was slaughtered. Such was the massacre of Sulla, coming with an interval of two or three years after those of Marius, between which was the blessed time in which Rome was without arms. In the time of Marius, Cicero was too young, and of no sufficient importance, on account of his birth or parentage, to fear anything. Nor is it probable that Marius would have turned against his townsmen. When Sulla's turn came, Cicero, though not absolutely connected with the Dictator, was, so to say, on his side in politics. In going back even to this period we may use the terms Liberals and Conservatives for describing the two parties. Marius was for the people; that is to say, he was opposed to the rule of the oligarchy, dispersed the Senate, and loved to feel that his own feet were on the necks of the nobility. Of liberty, or rights, or popular institutions he recked nothing; but not the less was he supposed to be on the people's side. Sulla, on the other hand, had been born a patrician, and affected to preserve the old traditions of oligarchic rule; and, indeed, though he took all the power of the State into his own hands, he did restore, and for a time preserve, these old traditions. It must be presumed that there was at his heart something of love for old Rome. The proscriptions began toward the end of the year 82 B. C., and were continued through eight or nine fearful months—up to the beginning of June, 81 B. C. A day was fixed at which there should be no more slaughtering—no more slaughtering, that is, without special order in each case, and no more confiscation—except such as might be judged necessary by those who had not as yet collected their prey from past victims. Then Sulla, as Dictator, set himself to work to reorganize the old laws. There should still be Consuls and Praetors, but with restricted powers, lessened almost down to nothing. It seems hard to gather what was exactly the Dictator's scheme as the future depositary of power when he should himself have left the scene. He did increase the privileges of the Senate; but thinking of the Senate of Rome as he must have thought of it, esteeming those old men as lowly as he must have esteemed them, he could hardly have intended that imperial power should be maintained by dividing it among them. He certainly contemplated no follower to himself, no heir to his power, as Caesar did. When he had been practically Dictator about three years—though he did not continue the use of the objectionable name—he resigned his rule and walked down, as it were, from his throne into private life. I know nothing in history more remarkable than Sulla's resignation; and yet the writers who have dealt with his name give no explanation of it. Plutarch, his biographer, expresses wonder that he should have been willing to descend to private life, and that he who made so many enemies should have been able to do so with security. Cicero says nothing of it. He had probably left Rome before it occurred, and did not return till after Sulla's death. It seems to have been accepted as being in no especial way remarkable. [57] At his own demand, the plenary power of Dictator had been given to him—power to do all as he liked, without reference either to the Senate or to the people, and with an added proviso that he should keep it as long as he thought fit, and lay it down when it pleased him. He did lay it down, flattering himself, probably, that, as he had done his work, he would walk out from his dictatorship like some Camillus of old. There had been no Dictator in Rome for more than a century and a quarter—not since the time of Hannibal's great victories; and the old dictatorships lasted but for a few months or weeks, after which the Dictator, having accomplished the special task, threw up his office. Sulla now affected to do the same; and Rome, after the interval of three years, accepted the resignation in the old spirit. It was natural to them, though only by tradition, that a Dictator should resign—so natural that it required no special wonder. The salt of the Roman Constitution was gone, but the remembrance of the savor of it was still sweet to the minds of the Romans.

It seems certain that no attempt was made to injure Sulla when he ceased to be nominally at the head of the army, but it is probable that he did not so completely divest himself of power as to be without protection. In the year after his abdication he died, at the age of sixty-one, apparently strong as regards general health, but, if Plutarch's story be true, affected with a terrible cutaneous disease. Modern writers have spoken of Sulla as though they would fain have praised him if they dared, because, in spite of his demoniac cruelty, he recognized the expediency of bringing the affairs of the Republic again into order. Middleton calls him the "only man in history in whom the odium of the most barbarous cruelties was extinguished by the glory of his great acts. " Mommsen, laying the blame of the proscriptions on the head of the oligarchy, speaks of Sulla as being either a sword or a pen in the service of the State, as a sword or a pen would be required, and declares that, in regard to the total "absence of political selfishness—although it is true in this respect only—Sulla deserves to be named side by side with Washington. "[58] To us at present who are endeavoring to investigate the sources and the nature of Cicero's character, the attributes of this man would be but of little moment, were it not that Cicero was probably Cicero because Sulla had been Sulla. Horrid as the proscriptions and confiscations were to Cicero—and his opinion of them was expressed plainly enough when it was dangerous to express them[59]—still it was apparent to him that the cause of order (what we may call the best chance for the Republic) lay with the Senate and with the old traditions and laws of Rome, in the re-establishment of which Sulla had employed himself. Of these institutions Mommsen speaks with a disdain which we now cannot but feel to be justified. "On the Roman oligarchy of this period, " he says "no judgment can be passed save one of inexorable and remorseless condemnation; and, like everything connected with it, the Sullan constitution is involved in that condemnation. "[60] We have to admit that the salt had gone out from it, and that there was no longer left any savor by which it could be preserved. But the German historian seems to err somewhat in this, as have also some modern English historians, that they have not sufficiently seen that the men of the day had not the means of knowing all that they, the historians, know. Sulla and his Senate thought that by massacring the Marian faction they had restored everything to an equilibrium. Sulla himself seems to have believed that when the thing was accomplished Rome would go on, and grow in power and prosperity as she had grown, without other reforms than those which he had initiated. There can be no doubt that many of the best in Rome — the best in morals, the best in patriotism, and the best in erudition — did think that, with the old forms, the old virtue would come back. Pompey thought so, and Cicero. Cato thought so, and Brutus. Caesar, when he came to think about it, thought the reverse. But even now to us, looking back with so many things made clear to us, with all the convictions which prolonged success produces, it is doubtful whether some other milder change — some such change as Cicero would have advocated — might not have prevented the tyranny of Augustus, the mysteries of Tiberius, the freaks of Caligula, the folly of Claudius, and the madness of Nero.

It is an uphill task, that of advocating the cause of a man who has failed. The Caesars of the world are they who make interesting stories. That Cicero failed in the great purpose of his life has to be acknowledged. He had studied the history of his country, and was aware that hitherto the world had produced nothing so great as Roman power; and he knew that Rome had produced true patriotism. Her Consuls, her Censors, her Tribunes, and her Generals had, as a rule, been true to Rome, serving their country, at any rate till of late years, rather than themselves. And he believed that liberty had existed in Rome, though nowhere else. It would be well if we could realize the idea of liberty which Cicero entertained. Liberty was very dear to him — dear to him not only as enjoying it himself, but as a privilege for the enjoyment of others. But it was only the liberty of a few. Half the population of the Roman cities were slaves, and in Cicero's time the freedom of the city, which he regarded as necessary to liberty, belonged only to a small proportion of the population of Italy. It was the liberty of a small privileged class for which he was anxious. That a Sicilian should be free under a Roman Proconsul, as a Roman citizen was entitled to be, was abhorrent to his doctrine. The idea of cosmopolitan freedom—an idea which exists with us, but is not common to very many even now—had not as yet been born: that care for freedom which springs from a desire to do to others as we would that they should do to us. It required Christ to father that idea; and Cicero, though he was nearer to Christianity than any who had yet existed, had not reached it. But this liberty, though it was but of a few, was so dear to him that he spent his life in an endeavor to preserve it. The kings had been expelled from Rome because they had trampled on liberty. Then came the Republic, which we know to have been at its best no more than an oligarchy; but still it was founded on the idea that everything should be done by the votes of the free people. For many years everything was done by the votes of the free people. Under what inducements they had voted is another question. Clients were subject to their patrons, and voted as they were told. We have heard of that even in England, where many of us still think that such a way of voting is far from objectionable. Perhaps compulsion was sometimes used—a sort of "rattening" by which large bodies were driven to the poll to carry this or the other measure. Simple eloquence prevailed with some, and with others flattery. Then corruption became rampant, as was natural, the rich buying the votes of the poor; and votes were bought in various ways—by cheap food as well as by money, by lavish expenditure in games, by promises of land, and other means of bribery more or less overt. This was bad, of course. Every freeman should have given a vote according to his conscience. But in what country—the millennium not having arrived in any—has this been achieved? Though voting in England has not always been pure, we have not wished to do away with the votes of freemen and to submit everything to personal rule. Nor did Cicero.

He knew that much was bad, and had himself seen many things that were very evil. He had lived through the dominations of Marius and Sulla, and had seen the old practices of Roman government brought down to the pretence of traditional forms. But still, so he thought, there was life left in the old forms, if they could be revivified by patriotism, labor, and intelligence. It was the best that he could imagine for the State—infinitely better than the chance of falling into the bloody hands of one Marius and one Sulla after another.

Mommsen tells us that nothing could be more rotten than the condition of oligarchical government into which Rome had fallen; and we are inclined to agree with Mommsen, because we have seen what followed. But that Cicero, living and seeing it all as a present spectator, should have hoped better things, should not, I think, cause us to doubt either Cicero's wisdom or his patriotism. I cannot but think that, had I been a Roman of those days, I should have preferred Cicero, with his memories of the past, to Caesar, with his ambition for the future.

Looking back from our standing-point of to-day, we know how great Rome was—infinitely greater, as far as power is concerned, than anything else which the world has produced. It came to pass that "Urbis et orbis" was not a false boast. Gradually growing from the little nest of robbers established on the banks of the Tiber, the people of Rome learned how to spread their arms over all the known world, and to conquer and rule, while they drew to themselves all that the ingenuity and industry of other people had produced. To do this, there must have been not only courage and persistence, but intelligence, patriotism, and superior excellence in that art of combination of which government consists. But yet, when we look back, it is hard to say when were the palmy days of Rome. When did those virtues shine by which her power was founded? When was that wisdom best exhibited from which came her capacity for ruling? Not in the time of her early kings, whose mythic virtues, if they existed, were concerned but in small matters; for the Rome of the kings claimed a jurisdiction extending as yet but a few miles from the city. And from the time of their expulsion, Rome, though she was rising in power, was rising slowly, and through such difficulties that the reader of history, did he not know the future, would think from time to time that the day of her destruction had come upon her. Not when Brennus was at Rome with his Gauls, a hundred and twenty-five years after the expulsion of the kings, could Rome be said to have been great; nor when, fifty or sixty years afterward, the Roman army—the only army which Rome then possessed—had to lay down its arms in the Caudine Forks and pass under the Samnite yoke. Then, when the Samnite wars were ended, and Rome was mistress in Italy—mistress, after all, of no more than Southern Italy—the Punic wars began. It could hardly have been during that long contest with Carthage, which was carried on for nearly fifty years, that the palmy days of Rome were at their best. Hannibal seems always to be the master. Trebia, Thrasymene and Canne, year after year, threaten complete destruction to the State. Then comes the great Scipio; and no doubt, if we must mark an era of Roman greatness, it would be that of the battle of Zama and the submission of Carthage, 201 years before Christ. But with Scipio there springs up the idea of personal ambition; and in the Macedonian and Greek wars that follow, though the arm of Rome is becoming stronger every day, and her shoulders broader, there is already the glamour of her decline in virtue. Her dealings with Antiochus, with Pyrrhus, and with the Achaeans, though successful, were hardly glorious. Then came the two Gracchi, and the reader begins to doubt whether the glory of the Republic is not already over. They demanded impossible reforms, by means as illegal as they were impossible, and were both killed in popular riots. The war with Jugurtha followed, in which the Romans were for years unsuccessful, and during which German hordes from the north rushed into Gaul and destroyed an army of 80,000 Romans. This brings us to Marius and to Sulla, of whom we have already spoken, and to that period of Roman politics which the German historian describes as being open to no judgment "save one of inexorable and remorseless condemnation. "

But, in truth, the history of every people and every nation will be subject to the same criticism, if it be regarded with the same severity. In all that man has done as yet in the way of government, the seeds of decay are apparent when looked back upon from an age in advance. The period of Queen Elizabeth was very great to us; yet by what dangers were we enveloped in her days! But for a storm at sea, we might have been subjected to Spain. By what a system of falsehood and petty tyrannies were we governed through the reigns of James I. and Charles I.! What periods of rottenness and danger there have been since! How little glorious was the reign of Charles II.! how full of danger that of William! how mean those of the four Georges, with the dishonesty of ministers such as Walpole and Newcastle! And to-day, are there not many who are telling us that we are losing the liberties which our forefathers got for us, and that no judgment can be passed on us "save one of inexorable and remorseless condemnation? " We are a great nation, and the present threatenings are probably vain. Nevertheless, the seeds of decay are no doubt inherent in our policies and our practices—so manifestly inherent that future historians will pronounce upon them with certainty.

But Cicero, not having the advantage of distance, having simply in his mind the knowledge of the greatness which had been achieved, and in his heart a true love for the country which had achieved it, and which was his own, encouraged himself to think that the good might be recovered and the bad eliminated. Marius and Sulla— Pompey also, toward the end of his career, if I can read his character rightly—Caesar, and of course Augustus, being all destitute of scruple, strove to acquire, each for himself, the power which the weak hands of the Senate were unable to grasp. However much, or however little, the country of itself might have been to any of them, it seemed good to him, whether for the country's sake or for his own, that the rule should be in his own hands. Each had the opportunity, and each used it, or tried to use it. With Cicero there is always present the longing to restore the power to the old constitutional possessors of it. So much is admitted, even by his bitter enemies; and I am sometimes at a loss whether to wonder most that a man of letters, dead two thousand years ago, should have enemies so bitter or a friend so keenly in earnest about him as I am. Cicero was aware quite as well as any who lived then, if he did not see the matter clearer even than any others, that there was much that was rotten in the State. Men who had been murderers on behalf of Marius, and then others who had murdered on behalf of Sulla—among whom that Catiline, of whom we have to speak presently, had been one— were not apt to settle themselves down as quiet citizens. The laws had been set aside. Even the law courts had been closed. Sulla had been law, and the closests of his favorites had been the law courts. Senators had been cowed and obedient. The Tribunes had only been mock Tribunes. Rome, when Cicero began his public life, was still trembling. The Consuls of the day were men chosen at Sulla's command. The army was Sulla's army. The courts were now again opened by Sulla's permission. The day fixed by Sulla when murderers might no longer murder—or, at any rate, should not be paid for murdering—had arrived. There was not, one would say, much hope for good things. But Sulla had reproduced the signs of order, and the best hope lay in that direction. Consuls, Praetors, Quaestors, Aediles, even Tribunes, were still there. Perhaps it might be given to him, to Cicero, to strengthen the hands of such officers. At any rate, there was no better course open to him by which he could serve his country.

The heaviest accusation brought against Cicero charges him with being insincere to the various men with whom he was brought in contact in carrying out the purpose of his life, and he has also been accused of having changed his purpose. It has been alleged that, having begun life as a democrat, he went over to the aristocracy as soon as he had secured his high office of State. As we go on, it will be my object to show that he was altogether sincere in his purpose, that he never changed his political idea, and that, in these deviations as to men and as to means, whether, for instance, he was ready to serve Caesar or to oppose him, he was guided, even in the insincerity of his utterances, by the sincerity of his purpose. I think that I can remember, even in Great Britain, even in the days of Queen Victoria, men sitting check by jowl on the same Treasury bench who have been very bitter to each other with anything but friendly words. With us fidelity in friendship is, happily, a virtue. In Rome expediency governed everything. All I claim for Cicero is, that he was more sincere than others around him.

NOTES:

[52] It was then that the foreign empire commenced, in ruling which the simplicity and truth of purpose and patriotism of the Republic were lost.

[53] The reverses of fortune to which Marius was subjected, how he was buried up to his neck in the mud, hiding in the marshes of Minturne, how he would have been killed by the traitorous magistrates of that city but that he quelled the executioners by the fire of his eyes; how he sat and glowered, a houseless exile, among the ruins of Carthage—all which things happened to him while he was running from the partisans of Sulla—are among the picturesque episodes of history. There is a tragedy called the *Wounds of Civil War*, written by Lodge, who was born some eight years before Shakspeare, in which the story of Marius is told with some exquisite poetry, but also with some ludicrous additions. The Gaul who is hired to kill Marius, but is frightened by his eyes, talks bad French mingled with bad English, and calls on Jesus in his horror!

[54] Brutus, ca. xc.

[55] Florus tells us that there were 2000 Senators and Knights, but that any one was allowed to kill just whom he would. "Quis autem illos potest computare quos in erbe passim quisquis voluit occidit" (lib. iii., ca. 21).

[56] About £487 10s. In Smith's Dictionary of Greek and Roman Antiquities the Attic talent is given as being worth £243 15s.

Mommsen quotes the price as 12,000 denarii, which would amount to about the same sum.

[57] Suetonius speaks of his death. Florus mentions the proscriptions and abdication. Velleius Paterculus is eloquent in describing the horrors of the massacres and confiscation. Dio Cassius refers again and again to the Sullan cruelty. But none of them give a reason for the abdication of Sulla.

[58] Vol. iii., p. 386. I quote from Mr. Dickson's translation, as I do not read German.

[59] In defending Roscius Amerinus, while Sulla was still in power, he speaks of the Sullan massacres as "pugna Cannensis, " a slaughter as foul, as disgraceful, as bloody as had been the defeat at Canne.

[60] Mommsen, vol. iii., p. 385.

CHAPTER IV.

HIS EARLY PLEADINGS. —SEXTUS ROSCIUS AMERINUS. —HIS
INCOME.

[Sidenote: B.C. 80, *aetat.* 27]

We now come to the beginning of the work of Cicero's life. This at first consisted in his employment as an advocate, from which he gradually rose into public or political occupation, as so often happens with a successful barrister in our time. We do not know with absolute certainty even in what year Cicero began his pleadings, or in what cause. It may probably have been in 81 B. C., when he was twenty-five, or in his twenty-sixth year. Of the pleadings of which we know the particulars, that in the defence of Sextus Roscius Amerinus, which took place undoubtedly in the year 80 B. C., etat twenty-seven, was probably the earliest. As to that, we have his speech nearly entire, as we have also one for Publius Quintius, which has generally been printed first among the orator's works. It has, however, I think, been made clear that that spoken for Sextus Roscius came before it. It is certain that there had been others before either of them. In that for Sextus he says that he had never spoken before in any public cause, [61] such as was the accusation in which he was now engaged, from which the inference has to be made that he had been engaged in private causes; and in that for Quintius he declares that there was wanting to him in that matter an aid which he had been accustomed to enjoy in others. [62] No doubt he had tried his 'prentice hand in cases of less importance. That of these two the defence of Sextus Roscius came first, is also to be found in his own words. More than once, in pleading for Quintius, he speaks of the proscriptions and confiscations of Sulla as evils then some time past. These were brought nominally to a close in June, 81; but it has been supposed by those who have placed this oration first that it was spoken in that very year. This seems to have been impossible. "I am most unwilling, " says he, "to call to mind that subject, the very memory of which should be wiped out from our thoughts. "[63] When the tone of the two speeches is compared, it will become evident that that for Sextus Roscius was spoken the first. It was, as I have said, spoken in his twenty-seventh year, B.C. 80, the year after the proscription lists had been closed, when Sulla was still Dictator, and when the sales of confiscated goods, though no longer legal, were still carried on under assumed authority. As to such violation of Sulla's own enactment, Cicero excuses the Dictator in this very speech, likening him to Great Jove the Thunderer. Even "Jupiter Optimus Maximus, " as he is whose nod the heavens, the earth, and seas obey—even he cannot so look after his numerous affairs but that the winds and the storms will be too strong sometimes, or the heat too great, or the cold too bitter. If so, how can we wonder that Sulla, who has to rule the State, to govern, in fact, the world, should not be able himself to see to everything? Jove probably found it convenient not to see many things. Such must certainly have been the case with Sulla.

I will venture, as other biographers have done before, to tell the story of Sextus Roscius of Ameria at some length, because it is in itself a tale of powerful romance, mysterious, grim, betraying guilt of the deepest dye, misery most profound, and audacity unparalleled; because, in a word, it is as interesting as any novel that modern fiction has produced; and also, I will tell it, because it lets in a flood of light upon the condition of Rome at the time. Our hair is made to stand on end when we remember that men had to pick their steps in such a State as this, and to live if it were possible, and, if not, then to be ready to die. We come in upon the fag-end of the proscription, and see, not the bloody wreath of Sulla as he triumphed on his Marian foes, not the cruel persecution of the ruler determined to establish his order of things by slaughtering every foe, but the necessary accompaniments of such ruthless deeds—those attendant villanies for which the Jupiter Optimus Maximus of the day had neither ears nor eyes. If in history we can ever get a glimpse at the real life of the people, it is always more interesting than any account of the great facts, however grand.

The Kalends of June had been fixed by Sulla as the day on which the slaughter legalized by the proscriptions should cease. In the September following an old gentleman named Sextus Roscius was murdered in the streets of Rome as he was going home from supper one night, attended by two slaves. By whom he was murdered, probably more than one or two knew then, but nobody knows now. He was a man of reputation, well acquainted with the Metelluses and Messalas of the day, and passing rich. His name had been down on no proscription list, for he had been a friend of Sulla's friends. He was supposed, when he was murdered, to be worth about six million of sesterces, or something between fifty and sixty thousand pounds of our money. Though there was at that time much money in Rome,

The Life of Cicero, Volume I

this amounted to wealth; and though we cannot say who murdered the man, we may feel sure that he was murdered for his money.

Immediately on his death his chattels were seized and sold—or divided, probably, without being sold—including his slaves, in whom, as with every rich Roman, much of his wealth was invested; and his landed estates—his farms, of which he had many—were also divided. As to the actual way in which this was done, we are left much in the dark. Had the name of Sextus Roscius been on one of the lists, even though the list would then have been out of date, we could have understood that it should have been so. Jupiter Optimus Maximus could not see everything, and great advantages were taken. We must only suppose that things were so much out of order that they who had been accustomed to seize upon the goods of the proscribed were able to stretch their hands so as to grasp almost anything that came in their way. They could no longer procure a rich man's name to be put down on the list, but they could pretend that it had been put down. At any rate, certain persons seized and divided the chattels of the murdered man as though he had been proscribed.

Old Roscius, when he was killed, had one son, of whom we are told that he lived always in the country at Ameria, looking after his father's farms, never visiting the capital, which was distant from Ameria something under fifty miles; a rough, uncouth, and probably honest man—one, at any rate, to whom the ways of the city were unknown, and who must have been but partially acquainted with the doings of the time. [64] As we read the story, we feel that very much depends on the character of this man, and we are aware that our only description of him comes from his own advocate. Cicero would probably say much which, though beyond the truth, could not be absolutely refuted, but would state as facts nothing that was absolutely false. Cicero describes him as a middle-aged man, who never left his farm, doing his duty well by his father, as whose agent he acted on the land—a simple, unambitious, ignorant man, to whom one's sympathies are due rather than our antipathy, because of his devotion to agriculture. He was now accused of having murdered his father. The accusation was conducted by one Erucius, who in his opening speech—the speech made before that by Cicero—had evidently spoken ill of rural employments. Then Cicero reminds him, and the judges, and the Court how greatly agriculture had been honored in the old days, when Consuls were taken from the ploughs. The imagination, however, of the reader pictures to itself a man who could hardly have been a Consul at any time—one

62

silent, lonely, uncouth, and altogether separate from the pleasant intercourses of life. Erucius had declared of him that he never took part in any festivity. Cicero uses this to show that he was not likely to have been tempted by luxury to violence. Old Roscius had had two sons, of whom he had kept one with him in Rome—the one, probably, whose society had been dearest to him. He, however, had died, and our Roscius—Sextus Roscius Amerinus, as he came to be called when he was made famous by the murder—was left on one of the farms down in the country. The accusation would probably not have been made, had he not been known to be a man sullen, silent, rough, and unpopular—as to whom such a murder might be supposed to be credible.

Why should any accusation have been made unless there was clear evidence as to guilt? That is the first question which presents itself. This son received no benefit from his father's death. He had in fact been absolutely beggared by it—had lost the farm, the farming utensils, every slave in the place, all of which had belonged to his father, and not to himself. They had been taken, and divided; taken by persons called "Sectores, " informers or sequestrators, who took possession of and sold—or did not sell—confiscated goods. Such men in this case had pounced down upon the goods of the murdered man at once and swallowed them all up, not leaving an acre or a slave to our Roscius. Cicero tells us who divided the spoil among them. There were two other Rosciuses, distant relatives, probably, both named Titus; Titus Roscius Magnus, who sojourned in Rome, and who seems to have exercised the trade of informer and assassin during the proscriptions, and Titus Roscius Capito, who, when at home, lived at Ameria, but of whom Cicero tells us that he had become an apt pupil of the other during this affair. They had got large shares, but they shared also with one Chrysogonus, the freedman and favorite of Sulla, who did the dirty work for Jupiter Optimus Maximus when Jupiter Optimus Maximus had not time to do it himself. We presume that Chrysogonus had the greater part of the plunder. As to Capito, the apt pupil, we are told again and again that he got three farms for himself.

Again, it is necessary to say that all these facts come from Cicero, who, in accordance with the authorized practice of barristers, would scruple at saying nothing which he found in his instructions. How instructions were conveyed to an advocate in those days we do not quite know. There was no system of attorneys. But the story was probably made out for the "patronus" or advocate by an underling, and in some way prepared for him. That which was thus prepared he exaggerated as the case might seem to require. It has to be understood of Cicero that he possessed great art and, no doubt, great audacity in such exaggeration; in regard to which we should certainly not bear very heavily upon him now, unless we are prepared to bear more heavily upon those who do the same thing in our own enlightened days. But Cicero, even as a young man, knew his business much too well to put forward statements which could be disproved. The accusation came first; then the speech in defence; after that the evidence, which was offered only on the side of the accuser, and which was subject to cross-examination. Cicero would have no opportunity of producing evidence. He was thus exempted from the necessity of proving his statements, but was subject to have them all disproved. I think we may take it for granted that the property of the murdered man was divided as he tells us.

If that was so, why should any accusation have been made? Our Sextus seems to have been too much crushed by the dangers of his position to have attempted to get back any part of his father's wealth. He had betaken himself to the protection of a certain noble lady, one Metella, whose family had been his father's friends, and by her and her friends the defence was no doubt managed. "You have my farms, " he is made to say by his advocate; "I live on the charity of another. I abandon everything because I am placid by nature, and because it must be so. My house, which is closed to me, is open to you: I endure it. You have possessed yourself of my whole establishment; I have not one single slave. I suffer all this, and feel that I must suffer it. What do you want more? Why do you persecute me further? In what do you think that I shall hurt you? How do I interfere with you? In what do I oppose you? Is it your wish to kill a man for the sake of plunder? You have your plunder. If for the sake of hatred, what hatred can you feel against him of whose land you have taken possession before you had even known him? "[65] Of all this, which is the advocate's appeal to pity, we may believe as little as we please. Cicero is addressing the judge, and desires only an acquittal. But the argument shows that no overt act in quest of restitution had as yet been made. Nevertheless, Chrysogonus feared such action, and had arranged with the two Tituses that something should be done to prevent it. What are we to think of the condition of a city in which not only could a man be murdered for his wealth walking home from supper—that, indeed, might happen in London if there existed the means of getting at the man's money when the man was dead—but in which such a plot could be concerted in order that the robbery might be consummated?

"We have murdered the man and taken his money under the false plea that his goods had been confiscated. Friends, we find, are interfering—these Metellas and Metelluses, probably. There is a son who is the natural heir. Let us say that he killed his own father. The courts of law, which have only just been reopened since the dear days of proscription, disorder, and confiscation, will hardly yet be alert enough to acquit a man in opposition to the Dictator's favorite. Let us get him convicted, and, as a parricide, sewed up alive in a bag and thrown into the river"—as some of us have perhaps seen cats drowned, for such was the punishment—"and then he at least will not disturb us. " It must have thus been that the plot was arranged.

It was a plot so foul that nothing could be fouler; but not the less was it carried out persistently with the knowledge and the assistance of many. Erucius, the accuser, who seems to have been put forward on the part of Chrysogonus, asserted that the man had caused his father to be murdered because of hatred. The father was going to disinherit the son, and therefore the son murdered the father. In this there might have been some probability, had there been any evidence of such an intention on the father's part. But there was none. Cicero declares that the father had never thought of disinheriting his son. There had been no quarrel, no hatred. This had been assumed as a reason —falsely. There was in fact no cause for such a deed; nor was it possible that the son should have done it. The father was killed in Rome when, as was evident, the son was fifty miles off. He never left his farm. Erucius, the accuser, had said, and had said truly, that Rome was full of murderers. [66] But who was the most likely to have employed such a person: this rough husbandman, who had no intercourse with Rome, who knew no one there, who knew little of Roman ways, who had nothing to get by the murder when committed, or they who had long been concerned with murderers, who knew Rome, and who were now found to have the property in their hands?

The two slaves who had been with the old man when he was killed, surely they might tell something? Here there comes out incidentally the fact that slaves when they were examined as witnesses were tortured, quite as a matter of course, so that their evidence might be extracted. This is spoken of with no horror by Cicero, nor, as far as I can remember, by other Roman writers. It was regarded as an established rule of life that a slave, if brought into a court of law, should be made to tell the truth by such appliances. This was so common that one is tempted to hope, and almost to suppose that the "question" was not ordinarily administered with circumstances of extreme cruelty. We hear, indeed, of slaves having their liberty given them in order that, being free, they may not be forced by torture to tell the truth; [67] but had the cruelty been of the nature described by Scott in "Old Mortality, " when the poor preacher's limbs were mangled, I think we should have heard more of it. Nor was the torture always applied, but only when the expected evidence was not otherwise forth-coming. Cicero explains, in the little dialogue given below, how the thing was carried on. [68] "You had better tell the truth now, my friend: Was it so and so? " The slave knows that, if he says it was so, there is the cross for him, or the "little horse; " but that, if he will say the contrary, he will save his joints from racking. And yet the evidence went for what it was worth.

In this case of Roscius there had certainly been two slaves present; but Cicero, who, as counsel for the defence, could call no witnesses, had not the power to bring them into court; nor could slaves have been made to give evidence against their masters. These slaves, who had belonged to the murdered man, were now the property either of Chrysogonus or of the two Tituses. There was no getting at their evidence but by permission of their masters, and this was withheld. Cicero demands that they shall be produced, knowing that the demand will have no effect. "The man here, " he says, pointing to the accused, "asks for it, prays for it. What will you do in this case? Why do you refuse? "[69]

By this time the reader is brought to feel that the accused person cannot possibly have been guilty; and if the reader, how much more the hearer? Then Cicero goes on to show who in truth were guilty. "Doubt now if you can, judges, by whom Roscius was killed: whether by him who, by his father's death, is plunged into poverty and trouble—who is forbidden even to investigate the truth—or by those who are afraid of real evidence, who themselves possess the plunder, who live in the midst of murder, and on the proceeds of murder. "[70]

Then he addresses one of the Tituses, Titus Magnus, who seems to have been sitting in the court, and who is rebuked for his impudence in doing so: "Who can doubt who was the murderer—you who have got all the plunder, or this man who has lost everything? But if it be added to this that you were a pauper before—that you have been known as a greedy fellow, as a dare-devil, as the avowed enemy of him who has been killed—then need one ask what has brought you to do such a deed as this? "[71]

He next tells what took place, as far as it was known, immediately after the murder. The man had been killed coming home from supper, in September, after it was dark, say at eight or nine o'clock, and the fact was known in Ameria before dawn. Travelling was not then very quick; but a messenger, one Mallius Glaucia, a man on very close terms with Titus Magnus, was sent down at once in a light gig to travel through the night and take the information to Titus Capito Why was all this hurry? How did Glaucia hear of the murder so quickly? What cause to travel all through the night? Why was it necessary that Capito should know all about it at once? "I cannot think, " says Cicero, "only that I see that Capito has got three of the farms out of the thirteen which the murdered man owned! " But Capito is to be produced as a witness, and Cicero gives us to understand what sort of cross-examination he will have to undergo.

In all this the reader has to imagine much, and to come to conclusions as to facts of which he has no evidence. When that hurried messenger was sent, there was probably no idea of accusing the son. The two real contrivers of the murder would have been more on their guard had they intended such a course. It had been conceived that when the man was dead and his goods seized, the fear of Sulla's favorite, the still customary dread of the horrors of the time, would cause the son to shrink from inquiry. Hitherto, when men had been killed and their goods taken, even if the killing and the taking had not been done strictly in accordance with Sulla's ordinance, it had been found safer to be silent and to endure; but this poor wretch, Sextus, had friends in Rome—friends who were friends of Sulla—of whom Chrysogonus and the Tituses had probably not bethought themselves. When it came to pass that more stir was made than they had expected, then the accusation became necessary.

But, in order to obtain the needed official support and aid, Chrysogonus must be sought. Sulla was then at Volaterra, in Etruria perhaps 150 miles north-west from Rome, and with him was his favorite Chrysogonus. In four days from the time of this murder the news was earned thither, and, so Cicero states, by the same messenger—by Glaucia—who had taken it to Ameria. Chrysogonus immediately saw to the selling of the goods, and from this Cicero implies that Chrysogonus and the two Tituses were in partner- ship.

But it seems that when the fact of the death of old Roscius was known at Ameria—at which place he was an occasional resident himself, and the most conspicuous man in the place—the inhabitants, struck with horror, determined to send a deputation to Sulla. Something of what was being done with their townsman's property was probably known, and there seems to have been a desire for justice. Ten townsmen were chosen to go to Sulla, and to beg that he would personally look into the matter. Here, again, we are very much in the dark, because this very Capito, to whom these farms were allotted as his share, was not only chosen to be one of the ten, but actually became their spokesman and their manager. The great object was to keep Sulla himself in the dark, and this Capito managed to do by the aid of Chrysogonus. None of the ten were allowed to see Sulla. They are hoaxed into believing that Chrysogonus himself will look to it, and so they go back to Ameria, having achieved nothing. We are tempted to believe that the deputation was a false deputation, each of whom probably had his little share, so that in this way there might be an appearance of justice. If it was so, Cicero has not chosen to tell that part of the story, having, no doubt, some good advocate's reason for omitting it.

So far the matter had gone with the Tituses, and with Chrysogonus who had got his lion's share. Our poor Roscius, the victim, did at first abandon his property, and allow himself to be awed into silence. We cannot but think that he was a poor creature, and can fancy that he had lived a wretched life during all the murders of the Sullan proscriptions. But in his abject misery he had found his way up among the great friends of his family at Rome, and had there been charged with the parricide, because Chrysogonus and the Tituses began to be afraid of what these great friends might do.

This is the story as Cicero has been able to tell it in hiss speech. Beyond that, we only know that the man was acquitted. Whether he got back part of his father's property there is nothing to inform us. Whether further inquiry was made as to the murder; whether evil befell those two Tituses or Chrysogonus was made to disgorge, there has been no one to inform us. The matter was of little importance in Rome, where murders and organized robberies of the kind were the common incidents of every-day life. History would have meddled with nothing so ordinary had not it happened that the case fell into the hands of a man so great a master of his language that it has been worth the while of ages to perpetuate the speech which he made in the matter. But the story, as a story of Roman life, is interesting, and it gives a slight aid to history in explaining the condition of things which Sulla had produced.

The attack upon Chrysogonus is bold, and cannot but have been offensive to Sulla, though Sulla is by name absolved from immediate blame. Chrysogonus himself, the favorite, he does not spare, saying words so bitter of tone that one would think that the judges—Sulla's judges—would have stopped him, had they been able. "Putting aside Sextus Roscius, " he says, "I demand, first of all, why the goods of an esteemed citizen were sold; then, why have the goods been sold of one who had not himself been proscribed, and who had not been killed while defending Sulla's enemies? It is against those only that the law is made. Then I demand why they were sold when the legal day for such sales had passed, and why they were sold for such a trifle. "[72] Then he gives us a picture of Chrysogonus flaunting down the streets. "You have seen him, judges, how, his locks combed and perfumed, he swims along the Forum "—he, a freedman, with a crowd of Roman citizens at his heels, that all may see that he thinks himself inferior to none—"the only happy man of the day, the only one with any power in his hands. "[73]

This trial was, as has been said, a "causa publica, " a criminal accusation of such importance as to demand that it should be tried before a full bench of judges. Of these the number would be uncertain, but they were probably above fifty. The Preter of the day—the Preter to whom by lot had fallen for that year that peculiar duty—presided, and the judges all sat round him. Their duty seems to have consisted in listening to the pleadings, and then in voting. Each judge could vote[74] "guilty, " "acquitted, " or "not proven, " as they do in Scotland. They were, in fact, jurymen rather than judges. It does not seem that any amount of legal lore was looked for specially in the judges, who at different periods had been taken from various orders of the citizens, but who at this moment, by a special law enacted by Sulla, were selected only from the Senators. We have ample evidence that at this period the judges in Rome were most corrupt. They were tainted by a double corruption: that of standing by their order instead of standing by the public—each man among them feeling that his turn to be accused might come—and that also of taking direct bribes. Cicero on various occasions—on this, for instance, and notably in the trial of Verres, to which we shall come soon—felt very strongly that his only means of getting a true verdict from the majority of judges was to frighten them into temporary honesty by the magnitude of the occasion. If a trial could be slurred through with indifferent advocates, with nothing to create public notice, with no efforts of genius to attract admiration, and a large attendance and consequent sympathy the judgment would, as a matter of course, be bought. In such a case as this of Sextus Roscius, the poor wretch would be condemned, sewed up in his bag, and thrown into the sea, a portion of the plunder would be divided among the judges, and nothing further would be said about it. But if an orator could achieve for himself such a reputation that the world would come and listen to him, if he could so speak that Rome should be made to talk about the trial, then might the judges be frightened into a true verdict. It may be understood, therefore, of what importance it was to obtain the services of a Cicero, or of a Hortensius, who was unrivalled at the Roman bar when Cicero began to plead.

There were three special modes of oratory in which Cicero displayed his powers. He spoke either before the judges—a large body of judges who sat collected round the Praetor, as in the case of Sextus Roscius—or in cases of civil law before a single judge, selected by the Praetor, who sat with an assessor, as in the case of Roscius the actor, which shall be mentioned just now. This was the recognized work of his life, in which he was engaged, at any rate, in his earlier years; or he spoke to the populace, in what was called the Concio, or assembly of the people—speeches made before a crowd called together for a special purpose, as were the second and third orations against Catiline; or in the Senate, in which a political rather than a judicial sentence was sought from the votes of the Senators. There was a fourth mode of address, which in the days of the Emperors became common, when the advocate spoke "ad Principem; " that is, to the Emperor himself, or to some ruler acting for him as sole judge. It was thus that Cicero pleaded before Caesar for Ligarius and for King Deiotarus, in the latter years of his life. In each of these a separate manner and a distinct line had to be adopted, in all of which he seems to have been equally happy, and equally powerful. In judging of his speeches, we are bound to remember that they were not probably uttered with their words arranged as we read them. Some of those we have were never spoken at all, as was the case with the five last Verrene orations, and with the second, by far the longest of the Philippics. Some, as was specially the case with the defence of Milo, the language of which is perhaps as perfect as that of any oration which has reached us from ancient or modern days, were only spoken in part; so that that which we read bears but small relation to that which was heard. All were probably retouched for publication. [75] That words so perfect in their construction should have flowed from a man's mouth, often with but little preparation, we cannot conceive. But we know from the evidence of the day, and from the character which remained of him through after Roman ages, how great was the immediate effect of his oratory. We can imagine him, in this case of Sextus Roscius, standing out in the open air in the Forum, with the movable furniture of the court around him, the seats on which the judges sat with the Praetor in the midst of them, all Senators in their white robes, with broad purple borders. There too were seated, we may suppose on lower benches, the friends of the accused and the supporters of the accusation, and around, at the back of the orator, was such a crowd as he by the character of his eloquence may have drawn to the spot. Cicero was still a young man; but his name had made itself known and we can imagine that some tidings had got abroad as to the bold words which would be spoken in reference to Sulla and Chrysogonus. The scene must have been very different from that of one of our dingy courts, in which the ermine is made splendid only by the purity and learning of the man who wears it. In Rome all exterior gifts were there. Cicero knew how to use them, so that the judges who made so large a part in the pageant should not dare to disgrace themselves because of its publicity. Quintilian gives his pupils much advice as to the way in which they should dress themselves[76] and hold their togas—changing the folds of the garment so as to suit the different parts of the speech—how they should move their arms, and hold their heads, and turn their necks; even how they should comb their hair when they came to stand in public and plead at the bar. All these arts, with many changes, no doubt, as years rolled on, had come down to him from days before Cicero; but he always refers to Cicero as though his were the palmy days of Roman eloquence. We can well believe that Cicero had studied many of these arts by his twenty-seventh year—that he knew how to hold his toga and how to drop it—how to make the proper angle with his elbow—how to comb his hair, and yet not be a fop—and to add to the glory of his voice all the personal graces which were at his command. Sextus Roscius Amerinus, with all his misfortunes, injustices, and miseries, is now to us no more than the name of a fable; but to those who know it, the fable is, I think, more attractive than most novels.

The Life of Cicero, Volume I

We know that Cicero pleaded other causes before he went to Greece in the year 79 B. C., especially those for Publius Quintius, of which we have his speech, and that for a lady of Arretium, in which he defended her right to be regarded as a free woman of that city. In this speech he again attacked Sulla, the rights of the lady in question having been placed in jeopardy by an enactment made by the Dictator; and again Cicero was successful. This is not extant. Then he started on his travels, as to which I have already spoken. While he was absent Sulla died, and the condition of the Republic during his absence was anything but hopeful. Lepidus was Consul during these two years, than whom no weaker officer ever held rule in Rome—or rebelled against Rome; and Sertorius, who was in truth a great man, was in arms against Rome in Spain, as a rebel, though he was in truth struggling to create a new Roman power, which should be purer than that existing in Italy. What Cicero thought of the condition of his country at this time we have no means of knowing. If he then wrote letters, they have not been preserved. His spoken words speak plainly enough of the condition of the courts of law, and let us know how resolved he was to oppose himself to their iniquities. A young man may devote himself to politics with as much ardor as a senior, but he cannot do so if he be intent on a profession. It is only when his business is so well grasped by him as to sit easily on him, that he is able to undertake the second occupation.

There is a rumor that Cicero, when he returned home from Greece, thought for awhile of giving himself up to philosophy, so that he was called Greek and Sophist in ridicule. It is not, however, to be believed that he ever for a moment abandoned the purpose he had formed for his own career. It will become evident as we go on with his life, that this so-called philosophy of the Greeks was never to him a matter of more than interesting inquiry. A full, active, human life, in which he might achieve for himself all the charms of high rank, gilded by intelligence, erudition, and refined luxury, in which also he might serve his country, his order, and his friends—just such a life as our leading men propose to themselves here, to-day, in our country—this is what Cicero had determined to achieve from his earliest years, and it was not likely that he should be turned from it by the pseudo logic of Greek philosophers, That the logic even of the Academy was false to him we have ample evidence, not only in his life but in his writings. There is a story that, during his travels, he consulted the oracle at Delphi as to his future career, and that on being told that he must look to his own genius and not to the opinion of the world at large, he determined to abandon the honors of the

72

Republic. That he should have talked among the young men of the day of his philosophic investigations till they laughed at him and gave him a nickname, may be probable, but it cannot have been that he ever thought of giving up the bar.

In the year of his return to Rome, when he was thirty, he married Terentia, a noble lady, of whom we are informed that she had a good fortune, and that her sister was one of the Vestal Virgins. [77] Her nobility is inferred from the fact that the virgins were, as a rule, chosen from the noble families, though the law required only that they should be the daughters of free parents, and of persons engaged in no mean pursuits. As to the more important question of Terentia's fortune there has never been a doubt. Plutarch, however, does not make it out to have been very great, assuming a sum which was equal to about £4200 of our money. He tells us at the same time that Cicero's own fortune was less than £4000. But in both of these statements, Plutarch, who was forced to take his facts where he could get them, and was not very particular in his authority, probably erred. The early education of Cicero, and the care taken to provide him with all that money could purchase, is, I think, conclusive of his father's wealth; and the mode of life adopted by Cicero shows that at no period did he think it necessary to live as men do live with small incomes.

We shall find, as we go on, that he spent his money freely, as men did at Rome who had the command of large means. We are aware that he was often in debt. We find that from his letters. But he owed money not as a needy man does, but as one who is speculative, sanguine, and quite confident of his own resources. The management of incomes was not so fixed a thing then as it is with us now. Speculation was even more rampant, and rising men were willing and were able to become indebted for enormous sums, having no security to offer but the promise of their future career. Caesar's debts during various times of his life were proverbial. He is said to have owed over £300,000 before he reached his first step in the public employment. Cicero rushed into no such danger as this. We know, indeed, that when the time came to him for public expenditure on a great scale, as, for instance, when he was filling the office of Aedile, he kept within bounds, and he did not lavish money which he did not possess. We know also that he refrained, altogether refrained, from the iniquitous habits of making large fortunes which were open to the great politicians of the Republic. To be Quaestor that he might be Aedile, Aedile that he might be Praetor and Consul, and Praetor and Consul that he might rob a province—pillage Sicily, Spain, or Asia, and then at last come back a rich man, rich enough to cope with all his creditors, and to bribe the judges should he be accused for his misdeeds—these were the usual steps to take by enterprising Romans toward power, wealth, and enjoyment. But it will be observed, in this sequence of circumstances, the robbery of the province was essential to success. This was sometimes done after so magnificent a fashion as to have become an immortal fact in history. The instance of Verres will be narrated in the next chapter but one. Something of moderation was more general, so that the fleeced provincial might still live, and prefer sufferance to the doubtful chances of recovery. A Pro- consul might rob a great deal, and still return with hands apparently clean, bringing with him a score of provincial Deputies to laud his goodness before the citizens at home. But Cicero robbed not at all. Even they who have been most hard upon his name, accusing him of insincerity and sometimes of want of patriotism, because his Roman mode of declaring himself without reserve in his letters has been perpetuated for us by the excellence of their language, even they have acknowledged that he kept his hands studiously clean in the service of his country, when to have clean hands was so peculiar as to be regarded as absurd.

There were other means in which a noble Roman might make money, and might do so without leaving the city. An orator might be paid for his services as an advocate. Cicero, had such a trade been opened to him, might have made almost any sum to which his imagination could have stretched itself. Such a trade was carried on to a very great extent. It was illegal, such payment having been forbidden by the "Lex Cincia De Muneribus, " passed more than a century before Cicero began his pleadings. [78] But the law had become a dead letter in the majority of cases. There can be no doubt that Hortensius, the predecessor and great rival of Cicero, took presents, if not absolute payment. Indeed, the myth of honorary work, which is in itself absurd, was no more practicable in Rome than it has been found to be in England, where every barrister is theoretically presumed to work for nothing. That the "Lex Cincia, " as far as the payment of advocates went, was absurd, may be allowed by us all. Services for which no regular payment can be exacted will always cost more than those which have a defined price. But Cicero would not break the law. It has been hinted rather than stated that he, like other orators of the day, had his price. He himself tells us that he took nothing; and no instance has been adduced that he had ever done so. He is free enough in accusing Hortensius of having accepted a beautiful statuette, an ivory sphinx of great value. What he knew of Hortensius, Hortensius would have known of him, had it been there to know; and what Hortensius or others had heard would certainly have been told. As far as we can learn, there is no ground for accusing Cicero of taking fees or presents beyond the probability that he would do so. I thiuk we are justified in believing that he did not do so, because those who watched his conduct closely found no opportunity of exposing him. That he was paid by different allied States for undertaking their protection in the Senate, is probable, such having been a custom not illegal. We know that he was specially charged with the affairs of Dyrrachium, and had probably amicable relations with other allied communities. This, however, must have been later in life, when his name was sufficiently high to insure the value of his services, and when he was a Senator.

Noble Romans also—noble as they were, and infinitely superior to the little cares of trade—were accustomed to traffic very largely in usury. We shall have a terrible example of such baseness on the part of Brutus—that Brutus whom we have been taught to regard as almost on a par with Cato in purity. To lend money to citizens, or more profitably to allied States and cities, at enormous rates of interest, was the ordinary resource of a Roman nobleman in quest of revenue. The allied city, when absolutely eaten to the bone by one noble Roman, who had plundered it as Proconsul or Governor, would escape from its immediate embarrassment by borrowing money from another noble Roman, who would then grind its very bones in exacting his interest and his principal. Cicero, in the most perfect of his works—the treatise De Officiis, an essay in which he instructs his son as to the way in which a man should endeavor to live so as to be a gentleman—inveighs both against trade and usury. When he tells us that they are to be accounted mean who buy in order that they may sell, we, with our later lights, do not quite agree with him, although he founds his assertion on an idea which is too often supported by the world's practice, namely, that men cannot do a retail business profitably without lying. [79] The doctrine, however, has always been common that retail trade is not compatible with noble bearing, and was practised by all Romans who aspired to be considered among the upper classes. That other and certainly baser means of making money by usury was, however, only too common. Crassus, the noted rich man of Rome in Caesar's day, who was one of the first Triumvirate, and who perished ignominiously in Parthia, was known to have gathered much of his wealth by such means. But against this Cicero is as staunchly severe as against shopkeeping. "First of all, " he says, "these profits are despicable which incur the hatred of men, such as those of gatherers of custom and lenders of money on usury. "[80]

Again, we are entitled to say that Cicero did not condescend to enrich himself by the means which he himself condemns, because, had he done so, the accusations made against him by his contemporaries would have reached our ears. Nor is it probable that a man in addressing his son as to rules of life would have spoken against a method of gathering riches which, had he practised it himself, must have been known to his son. His rules were severe as compared with the habits of the time. His dear friend Atticus did not so govern his conduct, or Brutus, who, when he wrote the De Officiis, was only less dear to him than Atticus. But Cicero himself seems to have done so faithfully. We learn from his letter that he owned house-property in Rome to a considerable extent, having probably thus invested his own money or that of his wife. He inherited also the family house at Arpinum. He makes it a matter for boasting that he had received in the course of his life by legacies nearly £200,000 (twenty million sesterces), in itself a source of great income, and one common with Romans of high position. [81] Of the extent of his income it is impossible to speak, or even make a guess. But we do know that he lived always as a rich man—as one who regards such a condition of life as essentially proper to him; and that though he was often in debt, as was customary with noble Romans, he could always write about his debts in a vein of pleasantry, showing that they were not a heavy burden to him; and we know that he could at all times command for himself villas, books, statues, ornaments, columns, galleries, charming shades, and all the delicious appendages of mingled wealth and intelligence. He was as might be some English marquis, who, though up to his eyes in mortgages, is quite sure that he will never want any of the luxuries befitting a marquis. Though we have no authority to tell us how his condition of life became what it was, it is necessary that we should understand that condition if we are to get a clear insight into his life. Of that condition we have ample evidence. He commenced his career as a youth upon whose behalf nothing was spared, and when he settled himself in Rome, with the purport of winning for himself the highest honors of the Republic, he did so with the means of living like a nobleman.

But the point on which it is most necessary to insist is this: that while so many—I may almost say all around him in his own order—were unscrupulous as to their means of getting money, he kept his hands clean. The practice then was much as it is now. A gentleman in our days is supposed to have his hands clean; but there has got abroad among us a feeling that, only let a man rise high enough, soil will not stick to him. To rob is base; but if you rob enough, robbery will become heroism, or, at any rate, magnificence. With Caesar his debts have been accounted happy audacity; his pillage of Gaul and Spain, and of Rome also, have indicated only the success of the great General; his cruelty, which in cold-blooded efficiency has equalled if not exceeded the blood-thirstiness of any other tyrant, has been called clemency. [82] I do not mean to draw a parallel between Caesar and Cicero. No two men could have been more different in their natures or in their career. But the one has been lauded because he was unscrupulous, and the other has incurred reproach because, at every turn and twist in his life, scruples dominated him. I do not say that he always did what he thought to be right. A man who doubts much can never do that. The thing that was right to him in the thinking became wrong to him in the doing. That from which he has shrunk as evil when it was within his grasp, takes the color of good when it has been beyond his reach. Cicero had not the stuff in him to rule the Rome and the Romans of his period; but he was a man whose hands were free from all stain, either of blood or money; and for so much let him, at any rate, have the credit.

Between the return of Cicero to Rome in 77 B. C. and his election as Quaestor in 75, in which period he married Terentia, he made various speeches in different causes, of which only one remains to us, or rather, a small part of one. This is notable as having been spoken in behalf of that Roscius, the great comic actor, whose name has become familiar to us on account of his excellence, almost as have those of Garrick, of Siddons, and of Talma. It was a pleading as to the value of a slave, and the amount of pecuniary responsibility attaching to Roscius on account of the slave, who had been murdered when in his charge. As to the murder, no question is made. The slave was valuable, and the injury done to his master was a matter of importance. He, having been a slave, could have no stronger a claim for an injury done to himself than would a dog or a horse. The slave, whose name was Panurge—a name which has since been made famous as having been borrowed by Rabelais, probably from this occurrence, and given to his demon of mischief—showed aptitude for acting, and was therefore valuable. Then one Flavius killed him; why or how we do not know; and, having killed him, settled with Roscius for the injury by giving him a small farm. But Roscius had only borrowed or hired the man from one Chaerea—or was in partnership with Chaerea as to the man—and on that account paid something out of the value of the farm for the loss incurred; but the owner was not satisfied, and after a lapse of time made a further claim. Hence arose the action, in pleading which Cicero was successful. In the fragment we have of the speech there is nothing remarkable except the studied clearness of the language; but it reminds us of the opinion which Cicero had expressed of this actor in the oration which he made for Publius Quintius, who was the brother-in-law of Roscius. "He is such an actor, " says Cicero, "that there is none other on the stage worthy to be seen; and such a man that among men he is the last that should have become an actor. "[83] The orator's praise of the actor is not of much importance. Had not Roscius been great in his profession, his name would not have come down to later ages. Nor is it now matter of great interest that the actor should have been highly praised as a man by his advocate; but it is something for us to know that the stage was generally held in such low repute as to make it seem to be a pity that a good man should have taken himself to such a calling.

In the year 76 B. C. Cicero became father of a daughter, whom we shall know as Tullia—who, as she grew up, became the one person whom he loved best in all the world—and was elected Quaestor. Cicero tells us of himself that in the preceding year he had solicited the Quaestorship, when Cotta was candidate for the Consulship and Hortensius for the Praetorship. There are in the dialogue De Claris Oratoribus—which has had the name of Brutus always given to it—some passages in which the orator tells us more of himself than in any other of his works. I will annex a translation of a small portion because of its intrinsic interest; but I will relegate it to an appendix, because it is too long either for insertion in the text or for a note. [84]

NOTES:

[61] Pro Sexto Roscio, ca. xxi. : "Quod antea causam publicam nullam dixerim. " He says also in the Brutus, ca. xc., "Itaque prima causa publica, pro Sex. Roscio dicta. " By "publica causa" he means a criminal accusation in distinction from a civil action.

[62] Pro Publio Quintio, ca. i: "Quod mihi consuevit in ceteris causis esse adjumento, id quoque in hac causa deficit. "

[63] Pro Publio Quintio, ca. xxi: "Nolo eam rem commemorando renovare, cujus omnino rei memoriam omnem tolli funditus ac deleri arbitor oportere. "

[64] Pro Roscio, ca. xlix. Cicero says of him that he would be sure to suppose that anything would have been done according to law of which he should be told that it was done by Sulla's order. "Putat homo imperitus noram, agricola et rusticus, ista omnia, que vos per Sullam gesta esse diciis, more, lege, jure gentium facta. "

[65] Pro Sexto Roscio, ca. 1.

[66] Pro Sexto Roscio, ca. xxix. : "Ejusmodi tempus erat, inquit, ut homines vulgo impune occiderentur. "

[67] Pro T. A. Milone, ca. xxi. : "Cur igitur cos manumisit? Metuebat scilicit ne indicarent; ne dolorem perferre non possent. "

[68] Pro T. A. Milone, ca. xxii. : "Heus tu, Ruscio, verbi gratia, cave sis mentiaris. Clodius insidias fecit Miloni? Fecit. Certa crux. Nullas fecit. Sperata libertas. "

[69] Pro Sexto Roscio, ca. xxviii.

[70] Ibid.

[71] Ibid, ca. xxxi.

[72] Pro Sexto Roscio, ca. xlv.

[73] Pro Sexto Roscio, ca. xlvi. The whole picture of Chrysogonus, of his house, of his luxuries, and his vanity, is too long for quotation, but is worth referring to by those who wish to see how bold and how brilliant Cicero could be.

[74] They put in tablets of wax, on which they recorded their judgement by inscribing letter, C, A, or NL—Condemno, Absolvo, or Non liquent—intending to show that the means of coming to a decision did not seem to be sufficient.

[75] Quintilian tells us, lib. x., ca. vii., that Cicero's speeches as they had come to his day had been abridged—by which he probably means only arranged—by Tiro, his slave and secretary and friend. "Nam Ciceronis ad praesens modo tempus aptatos libertus Tiro contraxit. "

[76] Quintilian, lib. xi., ca. iii. : "Nam et toga, et calecus, et capillus, tam nimia cura, quam negligentia, sunt reprehendenda. " — — "Sinistrum brachium eo usque allevandum est, ut quasi normalem illum angulum faciat. " Quint., lib. xii., ca. x., "ne hirta toga sit; " don't let the toga be rumpled; "non serica: " the silk here interdicted was the silk of effeminacy, not that silk of authority of which our barristers are proud. "Ne intonsum caput; non in gradus atque annulos comptum. " It would take too much space were I to give here all the lessons taught by this professor of deportment as to the wearing of the toga.

[77] A doubt has been raised whether he was not married when he went to Greece, as otherwise his daughter would seem to have become a wife earlier than is probable. The date, however, has been generally given as it is stated here.

[78] Tacitus, Annal., xl, 5, says, "Qua cavetiur antiquitus, ne quis, ob causam orandam, pecuniam donumve accipiat. "

[79] De Off, lib. i., ca. xlii. : "Sordidi etiam putandi, qui mercantur a mercatoribus, quod statim vendant. Nihil enim proficiunt, nisi admodum mentiantur. "

[80] De Off, lib. i, ca. xlii. : "Primum improbantur ii quaestus, qui in odia hominum incurrant: ut portitorum ut foeneratorum. " The Portitores were inferior collectors of certain dues, stationed at seaports, who are supposed to have been extremely vexatious in their dealings with the public.

[81] Philipp, 11-16.

[82] Let any who doubt this statement refer to the fate of the inhabitants of Alesia and Uxellodunum. Caesar did not slay or torture for the sake of cruelty, but was never deterred by humanity when expediency seemed to him to require victims. Men and

women, old and young, many or few, they were sacrificed without remorse if his purpose required it.

[83] Pro Pub. Quintio, ca. xxv.

[84] See Appendix B, Brutus, ca. xcii., xciii.

CHAPTER V.

CICERO AS QUAESTOR.

Cicero was elected Quaestor in his thirtieth year, B.C. 76. He was then nearly thirty-one. His predecessors and rivals at the bar, Cotta and Hortensius, were elected Consul and Praetor, respectively, in the same year. To become Quaestor at the earliest age allowed by the law (at thirty-one, namely) was the ambition of the Roman advocate who purposed to make his fortune by serving the State. To act as Quaestor in his thirty-second year, Aedile in his thirty-seventh, Praetor in his forty-first, and Consul in his forty-fourth year, was to achieve, in the earliest succession allowed by law, all the great offices of trust, power, and future emolument. The great reward of proconsular rapine did not generally come till after the last step, though there were notable instances in which a Propraetor with proconsular authority could make a large fortune, as we shall learn when we come to deal with Verres, and though Aediles, and even Quaestors, could find pickings. It was therefore a great thing for a man to begin as early as the law would permit, and to lose as few years as possible in reaching the summit. Cicero lost none. As he himself tells us in the passage to which I have referred in the last chapter, and which is to be found in the Appendix, he gained the good-will of men — that is, of free Romans who had the suffrage, and who could therefore vote either for him or against him — by the assiduity of his attention to the cases which he undertook, and by a certain brilliancy of speech which was new to them. [85] Putting his hand strenuously to the plough, allowing himself to be diverted by none of those luxuries to which Romans of his day were so wont to give way, he earned his purpose by a resolution to do his very best. He was "Novus Homo" — a man, that is, belonging to a family of which no member had as yet filled high office in the State. Against such there was a strong prejudice with the aristocracy, who did not like to see the good things of the Republic dispersed among an increased number of hands.

The power of voting was common to all Roman male citizens; but the power of influencing the electors had passed very much into the hands of the rich. The admiration which Cicero had determined to elicit would not go very far, unless it could be produced in a very high degree. A Verres could get himself made Praetor; a Lepidus some years since could receive the Consulship; or now an Antony, or almost a Catiline. The candidate would borrow money on the security of his own audacity, and would thus succeed—perhaps with some minor gifts of eloquence, if he could achieve them. With all this, the borrowing and the spending of money, that is, with direct bribery, Cicero would have nothing to do; but of the art of canvassing—that art by which he could at the moment make himself beloved by the citizens who had a vote to give—he was a profound master.

There is a short treatise, De Petitione Consulatus, on canvassing for the Consulship, of which mention may be made here, because all the tricks of the trade were as essential to him, when looking to be Quaestor, as when he afterward desired to be Consul, and because the political doings of his life will hurry us on too quickly in the days of his Consulship to admit of our referring to these lessons. This little piece, of which we have only a fragment, is supposed to have been addressed to Cicero by his brother Quintus, giving fraternal advice as to the then coming great occasion. The critics say that it was retouched by the orator himself. The reader who has studied Cicero's style will think that the retouching went to a great extent, or that the two brothers were very like each other in their power of expression.

The first piece of advice was no doubt always in Cicero's mind, not only when he looked for office, but whenever he addressed a meeting of his fellow-citizens. "Bethink yourself what is this Republic; what it is you seek to be in it, and who you are that seek it. As you go down daily to the Forum, turn the answer to this in your mind: 'Novus sum; consulatum peto; Roma est'—'I am a man of an untried family. It is the Consulship that I seek. It is Rome in which I seek it. '" Though the condition of Rome was bad, still to him the Republic was the greatest thing in the world, and to be Consul in that Republic the highest honor which the world could give.

There is nobility in that, but there is very much that is ignoble in the means of canvassing which are advocated. I cannot say that they are as yet too ignoble for our modern use here in England, but they are too ignoble to be acknowledged by our candidates themselves, or by their brothers on their behalf. Cicero, not having progressed far enough in modern civilization to have studied the beauty of truth, is held to be false and hypocritical. We who know so much more than he did, and have the doctrine of truth at our fingers' ends, are wise enough to declare nothing of our own shortcomings, but to attribute such malpractices only to others. "It is a good thing to be thought worthy of the rank we seek by those who are in possession of it. " Make yourself out to be an aristocrat, he means. "Canvass them, and cotton to them. Make them believe that in matters of politics you have always been with the aristocracy, never with the mob; " that if "you have at all spoken a word in public to tickle the people, you have done so for the sake of gaining Pompey. " As to this, it is necessary to understand Pompey's peculiar popularity at the moment, both with the Liberals and with the Conservatives. "Above all, see that you have with you the 'jeunesse dorée. ' They carry so much! There are many with you already. Take care that they shall know how much you think of them. "

He is especially desired to make known to the public the iniquities of Catiline, his opponent, as to whom Quintus says that, though he has lately been acquitted in regard to his speculations in Africa, he has had to bribe the judges so highly that he is now as poor as they were before they got their plunder. At every word we read we are tempted to agree with Mommsen that on the Roman oligarchy of the period no judgment can be passed save one, "of inexorable condemnation. "[86]

"Remember, " says Quintus, "that your candidature is very strong in that kind of friendship which has been created by your pleadings. Take care that each of those friends shall know what special business is allotted to him on the occasion; and as you have not troubled any of them yet, make them understand that you have reserved for the present moment the payment of their debts. " This is all very well; but the next direction mingles so much of business with its truth, that no one but Machiavelli or Quintus Cicero could have expressed it in words. "Men, " says Quintus, "are induced to struggle for us in these canvassings by three motives—by memory of kindness done, by the hope of kindness to come, and by community of political conviction. You must see how you are to catch each of these. Small favors will induce a man to canvass for you; and they who owe their safety to your pleadings, for there are many such, are aware that if they do not stand by you now they will be regarded by all the world as sorry fellows. Nevertheless, they should be made to feel that, as they are indebted to you, you will be glad to have an opportunity of becoming indebted to them. But as to those on whom you have a hold only by hope—a class of men very much more numerous, and likely to be very much more active—they are the men whom you should make to understand that your assistance will be always at their command. "

How severe, how difficult was the work of canvassing in Rome, we learn from these lessons. It was the very essence of a great Roman's life that he should live in public; and to such an extent was this carried that we wonder how such a man as Cicero found time for the real work of his life. The Roman patron was expected to have a levee every morning early in his own house, and was wont, when he went down into the Forum, to be attended by a crowd of parasites. This had become so much a matter of course that a public man would have felt himself deserted had he been left alone either at home or abroad. Rome was full of idlers—of men who got their bread by the favors of the great, who lounged through their lives—political quidnuncs, who made canvassing a trade—men without a conviction, but who believed in the ascendency of this or the other leader, and were ready to fawn or to fight in the streets, as there might be need. These were the Quirites of the day—men who were in truth fattened on the leavings of the plunder which was extracted from the allies; for it was the case now that a Roman was content to live on the industry of those whom his father had conquered. They would still fight in the legions; but the work of Rome was done by slaves, and the wealth of Rome was robbed from the Provinces. Hence it came about that there was a numerous class, to whom the name "assectatores" was given, who of course became specially prominent at elections. Quintus divides all such followers into three kinds, and gives instructions as to the special treatment to be applied to each. "There are those who come to pay their respects to you at your own house"—"Salutatores" they were called; "then those who go down with you into the Forum"—"Deductores; " "and after these the third, the class of constant followers"—"Assectatores, " as they were specially named. "As to the first, who are the least in consequence, and who, according to our present ways of living, come in great numbers, you should take care to let them know that their doing even so much as this is much esteemed by you. Let them perceive that you note it when they come, and say as much to their friends, who will repeat your words. Tell themselves often if it be possible. In this way men, when there are many candidates, will observe that there is one who has his eyes open to these courtesies, and they will give themselves heart and soul to him, neglecting all others. And mind you, when you find that a man does but pretend, do not let him perceive that you have perceived it. Should any one wish to excuse himself, thinking that he is suspected of indifference, swear that you have never doubted him, nor had occasion to doubt.

"As to the work of the 'Deductores, ' who go out with you—as it is much more severe than that of those who merely come to pay their compliments, let them understand that you feel it to be so, and, as far as possible, be ready to go into town with them at fixed hours. " Quintus here means that the "Deductores" are not to be kept waiting for the patron longer than can be helped. "The attendance of a daily crowd in taking you down to the Forum gives a great show of character and dignity.

"Then come the band of followers which accompanies you diligently wherever you go. As to those who do this without special obligation, take care that they should know how much you think of them. From those who owe it to you as a duty, exact it rigorously. See that they who can come themselves do come themselves, and that they who cannot, send others in their places. " What an idea does this give as to the labor of a candidate in Rome! I can imagine it to be worse even than the canvassing of an English borough, which to a man of spirit and honor is the most degrading of all existing employments not held to be absolutely disgraceful.

Quintus then goes on from the special management of friends to the general work of canvassing. "It requires the remembering of men's names"—"nomenclationem, " a happy word we do not possess—"flattery, diligence, sweetness of temper, good report, and a high standing in the Republic. Let it be seen that you have been at the trouble to remember people, and practise yourself to it so that the power may increase with you. There is nothing so alluring to the citizen as that. If there be a softness which you have not by nature, so affect it that it shall seem to be your own naturally. You have indeed a way with you which is not unbecoming to a good-natured man; but you must caress men—which is in truth vile and sordid at other times, but is absolutely necessary at elections. It is no doubt a mean thing to flatter some low fellow, but when it is necessary to make a friend it can be pardoned. A candidate must do it, whose face and look and tongue should be made to suit those he has to meet. What perseverance means I need not tell you. The word itself explains itself. As a matter of course, you shall not leave the city; but it is not enough for you to stick to your work in Rome and in the Forum. You must seek out the voters and canvass them separately; and take care that no one shall ask from another what it is that you want from him. Let it have been solicited by yourself, and often solicited. " Quintus seems to have understood the business well, and the elder brother no doubt profited by the younger brother's care.

It was so they did it at Rome. That men should have gone through all this in search of plunder and wealth does not strike us as being marvellous, or even out of place. A vile object justifies vile means. But there were some at Rome who had it in their hearts really to serve their country, and with whom it was at the same time a matter of conscience that, in serving their country, they would not dishonestly or dishonorably enrich themselves. There was still a grain of salt left. But even this could not make itself available for useful purpose without having recourse to tricks such as these!

[Sidenote: B.C. 75, aetat 32.]

In his proper year Cicero became Quaestor, and had assigned to him by lot the duty of looking after the Western Division of Sicily. For Sicily, though but one province as regarded general condition, being under one governor with proconsular authority, retained separate modes of government, or, rather, varied forms of subjection to Rome, especially in matters of taxation, according as it had or had not been conquered from the Carthaginians. [87] Cicero was quartered at Lilybaeum, on the west, whereas the other Quaestor was placed at Syracuse, in the east. There were at that time twenty Quaestors elected annually, some of whom remained in Rome; but most of the number were stationed about the Empire, there being always one as assistant to each Proconsul. When a Consul took the field with an army, he always had a Quaestor with him. This had become the case so generally that the Quaestor became, as it were, something between a private secretary and a senior lieutenant to a governor. The arrangement came to have a certain sanctity attached to it, as though there was something in the connection warmer and closer than that of mere official life; so that a Quaestor has been called a Proconsul's son for the time, and was supposed to feel that reverence and attachment that a son entertains for his father.

But to Cicero, and to young Quaestors in general, the great attraction of the office consisted in the fact that the aspirant having once become a Quaestor was a Senator for the rest of his life, unless he should be degraded by misconduct. Gradually it had come to pass that the Senate was replenished by the votes of the people, not directly, but by the admission into the Senate of the popularly elected magistrates. There were in the time of Cicero between 500 and 600 members of this body. The numbers down to the time of Sulla had been increased or made up by direct selection by the old Kings, or by the Censors, or by some Dictator, such as was Sulla; and the same thing was done afterward by Julius Caesar. The years between Sulla's Dictatorship and that of Caesar were but thirty— from 79 to 49 B. C. These, however, were the years in which Cicero dreamed that the Republic could be re-established by means of an honest Senate, which Senate was then to be kept alive by the constant infusion of new blood, accruing to it from the entrance of magistrates who had been chosen by the people. Tacitus tells us that it was with this object that Sulla had increased the number of Quaestors. [88]Cicero's hopes—his futile hopes of what an honest Senate might be made to do—still ran high, although at the very time in which he was elected Quaestor he was aware that the judges, then elected from the Senate, were so corrupt that their judgment could not be trusted. Of this popular mode of filling the Senate he speaks afterward in his treatise De Legibus. "From those who have acted as magistrates the Senate is composed—a measure altogether in the popular interest, as no one can now reach the highest rank"— namely, the Senate—"except by the votes of the people, all power of selecting having been taken away from the Censors. [89] In his pleadings for P. Sextus he makes the same boast as to old times, not with absolute accuracy, as far as we can understand the old constitution, but with the same passionate ardor as to the body. "Romans, when they could no longer endure the rule of kings, created annual magistrates, but after such fashion that the Council of the Senate was set over the Republic for its guidance. Senators were chosen for that work by the entire people, and the entrance to that order was opened to the virtue and to the industry of the citizens at large. "[90] When defending Cluentius, he expatiates on the glorious privileges of the Roman Senate. "Its high place, its authority, its splendor at home, its name and fame abroad, the purple robe, the ivory chair, the appanage of office, the fasces, the army with its command, the government of the provinces! "[91] On that splendor "apud exteras gentes, " he expatiates in one of his attacks upon Verres. [92] From all this will be seen Cicero's idea of the chamber into which he had made his way as soon as he had been chosen Quaestor.

In this matter, which was the pivot on which his whole life turned— the character, namely, of the Roman Senate—it cannot but be observed that he was wont to blow both hot and cold. It was his nature to do so, not from any aptitude for deceit, but because he was sanguine and vacillating—because he now aspired and now despaired. He blew hot and cold in regard to the Senate, because at times he would feel it to be what it was—composed, for the most part, of men who were time-serving and corrupt, willing to sell themselves for a price to any buyer; and then, again, at times he would think of the Senate as endowed with all those privileges which he names, and would dream that under his influence it would become what it should be—such a Senate as he believed it to have been in its old palmy days. His praise of the Senate, his description of what it should be and might be, I have given. To the other side of the picture we shall come soon, when I shall have to show how, at the trial of Verres, he declared before the judges themselves how terrible had been the corruption of the judgment-seat in Rome since, by Sulla's enactment, it had been occupied only by the Senators. One passage I will give now, in order that the reader may see by the juxtaposition of the words that he could denounce the Senate as loudly as he would vaunt its privileges. In the column on the left hand in the note I quote the words with which, in the first pleading against Verres, he declared "that every base and iniquitous thing done on the judgment-seat during the ten years since the power of judging had been transferred to the Senate should be not only denounced by him, but also proved; " and in that on the right I will repeat the noble phrases which he afterward used in the speech for Cluentius when he chose to speak well of the order. [93] Contra Verrem, Act. i, ca. xiii. : "Omnia non modo commemorabuntur, sed etiam, expositis certis rebus, agentur, quae inter decem annos, posteaquam judicia ad senatum translata sunt, in rebus judicandis nefarie flagitioseque facta sunt. "

It was on the Senate that they who wished well for Rome must depend—on the Senate, chosen, refreshed, and replenished from among the people; on a body which should be at the same time august and popular—as far removed on the one side from the tyranny of individuals as on the other from the violence of the mob; but on a Senate freed from its corruption and dirt, on a body of noble Romans, fitted by their individual character and high rank to rule and to control their fellow-citizens. This was Cicero's idea, and this the state of things which he endeavored to achieve. No doubt he dreamed that his own eloquence and his own example might do more in producing this than is given to men to achieve by such means. No doubt there was conceit in this—conceit and perhaps, vanity. It has to be admitted that Cicero always exaggerated his own powers. But the ambition was great, the purpose noble, and the course of his whole life was such as to bring no disgrace on his aspirations. He did not thunder against the judges for taking bribes, and then plunder a province himself. He did not speak grandly of the duty of a patron to his clients, and then open his hands to illicit payments. He did not call upon the Senate for high duty, and then devote himself to luxury and pleasure. He had a *beau ideal* of the manner in which a Roman Senator should live and work, and he endeavored to work and live up to that ideal. There was no period after his Consulship in which he was not aware of his own failure. Nevertheless, with constant labor, but with intermittent struggles, he went on, till, at the end, in the last fiery year of his existence, he taught himself again to think that even yet there was a chance. How he struggled, and in struggling perished, we shall see by-and-by.

What Cicero did as Quaestor in Sicily we have no means of knowing. His correspondence does not go back so far. That he was very active, and active for good, we have two testimonies, one of which is serious, convincing, and most important as an episode in his life. The other consists simply of a good story, told by himself of himself; not intended at all for his own glorification, but still carrying with it a certain weight. As to the first: Cicero was Quaestor in Lilybaeum in the thirty-second year of his life. In the thirty-seventh year he was elected Aedile, and was then called upon by the Sicilians to attack Verres on their behalf. Verres was said to have carried off from Sicily plunder to the amount of nearly £400,000, [94] after a misrule of three years' duration. All Sicily was ruined. Beyond its pecuniary losses, its sufferings had been excruciating; but not till the end had come of a Governor's proconsular authority could the almost hopeless chance of a criminal accusation against the tyrant be attempted. The tyrant would certainly have many friends in Rome. The injured provincials would probably have none of great mark. A man because he had been Quaestor was not, necessarily, one having influence, unless he belonged to some great family. This was not the case with Cicero. But he had made for himself such a character during his year of office that the Sicilians declared that, if they could trust themselves to any man at Rome, it would be to their former Quaestor. It had been a part of his duty to see that the proper supply of corn was collected in the island and sent to Rome. A great portion of the bread eaten in Rome was grown in Sicily, and much of it was supplied in the shape of a tax. It was the hateful practice of Rome to extract the means of living from her colonies, so as to spare her own laborers. To this, hard as it was, the Sicilians were well used. They knew the amount required of them by law, and were glad enough when they could be quit in payment of the dues which the law required; but they were seldom blessed by such moderation on the part of their rulers. To what extent this special tax could be stretched we shall see when we come to the details of the trial of Verres. It is no doubt only from Cicero's own words that we learn that, though he sent to Rome plenteous supplies, he was just to the dealer, liberal to the pawns, and forbearing to the allies generally; and that when he took his departure they paid him honors hitherto unheard of. [95] But I think we may take it for granted that this statement is true; firstly, because it has never been contradicted; and then from the fact that the Sicilians all came to him in the day of their distress.

As to the little story to which I have alluded, it has been told so often since Cicero told it himself, that I am almost ashamed to repeat it. It is, however, too emblematic of the man, gives us too close an insight both into his determination to do his duty and to his pride—conceit, if you will—at having done it, to be omitted. In his speech for Plancius[96] he tells us that by chance, coming direct from Sicily after his Quaestorship, he found himself at Puteoli just at the season when the fashion from Rome betook itself to that delightful resort. He was full of what he had done—how he had supplied Rome with corn, but had done so without injury to the Sicilians, how honestly he had dealt with the merchants, and had in truth won golden opinions on all sides—so much so that he thought that when he reached the city the citizens in a mob would be ready to receive him. Then at Puteoli he met two acquaintances. "Ah, " says one to him, "when did you leave Rome? What news have you brought? " Cicero, drawing his head up, as we can see him, replied that he had just returned from his province. "Of course, just back from Africa, " said the other. "Not so, " said Cicero, bridling in anger—"stomachans fastidiose, " as he describes it himself—"but from Sicily. " Then the other lounger, a fellow who pretended to know everything, put in his word. "Do you not know that our Cicero has been Quaestor at Syracuse? " The reader will remember that he had been Quaestor in the other division of the island, at Lilybaeum. "There was no use in thinking any more about it, " says Cicero. "I gave up being angry and determined to be like any one else, just one at the waters. " Yes, he had been very conceited, and well understood his own fault of character in that respect; but he would not have shown his conceit in that matter had he not resolved to do his duty in a manner uncommon then among Quaestors, and been conscious that ho had done it.

Perhaps there is no more certain way of judging a man than from his own words, if his real words be in our possession. In doing so, we are bound to remember how strong will be the bias of every man's mind in his own favor, and for that reason a judicious reader will discount a man's praise of himself. But the reader, to get at the truth, if he be indeed judicious, will discount them after a fashion conformable with the nature of the man whose character he is investigating. A reader will not be judicious who imagines that what a man says of his own praises must be false, or that all which can be drawn from his own words in his own dispraise must be true. If a man praise himself for honor, probity, industry, and patriotism, he will at any rate show that these virtues are dear to him, unless the course of his life has proved him to be altogether a hypocrite in such utterances. It has not been presumed that Cicero was a hypocrite in these utterances. He was honest and industrious; he did appreciate honor and love his country. So much is acknowledged; and yet it is supposed that what good he has told us of himself is false. If a man doubt of himself constantly; if in his most private intercourse and closest familiar utterances he admit occasionally his own human weakness; if he find himself to have failed at certain moments, and says so, the very feelings that have produced such confessions are proof that the highest points which have not been attained have been seen and valued. A man will not sorrowfully regret that he has won only a second place, or a third, unless he be alive to the glory of the first. But Cicero's acknowledgments have all been taken as proof against himself. All manner of evil is argued against him from his own words, when an ill meaning can be attached to them; but when he speaks of his great aspirations, he is ridiculed for bombast and vanity. On the strength of some perhaps unconsidered expression, in a letter to Atticus, he is condemned for treachery, whereas the sentences in which he has thoughtfully declared the purposes of his very soul are counted as clap-traps.

No one has been so frequently condemned out of his mouth as Cicero, and naturally. In these modern days we have contemporary records as to prominent persons. Of the characters of those who lived in long-past ages we generally fail to have any clear idea, because we lack those close chronicles which are necessary for the purpose. What insight have we into the personality of Alexander the Great, or what insight had Plutarch, who wrote about him? As to Samuel Johnson, we seem to know every turn of his mind, having had a Boswell. Alexander had no Boswell. But here is a man belonging to those past ages of which I speak who was his own Boswell, and after such a fashion that, since letters were invented, no records have ever been written in language more clear or more attractive. It is natural that we should judge out of his own mouth one who left so many more words behind him than did any one else, particularly one who left words so pleasant to read. And all that he wrote was after some fashion about himself. His letters, like all letters, are personal to himself. His speeches are words coming out of his own mouth about affairs in which he was personally engaged and interested. His rhetoric consists of lessons given by himself about his own art, founded on his own experience, and on his own observation of others. His so-called philosophy gives us the workings of his own mind. No one has ever told the world so much about another person as Cicero has told the world about Cicero. Boswell pales before him as a chronicler of minutiae. It may be a matter of small interest now to the bulk of readers to be intimately acquainted with a Roman who was never one of the world's conquerors. It may be well for those who desire to know simply the facts of the world's history, to dismiss as unnecessary the aspirations of one who lived so long ago. But if it be worth while to discuss the man's character, it must be worth while to learn the truth about it.

"Oh that mine adversary had written a book! " Who does not understand the truth of these words! It is always out of a man's mouth that you may most surely condemn him. Cicero wrote many books, and all about himself. He has been honored very highly. Middleton, in the preface to his own biography, which, with all its charms, has become a by-word for eulogy; quotes the opinion of Erasmus, who tells us that he loves the writings of the man "not only for the divine felicity of his style, but for the sanctity of his heart and morals. " This was the effect left on the mind of an accurate thinker and most just man. But then also has Cicero been spoken of with the bitterest scorn. From Dio Cassius, who wrote two hundred and twenty years after Christ, down to Mr. Froude, whose Caesar has just been published, he has had such hard things said of him by men who have judged him out of his own mouth, that the reader does not know how to reconcile what he now reads with the opinion of men of letters who lived and wrote in the century next after his death—with the testimony of such a man as Erasmus, and with the hearty praises of his biographer, Middleton. The sanctity of his heart and morals! It was thus that Erasmus was struck in reading his works. It is a feeling of that kind, I profess, that has induced me to take this work in hand—a feeling produced altogether by the study of his own words. It has seemed to be that he has loved men so well, has been so anxious for the true, has been so capable of honesty when dishonesty was common among all around him, has been so jealous in the cause of good government, has been so hopeful when there has been but little ground for hope, as to have deserved a reputation for sanctity of heart and morals.

Of the speeches made by Cicero as advocate after his Quaestorship, and before those made in the accusation of Verres, we have the fragment only of the second of two spoken in defence of Marcus Tullius Decula, whom we may suppose to have been distantly connected with his family. He does not avow any relationship. "What, " he says, in opening his argument, "does it become me, a Tullius, to do for this other Tullius, a man not only my friend, but my namesake? " It was a matter of no great importance, as it was addressed to judges not so called, but to "recuperatores, " judges chosen by the Praetor, and who acted in lighter cases.

NOTES:

[85] Brutus, ca. xciii. : "Animos hominum ad me dicendi novitate converteram. "

[86] It must be remembered that this advice was actually given when Cicero subsequently became a candidate for the Consulship, but it is mentioned here as showing the manner in which were sought the great offices of State.

[87] Cicero speaks of Sicily as divided into two provinces, "Quaestores utriusque provinciae" There was, however, but one Praetor or Proconsul. But the island had been taken by the Romans at two different times.

Lilybaeum and the west was obtained from the Carthaginians at the end of the first Punic war, whereas, Syracuse was conquered by Marcellus and occupied during the second Punic war.

[88] Tacitus, Ann., lib. xi., ca. xxii. : "Post, lege Sullae, viginti creati supplendo senatui, cui judica tradiderat. "

[89] De Legibus, iii, xii.

[90] Pro P. Sexto, lxv.

[91] Pro Cluentio, lvi.

[92] Contra Verrem, Act. iv., ca. xi. : "Ecquae civitas est, non modo in provinciis nostris, verum etiam in ultimis nationibus, aut tam potens, aut tam libera, aut etiam am immanis ac barbara; rex denique ecquis est, qui senatorem populi Romani tecto ac domo non invitet? "

[93] Contra Verrem, Act. i, ca. xiii. : "Omnia non modo commemorabuntur, sed etiam, expositis certis rebus, agentur, quae inter decem annos, posteaquam judicia ad senatum translata sunt, in rebus judicandis nefarie flagitioseque facta sunt. " Pro Cluentio, lvi. : "Locus, auctoritas, domi splendor, apud exteras nationes nomen et gratia, toga praetexta, cella curulis, insignia, fasces, exercitus, imperia, provincia. "

[94] Contra Verrem, Act. i., ca. xviii. : "Quadringenties sestertium ex Sicilia contra leges abstulisse. " In Smith's Dictionary of Grecian and Roman Antiquities we are told that a thousand sesterces is equal in our money to £8 17s. 1d. Of the estimated amount of this plunder we shall have to speak again.

[95] Pro Plancio, xxvi.

[96] Pro Plancio, xxvi.

CHAPTER VI.

VERRES

There are six episodes, or, as I may say, divisions in the life of Cicero to which special interest attaches itself. The first is the accusation against Verres, in which he drove the miscreant howling out of the city. The second is his Consulship, in which he drove Catiline out of the city, and caused certain other conspirators who were joined with the arch rebel to be killed, either legally or illegally. The third was his exile, in which he himself was driven out of Rome. The fourth was a driving out, too, though of a more honorable kind, when he was compelled, much against his will, to undertake the government of a province. The fifth was Caesar's passing of the Rubicon, the battle of Pharsalia, and his subsequent adherence to Caesar. The last was his internecine combat with Antony, which produced the Philippics, and that memorable series of letters in which he strove to stir into flames the expiring embers of the Republic. The literary work with which we are acquainted is spread, but spread very unequally, over his whole life. I have already told the story of Sextus Roscius Amerinus, having taken it from his own words. From that time onward he wrote continually; but the fervid stream of his eloquence came forth from him with unrivalled rapidity in the twenty last miserable months of his life.

We have now come to the first of those episodes, and I have to tell the way in which Cicero struggled with Verres, and how he conquered him. In 74 B. C. Verres was Praetor in Rome. At that period of the Republic there were eight Praetors elected annually, two of whom remained in the city, whereas the others were employed abroad, generally with the armies of the Empire. In the next year, 73 B. C., Verres went in due course to Sicily with proconsular or propraetorial authority, having the government assigned to him for twelve months. This was usual and constitutional, but it was not unusual, even if unconstitutional, that this period should be prolonged. In the case of Verres it was prolonged, so that he should hold the office for three years. He had gone through the other offices of the State, having been Quaestor in Asia and Aedile afterward in Rome, to the great misfortune of all who were subjected to his handling, as we shall learn by-and-by. The facts are mentioned here to show that the great offices of the Republic were open to such a man as Verres. They were in fact more

open to such a candidate than they would be to one less iniquitous —
to an honest man or a scrupulous one, or to one partially honest, or
not altogether unscrupulous. If you send a dog into a wood to get
truffles, you will endeavor to find one that will tear up as many
truffles as possible. A proconsular robber did not rob only for
himself; he robbed more or less for all Rome. Verres boasted that
with his three years of rule he could bring enough home to bribe all
the judges, secure all the best advocates, and live in splendid
opulence for the rest of his life. What a dog he was to send into a
wood for truffles!

To such a condition as this had Rome fallen when the deputies from
Sicily came to complain of their late governor, and to obtain the
services of Cicero in seeking for whatever reparation might be
possible. Verres had carried on his plunder during the years 73, 72,
71 B. C. During this time Cicero had been engaged sedulously as an
advocate in Rome. We know the names of some of the cases in which
he was engaged—those, for instance, for Publius Oppius, who,
having been Quaestor in Bithynia, was accused by his Proconsul of
having endeavored to rob the soldiers of their dues. We are told that
the poor province suffered greatly under these two officers, who
were always quarrelling as to a division of their plunder. In this case
the senior officer accused the younger, and the younger, by Cicero's
aid, was acquitted. Quintilian more than once refers to the speech
made for Oppius. Cicero also defended Varenus, who was charged
with having murdered his brother, and one Caius Mustius, of whom
we only know that he was a farmer of taxes. He was advocate also
for Sthenius, a Sicilian, who was accused before the Tribunes by
Verres. We shall hear of Sthenius again among the victims in Sicily.
The special charge in this case was that, having been condemned by
Verres as Praetor in Sicily, he had run away to Rome, which was
illegal. He was, however, acquitted. Of these speeches we have only
some short fragments, which have been quoted by authors whose
works have come down to us, such as Quintilian; by which we
know, at any rate, that Cicero's writings had been so far carefully
preserved, and that they were commonly read in those days. I will
translate here the concluding words of a short paper written by M.
du Rozoir in reference to Cicero's life at this period: "The assiduity
of our orator at the bar had obtained for him a high degree of favor
among the people, because they had seen how strictly he had
observed that Cincian law which forbade advocates to take either
money or presents for then pleadings—which law, however, the
advocates of the day generally did not scruple to neglect. "[97] It is a

good thing to be honest when honesty is in vogue; but to be honest when honesty is out of fashion is magnificent.

In the affair with Verres, there are two matters to interest the reader—indeed, to instruct the reader—if the story were sufficiently well told. The iniquity of Verres is the first—which is of so extravagant a nature as to become farcical by the absurdity of the extent to which he was not afraid to go in the furtherance of his avarice and lust. As the victims suffered two thousand years ago, we can allow ourselves to be amused by the inexhaustible fertility of the man's resources and the singular iniquity of his schemes. Then we are brought face to face with the barefaced corruption of the Roman judges—a corruption which, however, became a regular trade, if not ennobled, made, at any rate, aristocratic by the birth, wealth high names, and senatorial rank of the robbers. Sulla, for certain State purposes—which consisted in the maintenance of the oligarchy— had transferred the privileges of sitting on the judgment-seat from the Equites, or Knights, to the Senators. From among the latter a considerable number—thirty, perhaps, or forty, or even fifty—were appointed to sit with the Praetor to hear criminal cases of importance, and by their votes, which were recorded on tablets, the accused person was acquitted or condemned. To be acquitted by the most profuse corruption entailed no disgrace on him who was tried, and often but little on the judges who tried him. In Cicero's time the practice, with all its chances, had come to be well understood. The Provincial Governors, with their Quaestors and lieutenants, were chosen from the high aristocracy, which also supplied the judges. The judges themselves had been employed, or hoped to be employed, in similar lucrative service. The leading advocates belonged to the same class. If the proconsular thief, when he had made his bag, would divide the spoil with some semblance of equity among his brethren, nothing could be more convenient. The provinces were so large, and the Greek spirit of commercial enterprise which prevailed in them so lively, that there was room for plunder ample, at any rate, for a generation or two. The Republic boasted that, in its love of pure justice, it had provided by certain laws for the protection of its allied subjects against any possible faults of administration on the part of its own officers. If any injury were done to a province, or a city, or even to an individual, the province, or city, or individual could bring its grievance to the ivory chair of the Praetor in Rome and demand redress; and there had been cases not a few in which a delinquent officer had been condemned to banishment. Much, indeed, was necessary before the scheme as it was found to exist by Verres could work itself into perfection. Verres felt that in his time everything had been done for security as well as splendor. He would have all the great officers of State on his side. The Sicilians, if he could manage the case as he thought it might be managed, would not have a leg to stand upon. There was many a trick within his power before they could succeed in making good even their standing before the Praetor. It was in this condition of things that Cicero bethought himself that he might at one blow break through the corruption of the judgment-seat, and this he determined to do by subjecting the judges to the light of public opinion. If Verres could be tried under a bushel, as it were, in the dark, as many others had been tried, so that little or nothing should be said about the trial in the city at large, then there would be no danger for the judges. It could only be by shaming them, by making them understand that Rome would become too hot to hold them, that they could be brought to give a verdict against the accused. This it was that Cicero determined to effect, and did effect. And we see throughout the whole pleadings that he was concerned in the matter not only for the Sicilians, or against Verres. Could something be done for the sake of Rome, for the sake of the Republic, to redeem the courts of justice from the obloquy which was attached to them? Might it be possible for a man so to address himself not only to the judgment-seat, but to all Rome, as to do away with this iniquity once and forever? Could he so fill the minds of the citizens generally with horror at such proceedings as to make them earnest in demanding reform? Hortensius, the great advocate of the day, was not only engaged on behalf of Verres, but he was already chosen as Consul for the next year. Metellus, who was elected Praetor for the next year, was hot in defence of Verres. Indeed, there were three Metelluses among the friends of the accused, who had also on his side the Scipio of the day. The aristocracy of Rome was altogether on the side of Verres, as was natural. But if Cicero might succeed at all in this which he meditated, the very greatness of his opponents would help him. When it was known that he was to be pitted against Hortensius as an advocate, and that he intended to defy Hortensius as the coming Consul, then surely Rome would be awake to the occasion; and if Rome could be made to awake herself, then would this beautiful scheme of wealth from provincial plunder be brought to an end.

I will first speak of the work of the judges, and of the attempts made to hinder Cicero in the business he had undertaken. Then I will endeavor to tell something of the story of Verres and his doings. The subject divides itself naturally in this way. There are extant seven so-called orations about Verres, of which the two first apply to the manner in which the case should be brought before the courts. These two were really spoken, and were so effective that Verres—or probably Hortensius, on his behalf—was frightened into silence. Verres pleaded guilty, as we should say, which, in accordance with the usages of the court, he was enabled to do by retiring and going into voluntary banishment. This he did, sooner than stand his ground and listen to the narration of his iniquities as it would be given by Cicero in the full speech—the "perpetua oratio"—which would follow the examination of the witnesses. "What the orator said before the examination of the witnesses was very short. He had to husband his time, as it was a part of the grand scheme of Hortensius to get adjournment after adjournment because of certain sacred rites and games, during the celebration of which the courts could not sit. All this was arranged for in the scheme; but Cicero, in order that he might baffle the schemers, got through his preliminary work as quickly as possible, saying all that he had to say about the manner of the trial, about the judges, about the scheme, but dilating very little on the iniquities of the criminal. But having thus succeeded, having gained his cause in a great measure by the unexpected quickness of his operations, then he told his story. Then was made that "perpetua oratio" by which we have learned the extent to which a Roman governor could go on desolating a people who were intrusted to his protection. This full narration is divided into five parts, each devoted to a separate class of iniquity. These were never spoken, though they appear in the form of speeches. They would have been spoken, if required, in answer to the defence made by Hortensius on behalf of Verres after the hearing of the evidence. But the defence broke down altogether, in the fashion thus described by Cicero himself. "In that one hour in which I spoke"— this was the speech which we designate as the Actio Prima contra Verrem, the first pleading made against Verres, to which we shall come just now—"I took away all hope of bribing the judges from the accused—from this brazen-faced, rich, dissolute, and abandoned man. On the first day of the trial, on the mere calling of the names of the witnesses, the people of Rome were able to perceive that if this criminal were absolved, then there could be no chance for the Republic. On the second day his friends and advocates had not only lost all hope of gaining their cause, but all relish for going on with it. The third day so paralyzed the man himself that he had to bethink himself not what sort of reply he could make, but how he could escape the necessity of replying by pretending to be ill. "[98] It was in this way that the trial was brought to an end.

But we must go back to the beginning. When an accusation was to be made against some great Roman of the day on account of illegal public misdoings, as was to be made now against Verres, the conduct of the case, which would require probably great labor and expense, and would give scope for the display of oratorical excellence, was regarded as a task in which a young aspirant to public favor might obtain honor and by which he might make himself known to the people. It had, therefore, come to pass that there might be two or more accusers anxious to undertake the work, and to show themselves off as solicitous on behalf of injured innocence, or desirous of laboring in the service of the Republic. When this was the case, a court of judges was called upon to decide whether this man or that other was most fit to perform the work in hand. Such a trial was called "Divinatio, " because the judges had to get their lights in the matter as best they could without the assistance of witnesses—by some process of divination—with the aid of the gods, as it might be. Cicero's first speech in the matter of Verres is called In Quintum Caecilium Divinatio, because one Caecilius came forward to take the case away from him. Here was a part of the scheme laid by Hortensius. To deal with Cicero in such a matter would no doubt be awkward. His purpose, his diligence, his skill, his eloquence, his honesty were known. There must be a trial. So much was acknowledged; but if the conduct of it could be relegated to a man who was dishonest, or who had no skill, no fitness, no special desire for success, then the little scheme could be carried through in that way. So Caecilius was put forward as Cicero's competitor, and our first speech is that made by Cicero to prove his own superiority to that of his rival.

Whether Caecilius was or was not hired to break down in his assumed duty as accuser, we do not know. The biographers have agreed to say that such was the case, [99] grounding their assertion, no doubt, on extreme probability. But I doubt whether there is any evidence as to this. Cicero himself brings this accusation, but not in that direct manner which he would have used had he been able to prove it. The Sicilians, at any rate, said that it was so. As to the incompetency of the man, there was probably no doubt, and it might be quite as serviceable to have an incompetent as a dishonest accuser. Caecilius himself had declared that no one could be so fit as himself for the work. He knew Sicily well, having been born there.

He had been Quaestor there with Verres, and had been able to watch the governor's doings. No doubt there was—or had been in more pious days—a feeling that a Quaestor should never turn against the Proconsul under whom he had served, and to whom he had held the position almost of a son. [100]

But there was less of that feeling now than heretofore. Verres had quarrelled with his Quaestor. Oppius was called on to defend himself against the Proconsul with whom he had served. No one could know the doings of the governor of a province as well as his own Quaestor; and, therefore, so said Caecilius, he would be the preferable accuser. As to his hatred of the man, there could be no doubt as to that. Everybody knew that they had quarrelled. The purpose, no doubt, was to give some colorable excuse to the judges for rescuing Verres, the great paymaster, from the fangs of Cicero.

Cicero's speech on the occasion—which, as speeches went in those days, was very short—is a model of sagacity and courage. He had to plead his own fitness, the unfitness of his adversary, and the wishes in the matter of the Sicilians. This had to be done with no halting phrases. It was not simply his object to convince a body of honest men that, with the view of getting at the truth, he would be the better advocate of the two. We may imagine that there was not a judge there, not a Roman present, who was not well aware of that before the orator began. It was needed that the absurdity of the comparison between them should be declared so loudly that the judges would not dare to betray the Sicilians, and to liberate the accused, by choosing the incompetent man. When Cicero rose to speak, there was probably not one of them of his own party, not a Consul, a Praetor, an Aedile, or a Quaestor, not a judge, not a Senator, not a hanger-on about the courts, but was anxious that Verres with his plunder should escape. Their hope of living upon the wealth of the provinces hung upon it. But if he could speak winged words—words that should fly all over Rome, that might fly also among subject nations—then would the judges not dare to carry out this portion of the scheme.

"When, " he says, "I had served as Quaestor in Sicily, and had left the province after such a fashion that all the Sicilians had a grateful memory of my authority there, though they had older friends on whom they relied much, they felt that I might be a bulwark to them in their need. These Sicilians, harassed and robbed, have now come to me in public bodies, and have implored me to undertake their defence. 'The time has come, ' they say, 'not that I should look after the interest of this or that man, but that I should protect the very life and well-being of the whole province. ' I am inclined by my sense of duty, by the faith which I owe them, by my pity for them, by the example of all good Romans before me, by the custom of the Republic, by the old constitution, to undertake this task, not as pertaining to my own interests, but to those of my close friends. "[101] That was his own reason for undertaking the case. Then he reminds the judges of what the Roman people wished—the people who had felt with dismay the injury inflicted upon them by Sulla's withdrawal of all power from the Tribunes, and by the putting the whole authority of the bench into the hands of the Senators. "The Roman people, much as they have been made to suffer, regret nothing of that they have lost so much as the strength and majesty of the old judges. It is with the desire of having them back that they demand for the Tribunes their former power. It is this misconduct of the present judges that has caused them to ask for another class of men for the judgment-seat. By the fault and to the shame of the judges of to-day, the Censor's authority, which has hitherto always been regarded as odious and stern, even that is now requested by the people. "[102] Then he goes on to show that, if justice is intended, this case will be put into the hands of him whom the Sicilians have themselves chosen. Had the Sicilians said that they were unwilling to trust their affairs to Caecilius because they had not known him, but were willing to trust him, Cicero, whom they did know, would not even that have been reasonable enough of itself? But the Sicilians had known both of them, had known Caecilius almost as well as Cicero, and had expressed themselves clearly. Much as they desired to have Cicero, they were as anxious not to have Caecilius. Even had they held their tongues about this, everybody would have known it; but they had been far from holding their tongues. "Yet you offer yourself to these most unwilling clients, " he says, turning to Caecilius. "Yet you are ready to plead in a cause that does not belong to you! Yet you would defend those who would rather have no defender than such a one as you! "[103] Then he attacks Hortensius, the advocate for Verres. "Let him not think that, if I am to be employed here, the judges can be bribed without infinite danger to all concerned. In undertaking this cause of the Sicilians, I undertake also the cause of the people of Rome at large. It is not only that one wretched sinner should be crushed, which is what the Sicilians want, but that this terrible injustice should be stopped altogether, in compliance with the wishes of the people. "[104] When we remember how this was spoken, in the presence of those very judges, in the presence of Hortensius himself, in reliance only on the public opinion which he was to create by his own words, we cannot but acknowledge that it is very fine.

After that he again turns upon Caecilius. "Learn from me, " he says, "how many things are expected from him who undertakes the accusation of another. If there be one of those qualities in you, I will give up to you all that you ask. "[105] Caecilius was probably even now in alliance with Verres. He himself, when Quaestor, had robbed the people in the collection of the corn dues, and was unable therefore to include that matter in his accusation. "You can bring no charge against him on this head, lest it be seen that you were a partner with him in the business. "[106]

He ridicules him as to his personal insufficiency. "What, Caecilius! as to those practices of the profession without which an action such as this cannot be carried on, do you think that there is nothing in them? Need there be no skill in the business, no habit of speaking, no familiarity with the Forum, with the judgment-seats, and the laws? "[107] "I know well how difficult the ground is. Let me advise you to look into yourself, and to see whether you are able to do that kind of thing. Have you got voice for it, prudence, memory, wit? Are you able to expose the life of Verres, as it must be done, to divide it into parts and make everything clear? In doing all this, though nature should have assisted you" —as it has not at all, is of course implied — "if from your earliest childhood you had been imbued with letters; if you had learned Greek at Athens instead of at Lilybaeum—Latin in Rome instead of in Sicily—still would it not be a task beyond your strength to undertake such a case, so widely thought of, to complete it by your industry, and then to grasp it in your memory; to make it plain by your eloquence, and to support it with voice and strength sufficient? 'Have I these gifts, ' you will ask. Would that I had! But from my childhood I have done all that I could to attain them. "[108]

Cicero makes his points so well that I would fain go through the whole speech, were it not that a similar reason might induce me to give abridgments of all his speeches. It may not be that the readers of these orations will always sympathize with the orator in the matter which he has in hand—though his power over words is so great as to carry the reader with him very generally, even at this distance of time—but the neatness with which the weapon is used, the effectiveness of the thrust for the purpose intended, the certainty with which the nail is hit on the head—never with an expenditure of unnecessary force, but always with the exact strength wanted for the purpose—these are the characteristics of Cicero's speeches which carry the reader on with a delight which he will want to share with others, as a man when he has heard a good story instantly wishes to tell it again. And with Cicero we are charmed by the modernness, by the tone of to-day, which his language takes. The rapid way in which he runs from scorn to pity, from pity to anger, from anger to public zeal, and then instantly to irony and ridicule, implies a lightness of touch which, not unreasonably, surprises us as having endured for so many hundred years. That poetry should remain to us, even lines so vapid as some of those in which Ovid sung of love, seems to be more natural, because verses, though they be light, must have been labored. But these words spoken by Cicero seem almost to ring in our ears as having come to us direct from a man's lips. We see the anger gathering on the brow of Hortensius, followed by a look of acknowledged defeat. We see the startled attention of the judges as they began to feel that in this case they must depart from their intended purpose. We can understand how Caecilius cowered, and found consolation in being relieved from his task. We can fancy how Verres suffered—Verres whom no shame could have touched—when all his bribes were becoming inefficient under the hands of the orator.

Cicero was chosen for the task, and then the real work began. The work as he did it was certainly beyond the strength of any ordinary advocate. It was necessary that he should proceed to Sicily to obtain the evidence which was to be collected over the whole island. He must rate up, too, all the previous details of the life of this robber. He must be thoroughly prepared to meet the schemers on every point. He asked for a hundred and ten days for the purpose of getting up his case, but he took only fifty. We must imagine that, as he became more thoroughly versed in the intrigues of his adversaries, new lights came upon him. Were he to use the whole time allotted to him, or even half the time, and then make such an exposition of the criminal as he would delight to do were he to indulge himself with that "perpetua oratio" of which we hear, then the trial would be protracted till the coming of certain public games, during which the courts would not sit. There seem to have been three sets of games in his way—a special set for this year, to be given by Pompey, which were to last fifteen days; then the Ludi Romani, which were continued for nine days. Soon after that would come the games in honor of Victory—so soon that an adjournment over them would be obtained as a matter of course. In this way the trial would be thrown over into the next year, when Hortensius and one Metellus would be Consuls, and another Metellus would be the Praetor, controlling the judgment-seats.

Glabrio was the Praetor for this present year. In Glabrio Cicero could put some trust. With Hortensius and the two Metelluses in power, Verres would be as good as acquitted. Cicero, therefore, had to be on the alert, so that in this unexpected way, by sacrificing his own grand opportunity for a speech, he might conquer the schemers. We hear how he went to Sicily in a little boat from an unknown port, so as to escape the dangers contrived for him by the friends of Verres. [109] If it could be arranged that the clever advocate should be kidnapped by a pirate, what a pleasant way would that be of putting an end to these abominable reforms! Let them get rid of Cicero, if only for a time, and the plunder might still be divided. Against all this he had to provide. When in Sicily he travelled sometimes on foot, for the sake of caution—never with the retinue to which he was entitled as a Roman senator. As a Roman senator he might have demanded free entertainment at any town he entered, at great cost to the town. But from all this he abstained, and hurried back to Rome with his evidence so quickly that he was able to produce it before the judges, so as to save the adjournments which he feared.

Verres retired from the trial, pleading guilty, after hearing the evidence. Of the witness, and of the manner in which they told the story, we have no account. The second speech which we have—the Divinatio, or speech against Caecilius, having been the first—is called the Actio Prima contra Verrem—"the first process against Verres. " This is almost entirely confined to an exhortation to the judges. Cicero had made up his mind to make no speech about Verres till after the trial should be over. There would not be the requisite time. The evidence he must bring forward. And he would so appall these corrupt judges that they should not dare to acquit the accused. This Actio Prima contains the words in which he did appall the judges. As we read them, we pity the judges. There were fourteen, whose names we know. That there may have been many more is probable. There was the Praetor Urbanus of the day, Glabrio. With him were Metellus, one of the Praetors for the next year, and Caesonius, who, with Cicero himself, was Aedile designate. There were three Tribunes of the people and two military Tribunes. There was a Servilius, a Catulus, a Marcellus. Whom among these he suspected can hardly say. Certainly he suspected Metellus. To Servilius[110] he paid an ornate compliment in one of the written orations published after the trial was over, from whence we may suppose that he was well inclined toward him. Of Glabrio he spoke well. The body, as a body, was of such a nature that he found it necessary to appall them. It is thus that he begins: "Not by human wisdom, O ye judges, but by chance, and by the aid, as it were, of the gods themselves, an event has come to pass by which the hatred now felt for your order, and the infamy attached to the judgment seat, may be appeased; for an opinion has gone abroad, disgraceful to the Republic, full of danger to yourselves—which is in the mouths of all men not only here in Rome but through all nations—that by these courts as they are now constituted, a man, if he be only rich enough, will never be condemned, though he be ever so guilty. " What an exordium with which to begin a forensic pleading before a bench of judges composed of Praetors, Aediles, and coming Consuls! And this at a time, too, when men's minds were still full of Sulla's power; when some were thinking that they too might be Sullas; while the idea was still strong that a few nobles ought to rule the Roman Empire for their own advantage and their own luxury! What words to address to a Metellus, a Catulus, and a Marcellus! I have brought before you such a wretch, he goes on to say, that by a just judgment upon him you can recover your favor with the people of Rome, and your credit with other nations. "This is a trial in which you, indeed, will have to judge this man who is accused, but in which also the Roman people will have to judge you. By what is done to him will be determined whether a man who is guilty, and at the same time rich, can possibly be condemned in Rome. [111]If the matter goes amiss here, all men will declare, not that better men should be selected out of your order, which would be impossible, but that another order of citizens must be named from which to select the judges. "[112] This short speech was made. The witnesses were examined during nine days; then Hortensius, with hardly a struggle at a reply, gave way, and Verres stood condemned by his own verdict.

When the trial was over, and Verres had consented to go into exile, and to pay whatever fine was demanded, the "perpetua oratio" which Cicero thought good to make on the matter was published to the world. It is written as though it was to have been spoken, with counterfeit tricks of oratory—with some tricks so well done in the first part of it as to have made one think that, when these special words were prepared, he must have intended to speak them. It has been agreed, however, that such was not the case. It consists of a narration of the villainies of Verres, and is divided into what have been called five different speeches, to which the following appellations are given: De Praetura Urbana, in which we are told what Verres did when he was city Praetor, and very many things also which he did before he came to that office, De Jurisdictione Siciliensi, in which is described his conduct as a Roman magistrate on the island; De Re Frumentaria, setting forth the abomination of his exactions in regard to the corn tax; De Signis, detailing the robberies he perpetuated in regard to statues and other ornaments; and De Suppliciis, giving an account of the murders he committed and the tortures he inflicted. A question is sometimes mooted in conversation whether or no the general happiness of the world has been improved by increasing civilization When the reader finds from these stories, as told by a leading Roman of the day, how men were treated under the Roman oligarchy—not only Greek allies but Romans also—I think he will be inclined to answer the question in favour of civilization.

I can only give a few of the many little histories which have been preserved for us in this Actio Secunda; but perhaps these few may suffice to show how a great Roman officer could demean himself in his government. Of the doings of Verres before he went to Sicily I will select two. It became his duty on one occasion—a job which he seems to have sought for purpose of rapine—to go to Lampsacus, a town in Asia, as lieutenant, or legate, for Dolabella, who then had command in Asia. Lampsacus was on the Hellespont, an allied town of specially good repute. Here he is put up as a guest, with all the honors of a Roman officer, at the house of a citizen named Janitor. But he heard that another citizen, one Philodamus, had a beautiful daughter—an article with which we must suppose that Janitor was not equally well supplied. Verres, determined to get at the lady, orders that his creature Rubrius shall be quartered at the house of Philodamus. Philodamus, who from his rank was entitled to be burdened only with the presence of leading Romans, grumbles at this; but, having grumbled, consents, and having consented, does the best to make his house comfortable. He gives a great supper, at which the Romans eat and drink, and purposely create a tumult. Verres, we understand, was not there. The intention is that the girl shall be carried away and brought to him. In the middle of their cups the father is desired to produce his daughter; but this he refuses to do. Rubrius then orders the doors to be closed, and proceeds to ransack the house. Philodamus, who will not stand this, fetches his son, and calls his fellow-citizens around him. Rubrius succeeds in pouring boiling water over his host, but in the row the Romans get the worst of it. At last one of Verres's lictors—absolutely a Roman lictor—is killed, and the woman is not carried off. The man at least bore the outward signs of a lictor, but, according to Cicero, was in the pay of Verres as his pimp.

So far Verres fails; and the reader, rejoicing at the courage of the father who could protect his own house even against Romans, begins to feel some surprise that this case should have been selected. So far the lieutenant had not done the mischief he had intended, but he soon avenges his failure. He induces Dolabella, his chief, to have Philodamus and his son carried off to Laodicea, and there tried before Nero, the then Proconsul, for killing the sham lictor. They are tried at Laodicea before Nero, Verres himself sitting as one of the judges, and are condemned. Then in the market place of the town, in the presence of each other, the father and son are beheaded—a thing, as Cicero says, very sad for all Asia to behold. All this had been done some years ago; and, nevertheless, Verres had been chosen Praetor, and sent to Sicily to govern the Sicilians.

When Verres was Praetor at Rome—the year before he was sent to Sicily—it became his duty, or rather privilege, as he found it, to see that a certain temple of Castor in the city was given up in proper condition by the executors of a defunct citizen who had taken a contract for keeping it in repair. This man, whose name had been Junius, left a son, who was a Junius also under age, with a large fortune in charge of various trustees, tutors, as they were called, whose duty it was to protect the heir's interests. Verres, knowing of old that no property was so easily preyed on as that of a minor, sees at once that something may be done with the temple of Castor. The heir took oath, and to the extent of his property he was bound to keep the edifice in good repair. But Verres, when he made an inspection, finds everything to be in more than usually good order. There is not a scratch on the roof of which he can make use. Nothing has been allowed to go astray. Then "one of his dogs"—for he had boasted to his friend Ligur that he always went about with dogs to search out his game for him—suggested that some of the columns were out of the perpendicular. Verres does not know what this means; but the dog explains. All columns are, in fact, by strict measurement, more or less out of the perpendicular, as we are told that all eyes squint a little, though we do not see that they squint. But as columns ought to be perpendicular, here was a matter on which he might go to work. He does go to work. The trustees knowing their man—knowing also that in the present condition of Rome it was impossible to escape from an unjust Praetor without paying largely—went to his mistress and endeavored to settle the matter with her. Here we have an amusing picture of the way in which the affairs of the city were carried on in that lady's establishment; how she had her levee, took her bribes, and drove a lucrative trade. Doing, however, no good with her, the trustees settled with an agent to pay Verres two hundred thousand sesterces to drop the affair. This was something under £2000. But Verres repudiated the arrangement with scorn. He could do much better than that with such a temple and such a minor. He puts the repairs up to auction; and refusing a bid from the trustees themselves—the very persons who are the most interested in getting the work done, if there were work to do—has it knocked down to himself for five hundred and sixty thousand sesterces, or about £5000. [113] Then we are told how he had the pretended work done by the putting up of a rough crane. No real work is done, no new stones are brought, no money is spent. That is the way in which Verres filled his office as Praetor Urbanus; but it does not seem that any public notice is taken of his iniquities as long as he confined himself to little jobs such as this.

Then we come to the affairs of Sicily—and the long list of robberies is commenced by which that province was made desolate. It seems that nothing gave so grand a scope to the greed of a public functionary who was at the same time governor and judge as disputed wills. It was not necessary that any of the persons concerned should dispute the will among them. Given the facts that a man had died and left property behind him, then Verres would find means to drag the heir into court, and either frighten him into payment of a bribe or else rob him of his inheritance. Before he left Rome for the province he heard that a large fortune had been left to one Dio on condition that he should put up certain statues in the market-place. [114] It was not uncommon for a man to desire the reputation of adorning his own city, but to choose that the expense should be borne by his heir rather than by himself. Failing to put up the statues, the heir was required to pay a fine to Venus Erycina—to enrich, that is, the worship of that goddess, who had a favorite temple under Mount Eryx. The statues had been duly erected. But, nevertheless, here there was an opening. So Verres goes to work, and in the name of Venus brings an action against Dio. The verdict is given, not in favor of Venus but in favor of Verres.

This manner of paying honor to the gods, and especially to Venus, was common in Sicily. Two sons[115] received a fortune from their father, with a condition that, if some special thing were not done, a fine should be paid to Venus. The man had been dead twenty years ago. But "the dogs" which the Praetor kept were very sharp, and, distant as was the time, found out the clause. Action is taken against the two sons, who indeed gain their case; but they gain it by a bribe so enormous that they are ruined men. There was one Heraclius, [116] the son of Hiero, a nobleman of Syracuse, who received a legacy amounting to 3,000,000 sesterces—we will say £24,000—from a relative, also a Heraclius. He had, too, a house full of handsome silver plate, silk and hangings, and valuable slaves. A man, "Dives equom, dives pictai vestis et auri. " Verres heard, of course. He had by this time taken some Sicilian dogs into his service, men of Syracuse, and had learned from them that there was a clause in the will of the elder Heraclius that certain statues should be put up in the gymnasium of the city. They undertake to bring forward servants of the gymnasium who should say that the statues were never properly erected. Cicero tells us how Verres went to work, now in this court, now in that, breaking all the laws as to Sicilian jurisdiction, but still proceeding under the pretence of law, till he got everything out of the wretch—not only all the legacies from Heraclius, but every shilling, and every article left to the man by his father. There is a pretence of giving some of the money to the town of Syracuse; but for himself he takes all the valuables, the Corinthian vases, the purple hangings, what slaves he chooses. Then everything else is sold by auction. How he divided the spoil with the Syracusans, and then quarrelled with them, and how he lied as to the share taken by himself, will all be found in Cicero's narrative. Heraclius was of course ruined. For the stories of Epicrates and Sopater I must refer the reader to the oration. In that of Sopater there is the peculiarity that Verres managed to get paid by everybody all round.

The story of Sthenius is so interesting that I cannot pass it by. Sthenius was a man of wealth and high standing, living at Therma in Sicily, with whom Verres often took up his abode; for, as governor, he travelled much about the island, always in pursuit of plunder. Sthenius had had his house full of beautiful things. Of all these Verres possessed himself—some by begging, some by demanding, and some by absolute robbery. Sthenius, grieved as he was to find himself pillaged, bore all this. The man was Roman Praetor, and injuries such as these had to be endured. At Therma, however, in the public place of the city, there were some beautiful statues. For these Verres longed, and desired his host to get them for him.

Sthenius declared that this was impossible. The statues had, under peculiar circumstances, been recovered by Scipio Africanus from Carthage, and been restored by the Roman General to the Sicilians, from whom they had been taken, and had been erected at Therma. There was a peculiarly beautiful figure of Stesichorus, the poet, as an old man bent double, with a book in his hand—a very glorious work of art; and there was a goat—in bronze probably—as to which Cicero is at the pains of telling us that even he, unskilled as he was in such matters, could see its charms. No one had sharper eyes for such pretty ornaments than Cicero, or a more decided taste for them. But as Hortensius, his rival and opponent in this case, had taken a marble sphinx from Verres, he thought it expedient to show how superior he was to such matters. There was probably something of joke in this, as his predilections would no doubt be known to those he was addressing. [117]

In the matter Sthenius was incorruptible, and not even the Praetor could carry them away without his aid. Cicero, who is very warm in praise of Sthenius, declares that "here at last Verres had found one town, the only one in the world, from which he was unable to carry away something of the public property by force, or stealth, or open command, or favor. "[118]

The governor was so disgusted with this that he abandoned Sthenius, leaving the house which he had plundered of everything, and betook himself to that of one Agathinus, who had a beautiful daughter, Callidama, who, with her husband, Dorotheus, lived with her father They were enemies of Sthenius, and we are given to understand that Verres ingratiated himself with them partly for the sake of Callidama, who seems very quickly to have been given up to him, [119] and partly that he might instigate them to bring actions against Sthenius. This is done with great success; so that Sthenius is forced to run away, and betake himself, winter as it was, across the seas to Rome. It has already been told that when he was at Rome an action was brought against him by Verres for having run away when he was under judgment, in which Cicero defended him, and in which he was acquitted. In the teeth of his acquittal, Verres persecuted the man by every form of law which came to his hands as Praetor, but always in opposition to the law. There is an audacity about the man's proceedings, in his open contempt of the laws which it was his special duty to carry out, making us feel how confident he was that he could carry everything before him in Rome by means of his money. By robbery and concealing his robberies, by selling his judgments in such a way that he should maintain some reticence by ordinary precaution, he might have made much money, as other governors had done. But he resolved that it would pay him better to rob everywhere openly, and then, when the day of reckoning came, to buy the judges wholesale. As to shame at such doings, there was no such feelings left among Romans.

Before he comes to the story of Sthenius, Cicero makes a grandly ironical appeal to the bench before him: "Yes, O judges, keep this man; keep him in the State! Spare him, preserve him so that he, too, may sit with us as a judge here so that he, too, may, with impartiality, advise us, as a Senator, what may be best for us as to peace and war! Not that we need trouble ourselves as to his senatorial duties. His authority would be nothing. When would he dare, or when would he care, to come among us? Unless it might be in the idle month of February, when would a man so idle, so debauched, show himself in the Senate-house? Let him come and show himself. Let him advise us to attack the Cretans; to pronounce the Greeks of Byzantium free; to declare Ptolemy King. [120] Let him speak and vote as Hortensius may direct. This will have but little effect upon our lives or our property. But beyond this there is something we must look to; something that would be distrusted; something that every good man has to fear! If by chance this man should escape out of our hands, he would have to sit there upon that bench and be a judge. He would be called upon to pronounce on the lives of a Roman citizen. He would be the right-hand officer in the army of this man here, [121] of this man who is striving to be the lord and ruler of our judgment-seats. The people of Rome at least refuse this! This at least cannot be endured! "

The third of these narratives tells us how Verres managed in his province that provision of corn for the use of Rome, the collection of which made the possession of Sicily so important to the Romans. He begins with telling his readers—as he does too frequently—how great and peculiar is the task he has undertaken; and he uses an argument of which we cannot but admit the truth, though we doubt whether any modern advocate would dare to put it forward. We must remember, however, that Romans were not accustomed to be shamefaced in praising themselves. What Cicero says of himself all others said also of themselves; only Cicero could say it better than others. He reminds us that he who accuses another of any crime is bound to be especially free from that crime himself. "Would you charge any one as a thief? you must be clear from any suspicion of even desiring another man's property. Have you brought a man up for malice or cruelty? take care that you be not found hard-hearted. Have you called a man a seducer or an adulterer? be sure that your own life shows no trace of such vices. Whatever you would punish in another, that you must avoid yourself. A public accuser would be intolerable, or even a caviller, who should inveigh against sins for which he himself is called in question. But in this man I find all wickednesses combined. There is no lust, no iniquity, no shamelessness of which his life does not supply with ample evidence. " The nature of the difficulty to which Cicero is thus subjected is visible enough. As Verres is all that is bad, so must he, as accuser, be all that is good; which is more, we should say, than any man would choose to declare of himself! But he is equal to the occasion. "In regard to this man, O judges, I lay down for myself the law as I have stated it. I must so live that I must clearly seem to be, and always have been, the very opposite of this man, not only in my words and deeds, but as to that arrogance and impudence which you see in him. " Then he shows how opposite he is to Verres at any rate, in impudence! "I am not sorry to see, " he goes on to say, "that that life which has always been the life of my own choosing, has now been made a necessity to me by the law which I have laid down for myself. "[122] Mr. Pecksniff spoke of himself in the same way, but no one, I think, believed him. Cicero probably was believed. But the most wonderful thing is, that his manner of life justified what he said of himself. When others of his own order were abandoned to lust, iniquity, and shamelessness, he lived in purity, with clean hands, doing good as far as was in his power to those around him. A laugh will be raised at his expense in regard to that assertion of his that, even in the matter of arrogance, his conduct should be the opposite of that of Verres. But this will come because I have failed to interpret accurately the meaning of those words, "oris oculorumque illa contumacia ac superbia quam videtis. " Verres, as we can understand, had carried himself during the trial with a bragging, brazen, bold face, determined to show no shame as to his own doings. It is in this, which was a matter of manner and taste, that Cicero declares that he will be the man's opposite as well as in conduct. As to the ordinary boastings, by which it has to be acknowledged that Cicero sometimes disgusts his readers, it will be impossible for us to receive a just idea of his character without remembering that it was the custom of a Roman to boast. We wait to have good things said of us, or are supposed to wait. The Roman said them of himself. The "veni, vidi, vici" was the ordinary mode of expression in those times, and in earlier times among the Greeks.

[123] This is distasteful to us; and it will probably be distasteful to those who come after us, two or three hundred years hence, that this or that British statesman should have made himself an Earl or a Knight of the Garter. Now it is thought by many to be proper enough. It will shock men in future days that great peers or rich commoners should have bargained for ribbons and lieutenancies and titles. Now it is the way of the time. Though virtue and vice may be said to remain the same from all time to all time, the latitudes allowed and the deviations encouraged in this or the other age must be considered before the character of a man can be discovered. The boastings of Cicero have been preserved for us. We have to bethink ourselves that his words are 2000 years old. There is such a touch of humanity in them, such a feeling of latter-day civilization and almost of Christianity, that we are apt to condemn what remains in them of paganism, as though they were uttered yesterday. When we come to the coarseness of his attacks, his descriptions of Piso by-and-by, his abuse of Gabinius, and his invectives against Antony; when we read his altered opinions, as shown in the period of Caesar's dominion, his flattery of Caesar when in power, and his exultations when Caesar has been killed; when we find that he could be coarse in his language and a bully, and servile—for it has all to be admitted—we have to reflect under what circumstances, under what surroundings, and for what object were used the words which displease us. Speaking before the full court at this trial, he dared to say he knew how to live as a man and to carry himself as a gentleman. As men and gentlemen were then, he was justified.

The description of Verres's rapacity in regard to the corn tax is long and complex, and need hardly be followed at length, unless by those who desire to know how the iniquity of such a one could make the most of an imposition which was in itself very bad, and pile up the burden till the poor province was unable to bear it. There were three kinds of imposition as to corn. The first, called the "decumanum, " was simply a tithe.

The producers through the island had to furnish Rome with a tenth of their produce, and it was the Praetor's duty, or rather that of the Quaestor under the Praetor, to see that the tithe was collected. How Verres saw to this himself, and how he treated the Sicilian husbandmen in regard to the tithe, is so told that we are obliged to give the man credit for an infinite fertility of resources. Then there is the "emptum, " or corn bought for the use of Rome, of which there were two kinds. A second tithe had to be furnished at a price fixed by the Roman Senate, which price was considered to be below that of its real value, and then 800,000 bushels were purchased, or nominally purchased, at a price which was also fixed by the Senate, but which was nearer to the real value. Three sesterces a bushel for the first and four for the last, were the prices fixed at this time. For making these payments vast sums of money were remitted to Verres, of which the accounts were so kept that it was hard to say whether any found its way into the hands of the farmers who undoubtedly furnished the corn. The third corn tax was the "aestimatum". This consisted of a certain fixed quantity which had to be supplied to the Praetor for the use of his governmental establishment—to be supplied either in grain or in money. What such a one as Verres would do with his, the reader may conceive.

All this was of vital importance to Rome. Sicily and Africa were the granaries from which Rome was supplied with its bread. To get supplies from a province was necessary. Rich men have servants in order that they may live at ease themselves. So it was with the Romans to whom the provinces acted as servants. It was necessary to have a sharp agent, some Proconsul or Propraetor; but when there came one so sharp as Verres, all power of recreating supplies would for a time be destroyed. Even Cicero boasted that in a time of great scarcity, he, being then Quaestor in Sicily, had sent extraordinary store of corn over to the city. [124] But he had so done it as to satisfy all who were concerned.

Verres, in his corn dealings with the Sicilians, had a certain friend, companion, and minister—one of his favorite dogs, perhaps we may call him—named Apronius, whom Cicero specially describes. The description I must give, because it is so powerful; because it shows us how one man could in those days speak of another in open court before all the world; because it affords us an instance of the intensity of hatred which the orator could throw into his words; but I must hide it in the original language, as I could not translate it without offence. "[125]

Then we have a book devoted to the special pillage of statues and other ornaments, which, for the genius displayed in story-telling, is perhaps of all the Verrine orations the most amusing. The Greek people had become in a peculiar way devoted to what we generally call Art. We are much given to the collecting of pictures, china, bronze, and marbles, partly from love of such things, partly from pride in ornamenting our houses so as to excite the admiration of others, partly from a feeling that money so invested is not badly placed with a view to future returns. All these feelings operated with the Greeks to a much greater extent. Investments in consols and railway shares were not open to them. Money they used to lend at usury, no doubt, but with a great chance of losing it. The Greek colonists were industrious, were covetous, and prudent. From this it had come to pass that, as they made their way about the world—to the cities which they established round the Mediterranean—they collected in their new homes great store of ornamental wealth. This was done with much profusion at Syracuse, a Greek city in Sicily, and spread from them over the whole island. The temples of the gods were filled with the works of the great Greek artists, and every man of note had his gallery. That Verres, hog as he is described to have been, had a passion for these things, is manifest to us. He came to his death at last in defence of some favorite images. He had returned to Rome by means of Caesar's amnesty, and Marc Antony had him murdered because he would not surrender some treasures of art. When we read the De Signis—About Statues—we are led to imagine that the search after these things was the chief object of the man throughout his three years of office—as we have before been made to suppose that all his mind and time had been devoted to the cheating of the Sicilians in the matter of corn. But though Verres loved these trinkets, it was not altogether for himself that he sought them. Only one third of his plunder was for himself. Senators, judges, advocates, Consuls, and Praetors could be bribed with articles of *vertu* as well as with money.

There are eleven separate stories told of these robberies. I will give very shortly the details of one or two. There was one Marcus Heius, a rich citizen of Messana, in whose house Verres took great delight. Messana itself was very useful to him, and the Mamertines, as the people of Messana were called were his best friends in all Sicily: for he made Messana the depot of his plunder, and there he caused to be built at the expense of the Government an enormous ship called the *Cybea*, [126] in which his treasures were carried out of the island. He therefore specially favored Messana, and the district of Messana was supposed to have been scourged by him with lighter rods than those used elsewhere in Sicily. But this man Heius had a chapel, very sacred, in which were preserved four specially beautiful images. There was a Cupid by Praxiteles, and a bronze Hercules by Myro, and two Canoephrae by Polycletus These were treasures which all the world came to see, and which were open to be seen by all the world. These Verres took away, and caused accounts to be forged in which it was made to appear that he had bought them for trifling sums. It seems that some forced assent had been obtained from Heius as to the transaction. Now there was a plan in vogue for making things pleasant for a Proconsul retiring from his government, in accordance with which a deputation would proceed from the province to Rome to declare how well and kindly the Proconsul had behaved in his government. The allies, even when they had been, as it were, skinned alive by their governor, were constrained to send their deputations. Deputations were got up in Sicily from Messana and Syracuse, and with the others from Messana came this man Heius. Heius did not wish to tell about his statues; but he was asked questions, and was forced to answer. Cicero informs us how it all took place. "He was a man, " he said— this is what Cicero tells us that Heius said—"who was well esteemed in his own country, and would wish you"—you judges—"to think well of his religious spirit and of his personal dignity. He had come here to praise Verres because he had been required to do so by his fellow-citizens. He, however, had never kept things for sale in his own house; and had he been left to himself, nothing would have induced him to part with the sacred images which had been left to him by his ancestors as the ornaments of his own chapel. [127]

Nevertheless, he had come to praise Verres, and would have held his tongue had it been possible. "

Cicero finishes his catalogue by telling us of the manifold robberies committed by Verres in Syracuse, especially from the temples of the gods; and he begins his account of the Syracusan iniquities by drawing a parallel between two Romans whose names were well known in that city: Marcellus, who had besieged it as an enemy and taken it, and Verres, who had been sent to govern it in peace. Marcellus had saved the lives of the Syracusans; Verres had made the Forum to run with their blood. The harbor which had held its own against Marcellus, as we may read in our Livy, had been wilfully opened by Verres to Cilician pirates. This Syracuse which had been so carefully preserved by its Roman conqueror the most beautiful of all the Greek cities on the face of the earth—so beautiful that Marcellus had spared to it all its public ornaments—had been stripped bare by Verres. There was the temple of Minerva from which he had taken all the pictures. There were doors to this temple of such beauty that books had been written about them. He stripped the ivory ornaments from them, and the golden balls with which they had been made splendid. He tore off from them the head of the

Gorgon and carried it away, leaving them to be rude doors, Goth that he was!

And he took the Sappho from the Prytaneum, the work of Silanion! a thing of such beauty that no other man can have the like of it in his own private house; yet Verres has it—a man hardly fit to carry such a work of art as a burden, not possess it as a treasure of his own. "What, too! " he says, "have you not stolen Paean from the temple of Aesculapius—a statue so remarkable for its beauty, so well-known for the worship attached to it, that all the world has been wont to visit it? What! has not the image of Aristaeus been taken by you from the temple of Bacchus? Have you not even stolen the statue of Jupiter Imperator, so sacred in the eyes of all men—that Jupiter which the Greeks call Ourios? You have not hesitated to rob the temple of Proserpine of the lovely head in Parian marble. "[128] Then Cicero speaks of the worship due to all these gods as though he himself believed in their godhead. As he had begun this chapter with the Mamertines of Messana, so he ends it with an address to them. "It is well that you should come, you alone out of all the provinces, and praise Verres here in Rome. But what can you say for him? Was it not your duty to have built a ship for the Republic? You have built none such, but have constructed a huge private transport-vessel for Verres. Have you not been exempted from your tax on corn? Have you not been exempted in regard to naval and military recruits? Have you not been the receptacle of all his stolen goods? They will have to confess, these Mamertines, that many a ship laden with his spoils has left their port, and especially this huge transport-ship which they built for him! "

In the De Suppliciis—the treatise about punishments, as the last division of this process is called—Cicero tells the world how Verres exacted vengeance from those who were opposed to him, and with what horrid cruelty he raged against his enemies. The stories, indeed, are very dreadful. It is harrowing to think that so evil a man should have been invested with powers so great for so bad a purpose. But that which strikes a modern reader most is the sanctity attached to the name of a Roman citizen, and the audacity with which the Roman Proconsul disregarded that sanctity. "Cives Romanus" is Cicero's cry from the beginning to the end. No doubt he is addressing himself to Romans, and seeking popularity, as he always did. But, nevertheless, the demands made upon the outside world at large by the glory of that appellation are astonishing, even when put forward on such an occasion as this. One Gavius escapes from a prison in Syracuse, and, making his way to Messana, foolishly boasts that he would be soon over in Italy, out of the way of Praetor Verres and his cruelties. Verres, unfortunately, is in Messana, and soon hears from some of his friends, the Mamertines, what Gavius was saying. He at once orders Gavius to be flogged in public. "Cives Romanus sum! " exclaims Gavius, no doubt truly. It suits Verres to pretend to disbelieve this, and to declare that the man is a runagate slave. The poor wretch still cries "Cives Romanus! " and trusts alone to that appeal. Whereupon Verres puts up a cross on the sea-shore, and has the man crucified in sight of Italy, so that he shall be able to see the country of which he is so proud. Whether he had done anything to deserve crucifixion, or flogging, or punishment at all, we are not told. The accusation against Verres is not for crucifying the man, but for crucifying the Roman. It is on this occasion that Cicero uses the words which have become proverbial as to the iniquity of this proceeding. [129] During the telling of this story he explains this doctrine, claiming for the Roman citizen, all the world over, some such protection as freemasons are supposed to give each other, whether known or unknown. "Men of straw, " he says, "of no special birth, go about the world. They resort to places they have never seen before, where they know none, and none know them. Here, trusting to their claim solely, they feel themselves to be safe—not only where our magistrates are to be found, who are bound both by law and by opinion, not only among other Roman citizens who speak their language and follow the same customs, but abroad, over the whole world, they find this to be sufficient protection. "[130] Then he goes on to say that if any Praetor may at his will put aside this sanctity, all the provinces, all the kingdoms, all the free states, all the world abroad, will very soon lose the feeling.

But the most remarkable story is that told of a certain pirate captain. Verres had been remiss in regard to the pirates—very cowardly, indeed, if we are to believe Cicero. Piracy in the Mediterranean was at that time a terrible drawback to trade—that piracy that a year or two afterward Pompey was effectual in destroying. A governor in Sicily had, among other special duties, to keep a sharp lookout for the pirates. This Verres omitted so entirely that these scourges of the sea soon learned that they might do almost as they pleased on the Sicilian coasts. But it came to pass that on one day a pirate vessel fell by accident into the hands of the governor's officers. It was not taken, Cicero says, but was so overladen that it was picked up almost sinking. [131] It was found to be full of fine, handsome men, of silver both plated and coined, and precious stuffs. Though not "taken, " it was "found, " and carried into Syracuse. Syracuse is full of the news, and the first demand is that the pirates, according to Roman custom, shall all be killed. But this does not suit Verres. The slave-markets of the Roman Empire are open, and there are men among the pirates whom it will suit him better to sell than to kill. There are six musicians, "symphoniacos homines, " whom he sends as a present to a friend at Rome. But the people of Syracuse are very much in earnest. They are too sharp to be put off with pretences, and they count the number of slaughtered pirates. There are only some useless, weak, ugly old fellows beheaded from day to day; and being well aware how many men it must have taken to row and manage such a vessel, they demand that the full crew shall be brought to the block. "There is nothing in victory more sweet, " says Cicero, "no evidence more sure, than to see those whom you did fear, but have now got the better of, brought out to tortures or death. "[132] Verres is so much frightened by the resolution of the citizens that he docs not dare to neglect their wishes. There are lying in the prisons of Syracuse a lot of prisoners, Roman citizens, of whom he is glad to rid himself. He has them brought out, with their heads wrapped up so that they shall not be known, and has them beheaded instead of the pirates! A great deal is said, too, about the pirate captain—the arch-pirate, as he is called. There seems to have been some money dealings personally between him and Verres, on account of which Verres kept him hidden. At any rate, the arch-pirate was saved. "In such a manner this celebrated victory is managed. [133] The pirate ship is taken, and the chief pirate is allowed to escape. The musicians are sent to Rome. The men who are good-looking and young are taken to the Praetor's house. As many Roman citizens as will fill their places are carried out as public enemies, and are tortured and killed! All the gold and silver and precious stuffs are made a prize of by Verres! "

Such are the accusations brought against this wonderful man—the truth of which has, I think, on the whole been admitted. The picture of Roman life which it displays is wonderful, that such atrocities should have been possible; and equally so of provincial subjection, that such cruelties should have been endured. But in it all the greatest wonder is that there should have risen up a man so determined to take the part of the weak against the strong with no reward before him, apparently with no other prospect than that of making himself odious to the party to which he belonged. Cicero was not a Gracchus, anxious to throw himself into the arms of the people; he was an oligarch by conviction, born to oligarchy, bred to it, convinced that by it alone could the Roman Republic be preserved. But he was convinced also that unless these oligarchs could be made to do their duty the Republic could not stand. Therefore it was that he dared to defy his own brethren, and to make the acquittal of Verres an impossibility. I should be inclined to think that the day on which Hortensius threw up the sponge, and Verres submitted to banishment and fine, was the happiest in the orator's life. Verres was made to pay a fine which was very insufficient for his crimes, and then to retire into comfortable exile. From this he returned to Rome when the Roman exiles were amnestied, and was shortly afterward murdered by Antony, as has been told before.

NOTES:

[97] M. du Rozoir was a French critic, and was joined with M. Guéroult and M. de Guerle in translating and annotating the Orations of Cicero for M. Pauckoucke's edition of the Latin classics.

[98] In Verrem Actio Secunda, lib. i., vii.

[99] Plutarch says that Caecilius was an emancipated slave, and a Jew, which could not have been true, as he was a Roman Senator.

[100] De Oratore, lib. ii., c.xlix. The feeling is beautifully expressed in the words put into the mouth of Antony in the discussion on the charms and attributes of eloquence: "Qui mihi in liberum loco more majorum esse deberet. "

[101] In Q. Caec. Divinatio, ca. ii.

[102] Divinatio, ca. iii.

[103] Ibid., ca.vi.

[104] Ibid., ca. viii.

[105] Divinatio, ca. ix.

[106] Ibid., ca. xi.

[107] Ibid.

[108] Ibid., ca. xii.

[109] Actio Secunda, lib. ii., xl. He is speaking of Sthenius, and the illegality of certain proceedings on the part of Verres against him. "If an accused man could be condemned in the absence of the accuser, do you think that I would have gone in a little boat from Vibo to Vella, among all the dangers prepared for me by your fugitive slaves and pirates, when I had to hurry at the peril of my life, knowing that you would escape if I were not present to the day? "

[110] Actio Secunda, I. xxi.

[111] In Verrem, Actio Prima, xvi.

[112] In Verrem, Actio Prima, xvi.

[113] We are to understand that the purchaser at the auction having named the sum for which he would do the work, the estate of the minor, who was responsible for the condition of the temple, was saddled with that amount.

[114] In Verrem, Actio Secunda, lib. ii., vii.

[115] Ibid, ix.

[116] Ibid., lib. ii., xiv.

[117] See Appendix C.

[118] In Verrem, Actio Secunde, lib. ii., ca. xxxvi.

[119] Ibid. "Una nox intercesserat, quam iste Dorotheum sic diligebat, ut diceres, omnia inter eos esse communia. "—wife and all. "Iste" always means Verres in these narratives.

[120] These were burning political questions of the moment. It was as though an advocate of our days should desire some disgraced member of Parliament to go down to the House and assist the Government in protecting Turkey in Asia and invading Zululand.

[121] "Sit in ejus exercitu signifer. " The "ejus" was Hortensius, the coming Consul, too whom Cicero intended to be considered as pointing. For the passage, see In Verrem, Actio Secunda, lib. ii., xxxi.

[122] In Verrem, Actio Secunda, lib. iii., II.

[123] "Exegi monumentum aere perennius, " said Horace, gloriously. "Sum pius Aeneas" is Virgil's expression, put into the mouth of his hero. "Ipse Menaleas, " said Virgil himself. Homer and Sophocles introduce their heroes with self-sounded trumpetings:

[Greek: *Eiae Odysseus Daertiadaes os pasi doloisi Anthropoisi melo, kai meu kleos ouranon ikei.*]
Odyssey, book ix., 19 and 20.

[Greek: *Ho pasi kleinos Oidipous kaloumenos.*]
Oedipus Tyrannus, 8.

[124] Pro Plancio, xxvi. : "Fumenti in summa caritate maximum numerum miseram; negotiatoribus comis, mercatoribus justus, municipibus liberalis, sociis abstinens, omnibus eram visus in omni officio diligentissimus. "

[125] In Verrem, Actio Secunda, lib. iii., ix. : "is erit Apronius ille; qui, ut ipse non solum vita, sed etiam corpore atque ore significat, immensa aliqua vorago est ac gurges vitiorum turpitudinumque omnium. Hunc in omnibus stupris, hunc in fanorum expilationibus, hunc in impuris conviviis principera adhibebat; tantamque habebat morum similitudo conjuncnorum atque concordiam, ut Apronius, qui aliis inhumanus ac barbarus, isti uni commodus ac disertus videretur; ut quem omnes odissent neque videre vellent sine eo iste esse non posset; ut quum alii ne conviviis quidem iisdem quibus Apronius, hic iisdem etiam poculis uteretur, postremo, ut, odor Apronii teterrimus oris et corporis, quem, ut aiunt, ne bestiae quidem ferre possent, uni isti suavis et jucundus videretur. Ille erat in tribunali proximus; in cubiculo socius; in convivio dominus, ac tum maxime, quum, accubante praetextato praetoris filio, in convivio saltare nudus coeperat".

[126] A great deal is said of the *Cybea* in this and the last speech. The money expended on it was passed through the accounts as though

the ship had been built for the defence of the island from pirates, but it was intended solely for the depository of the governor's plunder.

[127] In Verrem, Actio Secunda, lib. iv., vii.

[128] In Verrem, Actio Secunda, lib. iv., lvii.

[129] In Verrem, Actio Secunda, lib. v., lxvi. : "Facinus est vinciri civem Romanum; scelus verberari; prope parricidium necari; quid dicam in crucem! "

[130] In Verrem, Actio Secunda, lib. v., lxv.

[131] In Verrem, Actio Secunda, lib. v., xx. : "Onere suo plane captam atque depressam. "

[132] In Verrem, Actio Secunda, lib. v., xxvi.

[133] Ibid., xxviii.

CHAPTER VII.

CICERO AS AEDILE AND PRAETOR.

[Sidenote: B.C. 69, *aetat.* 38.]

The year after the trial of Verres was that of Cicero's Aedileship. We know but little of him in the performance of the duties of this office, but we may gather that he performed them to the satisfaction of the people. He did not spend much money for their amusements, although it was the custom of Aediles to ruin themselves in seeking popularity after this fashion; and yet when, two years afterward, he solicited the Praetorship from the people, he was three times elected as first Praetor in all the comitia—three separate elections having been rendered necessary by certain irregularities and factious difficulties. To all the offices, one after another, he was elected in his first year—the first year possible in accordance with his age—and was elected first in honor, the first as Praetor, and then the first as Consul. This, no doubt, was partly due to his compliance with those rules for canvassing which his brother Quintus is said to have drawn out, and which I have quoted; but it proves also the trust which was felt in him by the people. The candidates, for the most part, were the candidates for the aristocracy. They were put forward with the idea that thus might the aristocratic rule of Rome be best maintained. Their elections were carried on by bribery, and the people were for the most part indifferent to the proceeding. Whether it might be a Verres, or an Antony, or a Hortensius, they took the money that was going. They allowed themselves to be delighted with the games, and they did as they were bid. But every now and then there came up a name which stirred them, and they went to the voting pens— ovilia—with a purpose of their own. When such a candidate came forward, he was sure to be first. Such had been Marius, and such had been the great Pompey, and such was Cicero. The two former were men successful in war, who gained the voices of the people by their victories. Cicero gained them by what he did inside the city. He could afford not to run into debt and ruin himself during his Aedileship, as had been common with Aediles, because he was able to achieve his popularity in another way. It was the chief duty of the Aediles to look after the town generally—to see to the temples of the gods, to take care that houses did not tumble down, to look to the cleansing of the streets, and to the supply of water. The markets were under them, and the police, and the recurrent festivals. An active man, with common-sense, such as was Cicero, no doubt did his duty as Aedile well.

He kept up his practice as an advocate during his years of office. We have left to us the part of one speech and the whole of another spoken during this period. The former was in favor of Fonteius, whom the Gauls prosecuted for plundering them as Propraetor, and the latter is a civil case on behalf of Caecina, addressed to the "Recuperatores, " as had been that for Marcus Tullius. The speech for Fonteius is remarkable as being as hard against the provincial Gauls as his speech against Verres had been favorable to the Sicilians. But the Gauls were barbarians, whereas the Sicilians were Greeks. And it should be always remembered that Cicero spoke as an advocate, and that the praise and censure of an advocate require to be taken with many grains of salt. Nothing that these wretched Gauls could say against a Roman citizen ought to be accepted in evidence! "All the Romans, " he says, "who have been in the province wish well to Fonteius. Would you rather believe these Gauls—led by what feeling? By the opinion of men! Is the opinion, then, of your enemies of greater weight than that of your fellow-citizens, or is it the greater credibility of the witnesses? Would you prefer, then, unknown men to known—dishonest men to honest—foreigners to your own countrymen—greedy men to those who come before you for nothing—men of no religion to those who fear the gods—those who hate the Empire and the name of Rome to allies and citizens who are good and faithful? "[134] In every word of this he begs the question so as to convince us that his own case was weak; and when he makes a final appeal to the pity of the judges we are sure that Fonteius was guilty. He tells the judges that the poor mother of the accused man has no other support than this son, and that there is a sister, one of the virgins devoted to the service of Vesta, who, being a vestal virgin, cannot have sons of her own, and is therefore entitled to have her brother preserved for her. When we read such arguments as these, we are sure that Fonteius had misused the Gauls. We believe that he was acquitted, because we are told that he bought a house in Rome soon afterward; but we feel that he escaped by the too great influence of his advocate. We are driven to doubt whether the power over words which may be achieved by a man by means of natural gifts, practice, and erudition, may not do evil instead of good. A man with such a tongue as that of Cicero will make the listener believe almost whatever he will; and the advocate is restrained by no horror of falsehood. In his profession alone it is considered honorable to be a bulwark to deception, and to make the worse appear the better cause. Cicero did so when the occasion seemed to him to require it, and has been accused of hypocrisy in consequence. There is a passage in one of the dialogues, De Oratore, which has been continually quoted against him because the word "fibs" has been used with approval. The orator is told how it may become him to garnish his good story with little white lies — "mendaciunculis. "[135] The advice does not indeed refer to facts, or to evidence, or to arguments. It goes no farther than to suggest that amount of exaggeration which is used by every teller of a good story in order that the story may be good. Such "mendaciuncula" are in the mouth of every diner-out in London, and we may pity the dinner-parties at which they are not used. Reference is made to them now because the use of the word by Cicero, having been misunderstood by some who have treated his name with severity, has been brought forward in proof of his falsehood. You shall tell a story about a very little man, and say that he is only thirty-six inches. You know very well that he is more than four feet high. That will be a "mendaciunculum, " according to Cicero. The phrase has been passed on from one enemy to another, till the little fibs of Cicero's recommending have been supposed to be direct lies suggested by him to all advocates, and therefore continually used by him as an advocate. They have been only the garnishing of his drolleries. As an advocate, he was about as false and about as true as an advocate of our own day. [136] That he was not paid, and that our English barristers are paid for the work they do, makes, I think, no difference either in the innocency or the falseness of the practice. I cannot but believe that, hereafter, an improved tone of general feeling will forbid a man of honor to use arguments which he thinks to be untrue, or to make others believe that which he does not believe himself. Such is not the state of things now in London, nor was it at Rome in Cicero's time. There are touches of eloquence in the plea for Fonteius, but the reader will probably agree with me that the orator was well aware that the late governor who was on his trial had misused those unfortunate Gauls.

In the year following that of Cicero's Aedileship were written the first of his epistles which have come to us. He was then not yet thirty-nine years old — B. C. 68 — and during that year and the next seven were written eleven letters, all to Atticus. Those to his other friends — Ad Familiares, as we have been accustomed to call them; Ad Diversos, they are commonly called now — began only with the close of his consular year. How it has come to pass that there have been preserved only those which were written after a period of life at which most men cease to be free correspondents, cannot be said with certainty. It has probably been occasioned by the fact that he caused his letters to be preserved as soon as he himself perceived how great would be their value. Of the nature of their value it is hardly possible to speak too highly. I am not prepared, indeed, to agree with the often quoted assertion of Cornelius Nepos that he who has read his letters to Atticus will not lack much of the history of those days. [137] A man who should have read them and nothing else, even in the days of Augustus, would not have learned much of the preceding age. But if not for the purpose of history, the letters generally have, if read aright, been all but enough for the purpose of biography. With a view to the understanding of the man's character, they have, I think, been enough. From them such a flood of light has been turned upon the writer that all his nobility and all his defects, all his aspirations and all his vacillations, have been made visible. We know how human he was, and how, too, he was only human — how he sighed for great events, and allowed himself to think sometimes that they could be accomplished by small manoeuvres — how like a man he could be proud of his work and boast — how like a man he could despair and almost die. But I wish it to be acknowledged, by those who read his letters in order that they may also read his character, that they were, when written, private letters, intended to tell the truth, and that if they are to be believed in reference to his weaknesses, they are also to be believed in reference to his strength. If they are singularly transparent as to the man — opening, especially to Atticus, the doors of his soul more completely than would even any girl of the nineteenth century when writing to her bosom friend — they must be taken as being more honestly true. To regard the aspirations as hypocritical, and only the meaner effusions of his mind as emblematic of the true man, is both unreasonable and uncharitable. Nor, I think, will that reader grasp the way to see the truth who cannot teach himself what has in Cicero's case, been the effect of daring to tell to his friend an unvarnished tale. When with us some poor thought does make its way across our minds, we do not sit down and write it to another, nor, if we did, would an immortality be awarded to the letter. If one of us were to lose his all — as Cicero lost his all when he was sent into exile — I think it might well be that he should for a time be unmanned; but he would either not write, or, in writing, would hide much of his feelings. On losing his Tullia, some father of to-day would keep it all in his heart, would not maunder out his sorrows. Even with our truest love for our friends, some fear is mingled which forbids the use of open words. Whether this be for good or for evil I will not say, but it is so. Cicero, whether he did or did not know that his letters would live, was impeded by no such fear. He said everything that there was within him—being in this, I should say, quite as unlike to other Romans of the day as he was to ourselves. In the collection as it has come to us there are about fifty letters—not from Cicero—written to Cicero by his brother, by Decimus Brutus, by Plancus, and others. It will, I think, be admitted that their tone is quite different from that used by himself. There are none, indeed, from Atticus—none written under terms of such easy friendship as prevailed when many were written by Cicero himself. It will probably be acknowledged that his manner of throwing himself open to his correspondent was peculiar to him. If this be so, he should surely have the advantage as well as the disadvantage of his own mode of utterance. The reader who allows himself to think that the true character of the man is to be read in the little sly things he said to Atticus, but that the nobler ideas were merely put forth to cajole the public, is as unfair to himself as he is to Cicero.

In reading the entire correspondence—the letters from Cicero either to Atticus or to others—it has to be remembered that in the ordinary arrangement of them made by Graevius[138] they are often incorrectly paced in regard to chronology. In subsequent times efforts have been made to restore them to their proper position, and so they should be read. The letters to Atticus and those Ad Diversos have generally been published separately. For the ordinary purpose of literary pleasure they may perhaps be best read in that way. The tone of them is different. The great bulk of the correspondence is political, or quasi-political. The manner is much more familiar, much less severe—though not on that account indicating less seriousness—in those written to Atticus than in the others. With one or two signal exceptions, those to Atticus are better worth reading. The character of the writer may perhaps be best gathered from divided perusal; but for a general understanding of the facts of Cicero's life, the whole correspondence should be taken as it was written. It has been published in this shape as well as in the other, and will be used in this shape in my effort to portray the life of him who wrote them. [139]

[Sidenote: B.C. 68, *aetat.* 39.]

We have three letters written when he was thirty-eight, in the year after his Aedileship. In the first he tells his friend of the death of his cousin, Lucius Cicero, who had travelled with him into Sicily, and alludes to the disagreements which had taken place between Pomponia, the sister of Atticus, and her husband, Quintus Cicero — our Cicero's brother. Marcus, in all that he says of his brother, makes the best of him. That Quintus was a scholar and a man of parts there can be no doubt; one, too, who rose to high office in the Republic. But he was arrogant, of harsh temper, cruel to those dependent on him, and altogether unimbued with the humanity which was the peculiar characteristic of his brother. "When I found him to be in the wrong, " says Cicero, in his first letter, " "I wrote to him as to a brother whom I loved; but as to one younger than myself, and whom I was bound to tell of his fault. " As is usual with correspondents, half the letter is taken up with excuses for not writing sooner; then he gives commissions for the purchase of statues for his Tusculan villa, of which we now hear for the first time, and tells his friend how his wife, Terentia, sends her love, though she is suffering from the gout. Tullia also, the dear little Tullia, "deliciae nostrae, "[140]sends her love. In the next, he says how a certain house which Atticus had intended to purchase had been secured by Fonteius for 130,000 sesterces — something over £1000, taking the sesterce at 2 d. This no doubt was part of the plunder which Fonteius had taken from the Gauls. Quintus is getting on better with his wife. Then he tells his friend very abruptly that his father died that year on the eighth day before the kalends of December — on the 24th of November. Some question as to the date of the old man's death had probably been asked. He gives further commissions as to statues, and declares of his Tusculan villa that he is happy only when he is there. In the third letter he promises that he will be ready to pay one Cincius £170 on a certain day, the price probably of more statues, and gives orders to his friend as to the buying of books. "All my prospect of enjoying myself at my ease depends on your goodness. " These were the letters he wrote when he had just ceased to be Aedile.

From the next two years five letters remain to us, chiefly noticeable from the continued commissions given by Cicero to Atticus for statues. Statues and more statues are wanted as ornaments for his Tusculanum. Should there be more than are needed for that villa, he will begin to decorate another that he has, the Formianum, near Caieta. He wants whatever Atticus may think proper for his "palaestra" and "gymnasium. " Atticus has a library or collection of maps for sale, and Cicero engages to buy them, though it seems that he has not at present quite got the money. He reserves, he says, all his little comings-in, "vindemiolas" — what he might make by selling his grapes as a lady in the country might get a little income from her spare butter—in order that he may have books as a resource for his old age. Again, he bids Atticus not to be afraid but what he, Cicero, will be able to buy them some day—which if he can do he will be richer than Crassus, and will envy no one his mansions or his lawns. He also declares that he has betrothed Tullia, then ten years old, to Caius Piso, son of Lucius Piso Frugi. The proposed marriage, which after three years of betrothal was duly solemnized, was considered to be in all respects desirable. Cicero thought very highly of his son-in-law, who was related to Calpurnius Piso, one of the Consuls of that year. So far everything was going well with our orator.

[Sidenote: B.C. 67, *aetat.* 40]

He was then candidate for the Praetorship, and was elected first, as has been already said. It was in that year, too that a law was passed in Rome, at the instance of one Gabinius, a tribune, authorizing Pompey to exterminate the pirates in the Mediterranean, and giving him almost unlimited power for this object. Pompey was not, indeed, named in this law. A single general, one who had been Consul, was to be approved by the Senate, with exclusive command by sea and for fifty miles on shore. He was to select as his own officers a hitherto unheard-of number, all of senatorial rank. It was well understood when the law was worded that Pompey alone could fill the place. The Senate opposed the scheme with all its power, although, seven years before, it had acknowledged the necessity of some measure for extirpating the pirates. But jealousies prevailed, and the Senate was afraid of Pompey. Gabinius, however, carried his law by the votes of the people, and Pompey was appointed.

Nothing tells us more clearly the wretched condition of things in Rome at this time than this infliction of pirates, under which their commerce was almost destroyed. Sulla had re-established the outside show of a strong government—a government which was strong enough to enable rich men to live securely in Rome; but he had done nothing to consolidate the Empire. Even Lucullus in the East had only partially succeeded, leaving Mithridates still to be dealt with by Pompey. Of what nature was the government of the provinces under Sulla's aristocracy we learn from the trials of Verres, and of Fonteius, and of Catiline. The Mediterranean swarmed with pirates, who taught themselves to think that they had nothing to fear from the hands of the Romans. Plutarch declares to us—no doubt with fair accuracy, because the description has been admitted by subsequent writers—how great was the horror of these depredations. [141] It is marvellous to us now that this should have been allowed—marvellous that pirates should reach such a pitch of importance that Verres had found it worth his while to sacrifice Roman citizens in their place. Pompey went forth with his officers, his fleets, and his money, and cleared the Mediterranean in forty days, as Plutarch says. Floras tells us that not a ship was lost by the Romans, and not a pirate left on the seas. [142]

In the history of Rome at this time we find men of mark whose characters, as we read, become clear to us, or appear to become clear. Of Marius and of Sulla we have a defined idea. Caesar, with his imperturbable courage, absence of scruples, and assurance of success, comes home to us. Cicero, I think, we certainly may understand. Catiline, Cato, Antony, and Brutus have left their portraits with us. Of Pompey I must acknowledge for myself that I have but a vague conception.

His wonderful successes seem to have been produced by so very little power of his own! He was not determined and venomous as was Marius; not cold-blooded and ruthless as was Sulla; certainly not confident as was Caesar; not humane as was Cicero; not passionate as Catiline; not stoic as was Cato; not reckless as was Antony, nor wedded to the idea of an oligarchy as was Brutus. Success came in his way, and he found it—found it again and again, till fortune seemed to have adopted him. Success lifted him higher and higher, till at last it seemed to him that he must be a Sulla whether he would or no. [143]

But he could not endure the idea of a rival Sulla. I doubt whether ambition would have prompted him to fight for the empire of the Republic, had he not perceived that that empire would fall into Caesar's hands did he not grasp it himself. It would have satisfied him to let things go, while the citizens called him "Magnus, " and regarded him as the man who could do a great thing if he would, if only no rivalship had been forced upon him. Caesar did force it on him, and then, as a matter of course, he fell. He must have understood warfare from his youth upward, knowing well the purposes of a Roman legion and of Roman auxiliaries. He had destroyed Sertorius in Spain, a man certainly greater than himself, and had achieved the honor of putting an end to the Servile war when Spartacus, the leader of the slaves and gladiators, had already been killed. He must have appreciated at its utmost the meaning of those words, "Cives Romanus". He was a handsome man, with good health, patient of labor, not given to luxury, reticent, I should say ungenerous, and with a strong touch of vanity; a man able to express but unable to feel friendship; with none of the highest attributes of manhood, but with all the second-rate attributes at their best; a capable, brave man, but one certain to fall crushed beneath the heel of such a man as Caesar, and as certain to leave such a one as Cicero in the lurch.

It is necessary that the reader should attempt to realize to himself the personal characteristics of Pompey, as from this time forward Cicero's political life—and his life now became altogether political—was governed by that of Pompey. That this was the case to a great extent is certain—to a sad extent, I think. The two men were of the same age; but Pompey had become a general among soldiers before Cicero had ceased to be a pupil among advocates. As Cicero was making his way toward the front, Pompey was already the first among Romans. He had been Consul seven years before his proper time, and had lately, as we have seen, been invested with extraordinary powers in that matter of putting down the pirates. In some sort the mantle of Sulla had fallen upon him. He was the leader of what we may call the conservative party. If, which I doubt, the political governance of men was a matter of interest to him, he would have had them governed by oligarchical forms. Such had been the forms in Rome, in which, though the votes of the people were the source of all power, the votes hardly went further than the selection of this or that oligarch. Pompey no doubt felt the expediency of maintaining the old order of things, in the midst of which he had been born to high rank, and had achieved the topmost place either by fortune or by merit. For any heartfelt conviction as to what might be best for his country or his countrymen, in what way he might most surely use his power for the good of the citizens generally, we must, I think, look in vain to that Pompey whom history has handed down to us. But, of all matters which interested Cicero, the governance of men interested him the most. How should the great Rome of his day rise to greater power than ever, and yet be as poor as in the days of her comparative insignificance? How should Rome be ruled so that Romans might be the masters of the world, in mental gifts as well as bodily strength, in arts as well as in arms—as by valor, so by virtue? He, too, was an oligarch by strongest conviction. His mind could conceive nothing better than Consuls, Praetors, Censors, Tribunes, and the rest of it; with, however, the stipulation that the Consuls and the Praetors should be honest men. The condition was no doubt an impossible one; but this he did not or would not see. Pompey himself was fairly honest. Up to this time he had shown no egregious lust for personal power. His hands were clean in the midst of so much public plunder. He was the leader of the conservative party. The "Optimates, " or "Boni, " as Cicero indifferently calls them—meaning, as we should say, the upper classes, who were minded to stand by their order—believed in him, though they did not just at that time wish to confide to him the power which the people gave him. The Senate did not want another Sulla; and yet it was Sulla who had reinstated the Senate. The Senate would have hindered Pompey, if it could, from his command against the pirates, and again from his command against Mithridates. But he, nevertheless, was naturally their head, as came to be seen plainly when, seventeen years afterward, Caesar passed the Rubicon, and Cicero in his heart acknowledged Pompey as his political leader while Pompey lived. This, I think, was the case to a sad extent, as Pompey was incapable of that patriotic enthusiasm which Cicero demanded. As we go on we shall find that the worst episodes in Cicero's political career were created by his doubting adherence to a leader whom he bitterly felt to be untrue to himself, and in whom his trust became weaker and weaker to the end.

Then came Cicero's Praetorship. In the time of Cicero there were eight Praetors, two of whom were employed in the city, and the six others in the provinces. The "Praetor Urbanus" was confined to the city, and was regarded as the first in authority.

This was the office filled by Cicero. His duty was to preside among the judges, and to name a judge or judges for special causes.

[Sidenote: B.C. 66, *aetat.* 41.]

Cicero at this time, when he and Pompey were forty or forty-one, believed thoroughly in Pompey. When the great General was still away, winding up the affairs of his maritime war against the pirates, there came up the continually pressing question of the continuation of the Mithridatic war. Lucullus had been absent on that business nearly seven years, and, though he had been at first grandly victorious, had failed at last. His own soldiers, tired of their protracted absence, mutinied against him, and Glabrio, a later Consul, who bad been sent to take the command out of his hands, had feared to encounter the difficulty. It was essential that something should be done, and one Manilius, a Tribune, a man of no repute himself, but whose name has descended to all posterity in the oration Pro Lege Manilia, proposed to the people that Pompey should have the command. Then Cicero first entered, as we may say, on political life. Though he had been Quaestor and Aedile, and was now Praetor, he had taken a part only in executive administration. He had had his political ideas, and had expressed them very strongly in that matter of the judges, which, in the condition of Rome, was certainly a political question of great moment. But this he had done as an advocate, and had interfered only as a barrister of to-day might do, who, in arguing a case before the judges, should make an attack on some alleged misuse of patronage. Now, for the first time, he made a political harangue, addressing the people in a public meeting from the rostra. This speech is the oration Pro Lego Manilia. This he explains in his first words. Hitherto his addresses had been to the judges—Judices; now it is to the people—Quirites: "Although, Quirites, no sight has ever been so pleasant to me as that of seeing you gathered in crowds—although this spot has always seemed to me the fittest in the world for action and the noblest for speech — nevertheless, not my own will, indeed, but the duties of the profession which I have followed from my earliest years have hitherto hindered me from entering upon this the best path to glory which is open to any good man. " It is only necessary for our purpose to say, in reference to the matter in question, that this command was given to Pompey in opposition to the Senate.

As to the speech itself, it requires our attention on two points. It is one of those choice morsels of polished Latinity which have given to Cicero the highest rank among literary men, and have, perhaps, made him the greatest writer of prose which the world has produced. I have sometimes attempted to make a short list of his *chefs d'oeuvre*—of his tidbits, as I must say, if I am bound to express myself in English. The list would never allow itself to be short, and so has become almost impossible; but, whenever the attempt has been made, this short oration in its integrity has always been included in it. My space hardly permits me to insert specimens of the author's style, but I will give in an appendix[144] two brief extracts as specimens of the beauty of words in Latin. I almost fancy that if properly read they would have a grace about them even to the ears of those to whom Latin is unknown. I venture to attach to them in parallel columns my own translation, acknowledging in despair how impossible I have found it to catch anything of the rhythm of the author. As to the beauty of the language I shall probably find no opponent. But a serious attack has been made on Cicero's character, because it has been supposed that his excessive praise was lavished on Pompey with a view of securing the great General's assistance in his candidature for the Consulship. Even Middleton repeats this accusation, and only faintly repels it. M. Du Rozoir, the French critic, declares that "in the whole oration there is not a word which was not dictated to Cicero the Praetor by his desire to become Consul, and that his own elevation was in his thoughts all through, and not that of Pompey. " The matter would be one to us but of little moment, were it not that Cicero's character for honesty as a politician depends on the truth or falsehood of his belief in Pompey. Pompey had been almost miraculously fortunate up to this period of his life's career. He had done infinitely valuable service to the State. He had already crushed the pirates. There was good ground for believing that in his hands the Roman arms would be more efficacious against Mithridates than in those of any other General. All that Cicero says on this head, whatever might have been his motive for saying it, was at any rate true.

A man desirous of rising in the service of his country of course adheres to his party. That Cicero was wrong in supposing that the Republic, which had in fact already fallen, could be re-established by the strength of any one man, could be bolstered up by any leader, has to be admitted; that in trusting to Pompey as a politician he leaned on a frail reed I admit; but I will not admit that in praising the man he was hypocritical or unduly self-seeking. In our own political contests, when a subordinate member of the Cabinet is zealously serviceable to his chief, we do not accuse him of falsehood because by that zeal he has also strengthened his own hands. How shall a patriot do the work of his country unless he be in high place? and how shall he achieve that place except by co-operation with those whom he trusts? They who have blamed Cicero for speaking on behalf of Pompey on this occasion, seem to me to ignore not only the necessities but the very virtues of political life.

One other remarkable oration Cicero made during his Praetorship — that, namely, in defence of Aulus Cluentius Habitus. As it is the longest, so is it the most intricate, and on account of various legal points the most difficult to follow of all his speeches. But there are none perhaps which tell us more of the condition, or perhaps I should say the possibilities, of life among the Romans of that day. The accusation against Roscius Amerinus was accompanied by horrible circumstances. The iniquities of Verres, as a public officer who had the power of blessing or of cursing a whole people, were very terrible; but they do not shock so much as the story here told of private life. That any man should have lived as did Oppianicus, or any woman as did Sassia, seems to prove a state of things worse than anything described by Juvenal a hundred and fifty years later. Cicero was no doubt unscrupulous as an advocate, but he could have gained nothing here by departing from verisimilitude. We must take the picture as given us as true, and acknowledge that, though law processes were common, crimes such as those of this man and of this woman were not only possible, but might be perpetrated with impunity. The story is too long and complicated to be even abridged; but it should be read by those who wish to know the condition of life in Italy during the latter days of the Republic.

[Sidenote: B.C. 65, aetat. 42.]

In the year after he was Praetor—in the first of the two years between his Praetorship and Consulship, B.C. 65—he made a speech in defence of one Caius Cornelius, as to which we hear that the pleadings in the case occupied four days. This, with our interminable "causes célèbres, " does not seem much to us, but Cicero's own speech was so long that in publishing it he divided it into two parts. This Cornelius had been Tribune in the year but one before, and was accused of having misused his power when in office. He had incurred the enmity of the aristocracy by attempts made on the popular side to restrain the Senate; especially by the stringency of a law proposed for stopping bribery at elections. Cicero's speeches are not extant. We have only some hardly intelligible fragments of them, which were preserved by Asconius, [145] a commentator on certain of Cicero's orations; but there is ground for supposing that these Cornelian orations were at the time matter of as great moment as those spoken against Verres, or almost as those spoken against Catiline. Cicero defended Cornelius, who was attacked by the Senate—by the rich men who desired office and the government of provinces. The law proposed for the restriction of bribery at elections no doubt attempted to do more by the severity of its punishment than can be achieved by such means: it was mitigated, but was still admitted by Cicero to be too rigorous. The rancor of the Senate against Cornelius seems to have been due to this attempt; but the illegality with which he was charged, and for which he was tried, had reference to another law suggested by him—for restoring to the people the right of pardon which had been usurped by the Senate. Caius Cornelius seems to have been a man honest and eager in his purpose to save the Republic from the greed of the oligarchs, but—as had been the Gracchi—ready in his eagerness to push his own authority too far in his attempt to restrain that of the Senate. A second Tribune, in the interest of the Senate, attempted to exercise an authority which undoubtedly belonged to him, by inhibiting the publication or reading of the proposed law. The person whose duty it was to read it was stopped; then Cornelius pushed aside the inferior officer, and read it himself. There was much violence, and the men who brought the accusation about Cornelius—two brothers named Cominii—had to hide themselves, and saved their lives by escaping over the roofs of the houses.

This took place when Cicero was standing for the Praetorship, and the confusion consequent upon it was so great that it was for awhile impossible to carry on the election. In the year after his Praetorship Cornelius was put upon his trial, and the two speeches were made.

The matter seems to have been one of vital interest in Rome. The contest on the part of the Senate was for all that made public life dear to such a body. Not to bribe—not to be able to lay out money in order that money might be returned ten-fold, a hundred-fold—would be to them to cease to be aristocrats. The struggles made by the Gracchi, by Livius Drusus, by others whose names would only encumber us here, by this Cornelius, were the expiring efforts of those who really desired an honest Republic. Such were the struggles made by Cicero himself; though there was present always to him an idea, with which, in truth, neither the demagogues nor the aristocrats sympathized, that the reform could be effected, not by depriving the Senate of its power, but by teaching the Senate to use it honestly. We can sympathize with the idea, but we are driven to acknowledge that it was futile.

Though we know that this was so, the fragments of the speeches, though they have been made intelligible to us by the "argument" or story of them prefixed by Asconius in his notes, cannot be of interest to readers. They were extant in the time of Quintilian, who speaks of them with the highest praise. [146] Cicero himself selects certain passages out of these speeches as examples of eloquence or rhythm, [147] thus showing the labor with which he composed them, polishing them by the exercise of his ear as well as by that of his intellect. We know from Asconius that this trial was regarded at the time as one of vital interest.

We have two letters from Cicero written in the year after his Praetorship, both to Atticus, the first of which tells us of his probable competition for the Consulship; the second informs his friend that a son is born to him—he being then forty-two years old—and that he is thinking to undertake the defence of Catiline, who was to be accused of peculation as Propraetor in Africa. "Should he be acquitted, " says Cicero, "I should hope to have him on my side in the matter of my canvass. If he should be convicted, I shall be able to bear that too. " There were to be six or seven candidates, of whom two, of course, would be chosen. It would be much to Cicero "to run, " as our phrase goes, with the one who among his competitors would be the most likely to succeed. Catiline, in spite of his then notorious character—in the teeth of the evils of his government in Africa—was, from his birth, his connections, and from his ability, supposed to have the best chance. It was open to Cicero to defend Catiline as he had defended Fonteius, and we know from his own words that he thought of doing so. But he did not; nor did Cicero join himself with Catiline in the canvassing. It is probable that the nature of Catiline's character and intentions were now becoming clearer from day to day. Catiline was tried and acquitted, having, it is said, bribed the judges.

NOTES:

[134] Pro Fonteio, xiii.

[135] De Oratore, lib. ii., lix. : "Perspicitis, hoc genus quam sit facetum, quam elegans, quam oratorium, sive habeas vere, quod narrare possis, quod tamen, est mendaciunculis aspergendum, sive fingas. " Either invent a story, or if you have an old one, add on something so as to make it really funny. Is there a parson, a bishop, an archbishop, who, if he have any sense of humor about him, does not do the same?

[136] Cicero, Pro Cluentio, l., explains very clearly his own idea as to his own speeches as an advocate, and may be accepted, perhaps, as explaining the ideas of barristers of to-day. "He errs, " he says, "who thinks that he gets my own opinions in speeches made in law courts; such speeches are what the special cases require, and are not to be taken as coming from the advocate as his own. "

[137] When the question is discussed, we are forced rather to wonder how many of the great historical doings of the time are not mentioned, or are mentioned very slightly, in Cicero's letters. Of

Pompey's treatment of the pirates, and of his battling in the East, little or nothing is said, nothing of Caesar's doings in Spain. Mention is made of Caesar's great operations in Gaul only in reference to the lieutenancy of Cicero's brother Quintus, and to the employment of his young friend Trebatius. Nothing is said of the manner of Caesar's coming into Rome after passing the Rubicon; nothing of the manner of fighting at Dyrrachium and Pharsalia; very little of the death of Pompey; nothing of Caesar's delay in Egypt. The letters deal with Cicero's personal doings and thoughts, and with the politics of Rome as a city. The passage to which allusion is made occurs in the life of Atticus, ca. xvi: "Quae qui legat non multum desideret historiam contextam illorum temporum. "

[138] Jean George Greefe was a German, who spent his life as a professor at Leyden, and, among other classical labors, arranged and edited the letters of Cicero. He died in 1703.

[139] It must be explained, however, that continued research and increased knowledge have caused the order of the letters, and the dates assigned to them, to be altered from time to time; and, though much has been done to achieve accuracy, more remains to be done. In my references to the letters I at first gave them, both to the arrangement made by Graevius and to the numbers assigned in the edition I am using; but I have found that the numbers would only mislead, as no numbering has been yet adopted as fixed. Arbitrary and even fantastic as is the arrangement of Graevius, it is better to confine myself to that because it has been acknowledged, and will enable my readers to find the letters if they wish to do so. Should Mr. Tyrell continue and complete his edition of the correspondence, he will go far to achieve the desired accuracy. A second volume has appeared since this work of mine has been in the press.

[140] The peculiarities of Cicero's character are nowhere so clearly legible as in his dealings with and words about his daughter. There is an effusion of love, and then of sorrow when she dies, which is un-Roman, almost feminine, but very touching.

[141] I annex a passage from our well known English translation: "The power of the pirates had its foundation in Cilicia. Their progress was the more dangerous, because at first it had been but little noticed. In the Mithridatic war they assumed new confidence and courage, on account of some services which they had rendered the king. After this, the Romans being engaged in civil war at the

very gates of their capital, the sea was left unguarded, and the pirates by degrees attempted higher things—not only attacking ships, but islands and maritime towns. Many persons distinguished for their wealth, birth and capacity embarked with them, and assisted in their depredations, as if their employment had been worthy the ambition of men of honor. They had in various places arsenals, ports, and watch-towers, all strongly fortified. Their fleets were not only extremely well manned, supplied with skilful pilots, and fitted for their business by their lightness and celerity, but there was a parade of vanity about them, more mortifying than their strength, in gilded sterns, purple canopies, and plated oars, as if they took a pride and triumphed in their villany. Music resounded, and drunken revels were exhibited on every coast. Here generals were made prisoners; and there the cities which the pirates had seized upon were paying their ransom, to the great disgrace of the Roman power. The number of their galleys amounted to a thousand, and the cities taken to four hundred. " The passage is taken from the life of Pompey.

[142] Florus, lib. iii., 6: "An felicitatem, quod ne una cuidam navis amissa est; an vero perpetuetatem, quod ampluis piratae non fuerunt. "

[143] Of the singular trust placed in Pompey there are very many proofs in the history of Rome at this period, but none, perhaps, clearer than the exception made in this favor in the wording of laws. In the agrarian law proposed by the Tribune Rullus, and opposed by Cicero when he was Consul, there is a clause commanding all Generals under the Republic to account for the spoils taken by them in war. But there is a special exemption in favor of Pompey. "Pompeius exceptus esto. " It is as though no Tribune dared to propose a law affecting Pompey.

[144] See Appendix D.

[145] Asconius Pedianus was a grammarian who lived in the reign of Tiberius, and whose commentaries on Cicero's speeches, as far as they go, are very useful in explaining to us the meaning of the orator. We have his notes on these two Cornelian orations and some others, especially on that of Pro Milone. There are also commentaries on some of the Verrine orations—not by Asconius, but from the pen of some writer now called Pseudo-Asconius, having been long

supposed to have come from Asconius. They, too, go far to elucidate much which would otherwise be dark to us.

[146] Quint., lib. viii., 3. The critic is explaining the effect of ornament in oratory—of that beauty of language which with the people has more effect than argument—and he breaks forth himself into perhaps the most eloquent passage in the whole Institute: "Cicero, in pleading for Cornelius, fought with arms which were as splendid as they were strong. It was not simply by putting the facts before the judges, by talking usefully, in good language and clearly, that he succeeded in forcing the Roman people to acknowledge by their voices and by their hands their admiration; it was the grandeur of his words, their magnificence, their beauty, their dignity, which produced that outburst. "

[147] Orator., lxvii. and lxx.

CHAPTER VIII.

CICERO AS CONSUL.

Hitherto everything had succeeded with Cicero. His fortune and his fame had gone hand-in-hand. The good-will of the citizens had been accorded to him on all possible occasions. He had risen surely, if not quickly, to the top of his profession, and had so placed himself there as to have torn the wreath from the brow of his predecessor and rival, Hortensius. On no memorable occasion had he been beaten. If now and then he had failed to win a cause in which he was interested, it was as to some matter in which, as he had said to Atticus in speaking of his contemplated defence of Catiline, he was not called on to break his heart if he were beaten. We may imagine that his life had been as happy up to this point as a man's life may be. He had married well. Children had been born to him, who were the source of infinite delight. He had provided himself with houses, marbles, books, and all the intellectual luxuries which well-used wealth could produce. Friends were thick around him. His industry, his ability, and his honesty were acknowledged. The citizens had given him all that it was in their power to give. Now at the earliest possible day, with circumstances of much more than usual honor, he was put in the highest place which his country had to offer, and knew himself to be the one man in whom his country at this moment trusted. Then came the one twelve-month, the apex of his fortunes; and after that, for the twenty years that followed, there fell upon him one misery after another—one trouble on the head of another trouble—so cruelly that the reader, knowing the manner of the Romans, almost wonders that he condescended to live.

[Sidenote: B.C. 64, *aetat.* 43]

He was chosen Consul, we are told, not by the votes but by the unanimous acclamation of the citizens. What was the exact manner of doing this we can hardly now understand. The Consuls were elected by ballot, wooden tickets having been distributed to the people for the purpose; but Cicero tells us that no voting tickets were used in his case, but that he was elected by the combined voice of the whole people. [148] He had stood with six competitors. Of these it is only necessary to mention two, as by them only was Cicero's life affected, and as out of the six, only they seem to have come prominently forward during the canvassing. These were Catiline the conspirator, as we shall have to call him in dealing with his name in the next chapter, and Caius Antonius, one of the sons of Marc Antony, the great orator of the preceding age, and uncle of the Marc Antony with whom we are all so well acquainted, and with whom we shall have so much to do before we get to the end of this work. Cicero was so easily the first that it may be said of him that he walked over the course. Whether this was achieved by the Machiavellian arts which his brother Quintus taught in his treatise De Petitione Consulatus, or was attributable to his general popularity, may be a matter of doubt. As far as we can judge from the signs which remain to us of the public feeling of the period, it seems that he was at this time regarded with singular affection by his countrymen. He had robbed none, and had been cruel to no one. He had already abandoned the profit of provincial government —to which he was by custom entitled after the lapse of his year's duty as Praetor—in order that he might remain in Rome among the people. Though one of the Senate himself—and full of the glory of the Senate, as he had declared plainly enough in that passage from one of the Verrine orations which I have quoted—he had generally pleaded on the popular side. Such was his cleverness, that even when on the unpopular side—as he may be supposed to have been when defending Fonteius—he had given a popular aspect to the cause in hand. We cannot doubt, judging from the loud expression of the people's joy at his election, that he had made himself beloved But, nevertheless, he omitted none of those cares which it was expected that a candidate should take. He made his electioneering speech "in toga candida"—in a white robe, as candidates did, and were thence so called. It has not come down to us, nor do we regret it, judging from the extracts which have been collected from the notes which Asconius wrote upon it. It was full of personal abuse of Antony and Catiline, his competitors. Such was the practice of Rome at this time, as it was also with us not very long since. We shall have more than enough of such eloquence before we have done our task. When we come to the language in which Cicero spoke of Clodius, his enemy, of Piso and Gabinius, the Consuls who allowed him to be banished, and of Marc Antony, his last great opponent—the nephew of the man who was now his colleague—we shall have very much of it. It must again be pleaded that the foul abuse which fell from other lips has not been preserved and that Cicero, therefore, must not be supposed to have been more foul mouthed than his rivals. We can easily imagine that he was more bitter than others, because he had more power to throw into his words the meaning which he intended them to convey.

Antony was chosen as Cicero's colleague. It seems, from such evidence as we are able to get on the subject, that Cicero trusted Antony no better than he did Catiline, but, appreciating the wisdom of the maxim, "divide et impera" — separate your enemies and you will get the better of them, which was no doubt known as well then as now — he soon determined to use Antony as his ally against Catiline, who was presumed to reckon Antony among his fellow-conspirators. Sallust puts into the mouth of Catiline a declaration to this effect, [149] and Cicero did use Antony for the purpose. The story of Catiline's conspiracy is so essentially the story of Cicero's Consulship, that I may be justified in hurrying over the other events of his year's rule; but still there is something that must be told. Though Catiline's conduct was under his eye during the whole year, it was not till October that the affairs in which we shall have to interest ourselves commenced.

Of what may have been the nature of the administrative work done by the great Roman officers of State we know very little; perhaps I might better say that we know nothing. Men, in their own diaries, when they keep them, or even in their private letters, are seldom apt to say much of those daily doings which are matter of routine to themselves, and are by them supposed to be as little interesting to others. A Prime-minister with us, were he as prone to reveal himself in correspondence as was Cicero with his friend Atticus, would hardly say when he went to the Treasury Chambers or what he did when he got there. We may imagine that to a Cabinet Minister even a Cabinet Council would, after many sittings, become a matter of course. A leading barrister would hardly leave behind him a record of his work in chambers. It has thus come to pass that, though we can picture to ourselves a Cicero before the judges, or addressing the people from the rostra, or uttering his opinion in the Senate, we know nothing of him as he sat in his office and did his consular work. We cannot but suppose that there must have been an office with many clerks. There must have been heavy daily work. The whole operation of government was under the Consul's charge, and to Cicero, with a Catiline on his hands, this must have been more than usually heavy. How he did it, with what assistance, sitting at what writing-table, dressed in what robes, with what surroundings of archives and red tape, I cannot make manifest to myself. I can imagine that there must have been much of dignity, as there was with all leading Romans, but beyond that I cannot advance even in fancying what was the official life of a Consul.

In the old days the Consul used, as a matter of course, to go out and do the fighting. When there was an enemy here, or an enemy there, the Consul was bound to hurry off with his army, north or south, to different parts of Italy. But gradually this system became impracticable. Distances became too great, as the Empire extended itself beyond the bounds of Italy, to admit of the absence of the Consuls. Wars prolonged themselves through many campaigns, as notably did that which was soon to take place in Gaul under Caesar. The Consuls remained at home, and Generals were sent out with proconsular authority. This had become so certainly the case, that Cicero on becoming Consul had no fear of being called on to fight the enemies of his country. There was much fighting then in course of being done by Pompey in the East; but this would give but little trouble to the great officers at home, unless it might be in sending out necessary supplies.

The Consul's work, however, was severe enough. We find from his own words, in a letter to Atticus written in the year but one after his Consulship, 61 B. C., that as Consul he made twelve public addresses. Each of them must have been a work of labor, requiring a full mastery over the subject in hand, and an arrangement of words very different in their polished perfection from the generality of parliamentary speeches to which we are accustomed. The getting up of his cases must have taken great time. Letters went slowly and at a heavy cost. Writing must have been tedious when that most common was done with a metal point on soft wax. An advocate who was earnest in a case had to do much for himself. We have heard how Cicero made his way over to Sicily, creeping in a little boat through the dangers prepared for him, in order that he might get up the evidence against Verres. In defending Aulus Cluentius when he was Praetor, Cicero must have found the work to have been immense. In preparing the attack upon Catiline it seems that every witness was brought to himself. There were four Catiline speeches made in the year of his Consulship, but in the same year many others were delivered by him. He mentions, as we shall see just now, twelve various speeches made in the year of his Consulship.

I imagine that the words spoken can in no case have been identical with those which have come to us—which were, as we may say, prepared for the press by Tiro, his slave and secretary. We have evidence as to some of them, especially as to the second Catiline oration, that time did not admit of its being written and learned by heart after the occurrence of the circumstances to which it alludes. It needs must have been extemporary, with such mental preparation as one night may have sufficed to give him. How the words may have been taken down in such a case we do not quite know; but we are aware that short-hand writers were employed, though there can hardly have been a science of stenography perfected as is that with us. [150]

The words which we read were probably much polished before they were published, but how far this was done we do not know. What we do know is that the words which he spoke moved, convinced, and charmed those who heard them, as do the words we read move, convince and charm us. Of these twelve consular speeches Cicero gives a special account to his friend. "I will send you, " he says, "the speechlings[151] which you require, as well as some others, seeing that those which I have written out at the request of a few young men please you also. It was an advantage to me here to follow the example of that fellow-citizen of yours in those orations which he called his Philippics. In these he brightened himself up, and discarded his 'nisi prius' way of speaking, so that he might achieve something more dignified, something more statesman-like. So I have done with these speeches of mine which may be called 'consulares, '" as having been made not only in his consular year but also with something of consular dignity. "Of these, one, on the new land laws proposed, was spoken in the Senate on the kalends of January. The second, on the same subject, to the people. The third was respecting Otho's law. [152]

The fourth was in defence of Rabirius. [153]

The fifth was in reference to the children of those who had lost their property and their rank under Sulla's proscription. [154]

The sixth was an address to the people, and explained why I renounced my provincial government. [155]

The seventh drove Catiline out of the city. The eighth was addressed to the people the day after Catiline fled. The ninth was again spoken to the people, on the day on which the Allobroges gave their evidence. Then, again, the tenth was addressed to the Senate on the fifth of December"—also respecting Catiline. "There arc also two short supplementary speeches on the Agrarian war. You shall have the whole body of them. As what I write and what I do are equally interesting to you, you will gather from the same documents all my doings and all my sayings. "

It is not to be supposed that in this list are contained all the speeches which he made in his consular year, but those only which he made as Consul—those to which he was desirous of adding something of the dignity of statesmanship, something beyond the weight attached to his pleadings as a lawyer. As an advocate, Consul though he was, he continued to perform his work; from whence we learn that no State dignity was so high as to exempt an established pleader from the duty of defending his friends. Hortensius, when Consul elect, had undertaken to defend Verres. Cicero defended Murena when he was Consul. He defended C. Calpurnius Piso also, who was accused, as were so many, of proconsular extortion; but whether in this year or in the preceding is not, I think, known. [156]

Of his speech on that occasion we have nothing remaining. Of his pleading for Murena we have, if not the whole, the material part, and, though nobody cares very much for Murena now, the oration is very amusing. It was made toward the end of the year, on the 20th of November, after the second Catiline oration, and before the third, at the very moment in which Cicero was fully occupied with the evidence on which he intended to convict Catiline's fellow-conspirators. As I read it I am carried away by wonder, rather than admiration, at the energy of the man who could at such a period of his life give up his time to master the details necessary for the trial of Murena.

Early in the year Cicero had caused a law to be passed—which, after him, was called the Lex Tullia—increasing the stringency of the enactments against bribery on the part of consular candidates. His intention had probably been to hinder Catiline, who was again about to become a candidate. But Murena, who was elected, was supposed to have been caught in the meshes of the net, and also Silanus, the other Consul designate. Cato, the man of stern nature, the great Stoic of the day, was delighted to have an opportunity of proceeding against some one, and not very sorry to attack Murena with weapons provided from the armory of Murena's friend, Cicero. Silanus, however, who happened to be cousin to Cato, was allowed to pass unmolested. Sulpicius, who was one of the disappointed candidates, Cato, and Postumius were the accusers. Hortensius, Crassus, and Cicero were combined together for the defence of Murena. But as we read the single pleading that has come to us, we feel that, unlike those Roman trials generally, this was carried on without any acrimony on either side. I think it must have been that Cato wished to have an opportunity of displaying his virtue, but it had been arranged that Murena was to be acquitted. Murena was accused, among other things, of dancing! Greeks might dance, as we hear from Cornelius Nepos, [157] but for a Roman Consul it would be disgraceful in the highest extreme. A lady, indeed, might dance, but not much. Sallust tells us of Sempronia—who was, indeed, a very bad female if all that he says of her be true—that she danced more elegantly than became an honest woman. [158]

She was the wife of a Consul. But a male Roman of high standing might not dance at all. Cicero defends his friend by showing how impossible it was—how monstrous the idea. "No man would dance unless drunk or mad. " Nevertheless, I imagine that Murena had danced.

Cicero seizes an opportunity of quizzing Cato for his stoicism, and uses it delightfully. Horace was not more happy when, in defence of Aristippus, he declared that any philosopher would turn up his nose at cabbage if he could get himself asked to the tables of rich men. [159] "There was one Zeno, " Cicero says, "who laid down laws. No wise man would forgive any fault. No man worthy of the name of man would allow himself to be pitiful. Wise men are beautiful, even though deformed; rich though penniless; kings though they be slaves. We who are not wise are mere exiles, runagates, enemies of our country, and madmen. Any fault is an unpardonable crime. To kill an old cock, if you do not want it, is as bad as to murder your father! "[160]

And these doctrines, he goes on to say, which are used by most of us merely as something to talk about, this man Cato absolutely believes, and tries to live by them. I shall have to refer back to this when I speak of Cicero's philosophy more at length; but his common-sense crops up continually in the expressions which he uses for defending the ordinary conditions of a man's life, in opposition to that impossible superiority to mundane things which the philosophers professed to teach their pupils. He turns to Cato and asks him questions, which he answers himself with his own philosophy: "Would you pardon nothing? Well, yes; but not all things. Would you do nothing for friendship? Sometimes, unless duty should stand in the way. Would you never be moved to pity? I would maintain my habit of sincerity, but something must no doubt be allowed to humanity. It is good to stick to your opinion, but only until some better opinion shall have prevailed with you. " In all this the humanity of our Cicero, as opposed equally to the impossible virtue of a Cato or the abominable vice of a Verres, is in advance of his age, and reminds us of what Christ has taught us.

But the best morsel in the whole oration is that in which he snubs the lawyers. It must be understood that Cicero did not pride himself on being a lawyer. He was an advocate, and if he wanted law there were those of an inferior grade to whom he could go to get it. In truth, he did understand the law, being a man of deep research, who inquired into everything. As legal points had been raised, he thus addresses Sulpicius, who seems to have affected a knowledge of jurisprudence, who had been a candidate for the Consulship, and who was his own intimate friend: "I must put you out of your conceit, " he says; "it was your other gifts, not a knowledge of the laws—your moderation, your wisdom, your justice—which, in my opinion, made you worthy of being loved. I will not say you threw away your time in studying law, but it was not thus you made yourself worthy of the Consulship. [161]

That power of eloquence, majestic and full of dignity which has so often availed in raising a man to the Consulship, is able by its words to move the minds of the Senate and the people and the judges. [162] But in such a poor science as that of law what honor can there be? Its details are taken up with mere words and fragments of words. [163] They forget all equity in points of law, and stick to the mere letter. "[164] He goes through a presumed scene of chicanery, which, Consul as he was, he must have acted before the judges and the people, no doubt to the extreme delight of them all. At last he says, "Full as I am of business, if you raise my wrath I will make myself a lawyer, and learn it all in three days. "[165] From these and many other passages in Cicero's writings and speeches, and also from, Quintilian, we learn that a Roman advocate was by no means the same as an English barrister. The science which he was supposed to have learned was simply that of telling his story in effective language. It no doubt came to pass that he had much to do in getting up the details of his story—what we may call the evidence—but he looked elsewhere, to men of another profession, for his law. The "juris consultus" or the "juris peritus" was the lawyer, and as such was regarded as being of much less importance than the "patronus" or advocate, who stood before the whole city and pleaded the cause. In this trial of Murena, who was by trade a soldier, it suited Cicero to belittle lawyers and to extol the army. When he is telling Sulpicius that it was not by being a lawyer that a man could become Consul, he goes on to praise the high dignity of his client's profession. "The greatest glory is achieved by those who excel in battle. All our empire, all our republic, is defended and made strong by them. "[166] It was thus that the advocate could speak! This comes from the man who always took glory to himself in declaring that the "toga" was superior to helmet and shield. He had already declared that they erred who thought that they were going to get his own private opinion in speeches made in law courts. [167] He knew how to defend his friend Murena, who was a soldier, and in doing so could say very sharp things, though yet in joke, against his friend Sulpicius, the lawyer. But in truth few men understood the Roman law better than did Cicero.

But we must go back to that agrarian law respecting which, as he tells us, four of his consular speeches were made. This had been brought forward by Rullus, one of the Tribunes, toward the end of the last year. The Tribunes came into office in December, whereas at this period of the Republic the Consuls were in power only on and from January 1st. Cicero, who had been unable to get the particulars of the new law till it had been proclaimed, had but a few days to master its details. It was, to his thinking, altogether revolutionary. We have the words of many of the clauses; and though it is difficult at this distance of time to realize what would have been its effect, I think we are entitled to say that it was intended to subvert all property. Property, speaking of it generally, cannot be destroyed The land remains, and the combined results of man's industry are too numerous, too large, and too lasting to become a wholesale prey to man's anger or madness. Even the elements when out of order can do but little toward perfecting destruction. A deluge is wanted — or that crash of doom which, whether it is to come or not, is believed by the world to be very distant. But it is within human power to destroy possession, and redistribute the goods which industry, avarice, or perhaps injustice has congregated. They who own property are in these days so much stronger than those who have none, that an idea of any such redistribution does not create much alarm among the possessors. The spirit of communism does not prevail among people who have learned that it is, in truth, easier to earn than to steal. But with the Romans political economy had naturally not advanced so far as with us. A subversion of property had to a great extent taken place no later than in Sulla's time. How this had been effected the story of the property of Roscius Amerinus has explained to us.

Under Sulla's enactments no man with a house, with hoarded money, with a family of slaves, with rich ornaments, was safe. Property had been made to change hands recklessly, ruthlessly, violently, by the illegal application of a law promulgated by a single individual, who, however, had himself been instigated by no other idea than that of re-establishing the political order of things which he approved. Rullus, probably with other motives, was desirous of effecting a subversion which, though equally great, should be made altogether in a different direction. The ostensible purpose was something as follows: as the Roman people had by their valor and wisdom achieved for Rome great victories, and therefore great wealth, they, as Roman citizens, were entitled to the enjoyment of what they had won; whereas, in fact, the sweets of victory fell to the lot only of a few aristocrats. For the reform of this evil it should be enacted that all public property which had been thus acquired, whether land or chattels, should be sold, and with the proceeds other lands should be bought fit for the use of Roman citizens, and be given to those who would choose to have it. It was specially suggested that the rich country called the Campania—that in which Naples now stands with its adjacent isles—should be bought up and given over to a great Roman colony. For the purpose of carrying out this law ten magistrates should be appointed, with plenipotentiary power both as to buying and selling. There were many underplots in this. No one need sell unless he chose to sell; but at this moment much land was held by no other title than that of Sulla's proscriptions. The present possessors were in daily fear of dispossession, by some new law made with the object of restoring their property to those who had been so cruelly robbed. These would be very glad to get any price in hand for land of which their tenure was so doubtful; and these were the men whom the "decemviri, " or ten magistrates, would be anxious to assist. We are told that the father-in-law of Rullus himself had made a large acquisition by his use of Sulla's proscriptions. And then there would be the instantaneous selling of the vast districts obtained by conquest and now held by the Roman State. When so much land would be thrown into the market it would be sold very cheap and would be sold to those whom the "decemviri" might choose to favor. We can hardly now hope to unravel all the intended details, but we may be sure that the basis on which property stood would have been altogether changed by the measure. The "decemviri" were to have plenary power for ten years. All the taxes in all the provinces were to be sold, or put up to market. Everything supposed to belong to the Roman State was to be sold in every province, for the sake of collecting together a huge sum of money, which was to be divided in the shape of land among the poorer Romans. Whatever may have been the private intentions of Rullus, whether good or bad, it is evident, even at this distance of time, that a redistribution of property was intended which can only be described as a general subversion. To this the new Consul opposed himself vehemently, successfully, and, we must needs say, patriotically.

The intense interest which Cicero threw into his work is as manifest in these agrarian orations as in those subsequently made as to the Catiline conspiracy. He ascends in his energy to a dignity of self-praise which induces the reader to feel that a man who could so speak of himself without fear of contradiction had a right to assert the supremacy of his own character and intellect. He condescends, on the other hand, to a virulence of personal abuse against Rullus which, though it is to our taste offensive, is, even to us, persuasive, making us feel that such a man should not have undertaken such a work. He is describing the way in which the bill was first introduced: "Our Tribunes at last enter upon their office. The harangue to be made by Rullus is especially expected. He is the projector of the law, and it was expected that he would carry himself with an air of special audacity. When he was only Tribune elect he began to put on a different countenance, to speak with a different voice, to walk with a different stop. We all saw how he appeared with soiled raiment, with his person uncared for, and foul with dirt, with his hair and beard uncombed and untrimmed. "[168] In Rome men under afflictions, particularly if under accusation, showed themselves in soiled garments so as to attract pity, and the meaning here is that Rullus went about as though under grief at the condition of his poor fellow-citizens, who were distressed by the want of this agrarian law. No description could be more likely to turn an individual into ridicule than this of his taking upon himself to represent in his own person the sorrows of the city. The picture of the man with the self-assumed garments of public woe, as though he were big enough to exhibit the grief of all Rome, could not but be effective. It has been supposed that Cicero was insulting the Tribune because he was dirty. Not so. He was ridiculing Rullus because Rullus had dared to go about in mourning—"sordidatus" —on behalf of his country.

But the tone in which Cicero speaks of himself is magnificent. It is so grand as to make us feel that a Consul of Rome, who had the cares of Rome on his shoulders, was entitled to declare his own greatness to the Senate and to the people. There are the two important orations—

that spoken first in the Senate, and then the speech to the people from which I have already quoted the passage personal to Rullus. In both of them he declares his own idea of a Consul, and of himself as Consul. He has been speaking of the effect of the proposed law on the revenues of the State, and then proceeds: "But I pass by what I have to say on that matter and reserve it for the people. I speak now of the danger which menaces our safety and our liberty. For what will there be left to us untouched in the Republic, what will remain of your authority and freedom, when Rullus, and those whom you fear much more than Rullus, [169] with this band of ready knaves, with all the rascaldom of Rome, laden with gold and silver, shall have seized on Capua and all the cities round? To all this, Senators"—Patres conscripti he calls them—"I will oppose what power I have. As long as I am Consul I will not suffer them to carry out their designs against the Republic.

"But you, Rullus, and those who are with you, have been mistaken grievously in supposing that you will be regarded as friends of the people in your attempts to subvert the Republic in opposition to a Consul who is known in very truth to be the people's friend I call upon you, I invite you to meet me in the assembly. Let us have the people of Rome as a judge between us. Let us look round and see what it is that the people really desire. We shall find that their is nothing so dear to them as peace and quietness and ease. You have handed over the city to me full of anxiety, depressed with fear, disturbed by these projected laws and seditious assemblies. " (It must be remembered that he had only on that very day begun his Consulship) "The wicked you have filled with hope, the good with fear. You have lobbed the Forum of loyalty and the Republic of dignity. But now, when in the midst of these troubles of mind and body, when in this great darkness the voice and the authority of the Consul has been heard by the people—when he shall have made it plain that there is no cause for fear, that no strange army shall enroll itself, no bands collect themselves; that there shall be no new colonies, no sale of the revenue no altered empire, no royal 'decemvirs, ' no second Rome no other centre of rule but this; that while I am Consul there shall be perfect peace, perfect ease—do you suppose that I shall dread the superior popularity of your new agrarian law? Shall I, do you think, be afraid to hold my own against you in an assembly of the citizens when I shall have exposed the iniqiuty of your designs, the fraud of this law, the plots which your Tribunes of the people, popular as they think themselves, have contrived against the Roman people? Shall I fear—I who have determined to be Consul after that fashion in which alone a man may do so in dignity and freedom, reaching to ask nothing for myself which any Tribune could object to have given to me? "[170]

This was to the Senate, but he is bolder still when he addresses the people. He begins by reminding them that it has always been the custom of the great officers of state, who have enjoyed the right of having in their houses the busts and images of their ancestors, in their first speech to the people to join with thanks for the favors done to themselves some records of the noble deeds done by their forefathers. [171] He, however, could do nothing of the kind: he had no such right: none in his family had achieved such dignity. To speak of himself might seem too proud, but to be silent would be ungrateful. Therefore would he restrain himself, but would still say something, so that he might acknowledge what he had received. Then he would leave it for them to judge whether he had deserved what they had done for him.

"It is long ago—almost beyond the memory of us now here—since you last made a new man Consul. [172] That high office the nobles had reserved for themselves, and defended it, as it were, with ramparts. You have secured it for me, so that in future it shall be open to any who may be worthy of it. Nor have you only made me a Consul, much as that is, but you have done so in such a fashion that but few among the old nobles have been so treated, and no new man—'novus ante me nemo. ' I have, if you will think of it, been the only new man who has stood for the Consulship in the first year in which it was legal, and who has got it. " Then he goes on to remind them, in words which I have quoted before, that they had elected him by their unanimous voices. All this, he says, had been very grateful to him, but he had quite understood that it had been done that he might labor on their behalf. That such labor was severe, he declares. The Consulship itself must be defended. His period of Consulship to any Consul must be a year of grave responsibility, but more so to him than to any other. To him, should he be in doubt, the great nobles would give no kind advice. To him, should he be overtasked, they would give no assistance. But the first thing he would look for should be their good opinion. To declare now, before the people, that he would exercise his office for the good of the people was his natural duty. But in that place, in which it was difficult to speak after such a fashion, in the Senate itself, on the very first day of his Consulship, he had declared the same thing—"popularem me futurum esse consulem. "[173]

The course he had to pursue was noble, but very difficult. He desired, certainly, to be recognized as a friend of the people, but he desired so to befriend them that he might support also at the same time the power of the aristocracy. He still believed, as we cannot believe now, that there was a residuum of good in the Senate sufficient to blossom forth into new powers of honest government. When speaking to the oligarchs in the Senate of Rullus and his land law, it was easy enough to carry them with him. That a Consul should oppose a Tribune who was coming forward with a "Lex agraria" in his hands, as the latest disciple of the Gracchi, was not out of the common order of things. Another Consul would either have looked for popularity and increased power of plundering, as Antony might have done, or have stuck to his order, as he would have called it—as might have been the case with the Cottas, Lepiduses and Pisos of preceding years. But Cicero determined to oppose the demagogue Tribune by proving himself to the people to be more of a demagogue than he. He succeeded, and Rullus with his agrarian law was sent back into darkness. I regard the second speech against Rullus as the *ne plus ultra*, the very *beau ideal* of a political harangue to the people on the side of order and good government.

I cannot finish this chapter, in which I have attempted to describe the lesser operations of Cicero's Consulship, without again alluding to the picture drawn by Virgil of a great man quelling the storms of a seditious rising by the gravity of his presence and the weight of his words. [174] The poet surely had in his memory some occasion in which had taken place this great triumph of character and intellect combined. When the knights, during Cicero's Consulship essayed to take their privileged places in the public theatre, in accordance with a law passed by Roscius Otho a few years earlier (B. C. 68), the founder of the obnoxious law himself entered the building. The people, enraged against a man who had interfered with them and their pleasures, and who had brought them, as it were under new restraints from the aristocracy, arose in a body and began to break everything that came to hand. "Tum pietate gravem! " The Consul was sent for. He called on the people to follow him out of the theatre to the Temple of Bellona, and there addressed to them that wonderful oration by which they were sent away not only pacified but in good-humor with Otho himself. "Iste regit dictis animos et pectora mulcet. " I have spoken of Pliny's eulogy as to the great Consul's doings of the year. The passage is short and I will translate it: [175] "But, Marcus Tullius, how shall I reconcile it to myself to be silent as to you, or by what special glory shall I best declare your excellence? How better than by referring to the grand testimony given to you by the whole nation, and to the achievements of your Consulship as a specimen of your entire life? At your voice the tribes gave up their agrarian law, which was as the very bread in their mouths. At your persuasion they pardoned Otho his law and bore with good-humor the difference of the seats assigned to them. At your prayer the children of the proscribed forbore from demanding their rights of citizenship. Catiline was put to flight by your skill and eloquence. It was you who silenced[176] M. Antony. Hail, thou who wert first addressed as the father of your country—the first who, in the garb of peace, hast deserved a triumph and won the laurel wreath of eloquence. " This was grand praise to be spoken of a man more than a hundred years after his death, by one who had no peculiar sympathies with him other than those created by literary affinity.

None of Cicero's letters have come to us from the year of his Consulship.

NOTES:

[148] De Lege Agraria, ii., 2: "Meis comitiis non tabellam, vindicem tacitae libertatis, sed vocem vivam prae vobis, indicem vestrarum erga me voluntatum ac studiorum tulistis. Itaque me——una voce universus populus Romanus consulem declaravit. "

[149] Sall., Conj. Catilinaria, xxi. : "Petere consularum C. Antonium, quem sibi collegam fore speraret, hominem et familiarem, et omnibus necessitudinibus circumventum. " Sallust would no doubt have put anything into Catiline's mouth which would suit his own purpose; but it was necessary for his purpose that he should confine himself to credibilities.

[150] Cicero himself tells us that many short-hand writers were sent by him—"Plures librarii, " as he calls them—to take down the words of the Agrarian law which Rullus proposed. De Lege Agra., ii., 5. Pliny, Quintilian, and Martial speak of these men as Notarii. Martial explains the nature of their business:

"Currant verba licet, manus est velocior illis;
Nondum lingua suum, dextra peregit opus. "—xiv., 208.

[151]Ad Att., ii., 1. "Oratiunculas, " he calls them. It would seem here that he pretends to have preserved these speeches only at the request of some admiring young friends. Demosthenes, of course, was the "fellow-citizen, " so called in badinage, because Atticus, deserting Rome, lived much at Athens.

[152] This speech, which has been lost, was addressed to the people with the view of reconciling them to a law in accordance with which the Equites were entitled to special seats in the theatre. It was altogether successful.

[153] This, which is extant, was spoken in defence of an old man who was accused of a political homicide thirty-seven years before—of having killed, that is, Saturninus the Tribune. Cicero was unsuccessful, but Rabirius was saved by the common subterfuge of an interposition of omens. There are some very fine passages in this oration.

[154] This has been lost. Cicero, though he acknowledged the iniquity of Sulla's proscriptions, showed that their effects could not now be reversed without further revolutions. He gained his point on this occasion.

[155] This has been lost. Cicero, in accordance with the practice of the time, was entitled to the government of a province when ceasing to be Consul. The rich province of Macedonia fell to him by lot, but he made it over to his colleague Antony, thus purchasing, if not Antony's co-operation, at any rate his quiescence, in regard to Catiline. He also made over the province of Gaul, which then fell to his lot, to Metellus, not wishing to leave the city. All this had to be explained to the people.

[156] It will be seen that he also defended Rabirius in his consular year, but had thought fit to include that among his consular speeches. Some doubt has been thrown, especially by Mr. Tyrrell, on the genuineness of Cicero's letter giving the list of his "orationculas consulares, " because the speeches Pro Murena and Pro Pisone are omitted, and as containing some "rather un-Ciceronian expressions. " My respect for Mr. Tyrrell's scholarship and judgment is so great that I hardly dare to express an opinion contrary to his; but I should be sorry to exclude a letter so Ciceronian in its feeling. And if we are to have liberty to exclude without evidence, where are we to stop?

[157] Corn. Nepo., Epaminondas, I.: "We know that with us" (Romans) "music is foreign to the employments of a great man. To dance would amount to a vice. But these things among the Greeks are not only pleasant but praiseworthy. "

[158] Conj. Catilinaria, xxv.

[159] Horace, Epis. i., xvii. :

> "Si sciret regibus uti
> Fastidiret olus qui me notat. "

[160] Pro Murena, xxix.

[161] Pro Murena, x. This Sulpicius was afterward Consul with M. Marcellus, and in the days of the Philippies was sent as one of a deputation to Antony. He died while on the journey. He is said to have been a man of excellent character, and a thorough-going conservative.

[162] Pro Murena, xi.

[163] Ibid., xi.

[164] Ibid., xii.

[165] Ibid., xiii.

[166] Ibid., xi.

[167] Pro Cluentio, 1.

[168] De Lege Agraria, ii., 5.

[169] He alludes here to his own colleague Antony, whom through his whole year of office he had to watch lest the second Consul should join the enemies whom he fears—should support Rullus or go over to Catiline. With this view, choosing the lesser of the two evils, he bribes Antony with the government of Macedonia.

[170] De Lege Agraria, i., 7 and 8.

[171] The "jus imagins" belonged to those whose ancestors was counted an Aedile, a Praetor, or a Consul. The descendants of such officers were entitled to have these images, whether in bronze, or marble, or wax, carried at the funerals of their friends.

[172] Forty years since, Marius who was also "novus homo, " and also, singularly enough, from Arpinum, had been made Consul, but not with the glorious circumstances as now detailed by Cicero.

[173] De Lege Agrana, 11, 1, 2, and 3.

[174] See Introduction.

[175] Pliny the elder, Hist. Nat., lib. vii., ca. xxxi.

[176] The word is "proscripsisti, " "you proscribed him. " For the proper understanding of this, the bearing of Cicero toward Antony during the whole period of the Philippics must be considered.

CHAPTER IX

CATILINE.

To wash the blackamoor white has been the favorite task of some modern historians. To find a paradox in character is a relief to the investigating mind which does not care to walk always in the well-tried paths, or to follow the grooves made plain and uninteresting by earlier writers. Tiberius and even Nero have been praised. The memories of our early years have been shocked by instructions to regard Richard III. and Henry VIII. as great and scrupulous kings. The devil may have been painted blacker than he should be, and the minds of just men, who will not accept the verdict of the majority, have been much exercised to put the matter right. We are now told that Catiline was a popular hero; that, though he might have wished to murder Cicero, he was, in accordance with the practice of his days, not much to be blamed for that; and that he was simply the follower of the Gracchi, and the forerunner of Caesar in his desire to oppose the oligarchy of Rome. [177] In this there is much that is true. Murder was common. He who had seen the Sullan proscriptions, as both Catiline and Cicero had done, might well have learned to feel less scrupulous as to blood than we do in these days. Even Cicero, who of all the Romans was the most humane—even he, no doubt, would have been well contented that Catiline should have been destroyed by the people. [178] Even he was the cause, as we shall see just now, of the execution of the leaders of the conspirators whom Catiline left behind him in the city—an execution of which the legality is at any rate very doubtful. But in judging even of bloodshed we have to regard the circumstances of the time in the verdicts we give. Our consciousness of altered manners and of the growth of gentleness force this upon us. We cannot execrate the conspirators who murdered Caesar as we would do those who might now plot the death of a tyrant; nor can we deal as heavily with the murderers of Caesar as we would have done then with Catilinarian conspirators in Rome, had Catiline's conspiracy succeeded. And so, too, in acknowledging that Catiline was the outcome of the Gracchi, and to some extent the preparation for Caesar, we must again compare him with them, his motives and designs with theirs, before we can allow ourselves to sympathize with him, because there was much in them worthy of praise and honor.

That the Gracchi were seditious no historian has, I think, denied. They were willing to use the usages and laws of the Republic where those usages and laws assisted them, but as willing to act illegally when the usages and laws ran counter to them. In the reforms or changes which they attempted they were undoubtedly rebels; but no reader comes across the tale of the death, first of one and then of the other, without a regret. It has to be owned that they were murdered in tumults which they themselves had occasioned. But they were honest and patriotic. History has declared of them that their efforts were made with the real purport of relieving their fellow-countrymen from what they believed to be the tyranny of oligarchs. The Republic even in their time had become too rotten to be saved; but the world has not the less given them the credit for a desire to do good; and the names of the two brothers, rebels as they were, have come down to us with a sweet savor about them. Caesar, on the other hand, was no doubt of the same political party. He too was opposed to the oligarchs, but it never occurred to him that he could save the Republic by any struggles after freedom. His mind was not given to patriotism of that sort—not to memories, not to associations. Even laws were nothing to him but as they might be useful. To his thinking, probably even in his early days, the state of Rome required a master. Its wealth, its pleasures, its soldiers, its power, were there for any one to take who could take them—for any one to hold who could hold them. Mr. Beesly, the last defender of Catiline, has stated that very little was known in Rome of Caesar till the time of Catiline's conspiracy, and in that I agree with him. He possessed high family rank, and had been Quaestor and Aedile; but it was only from this year out that his name was much in men's mouths, and that he was learning to look into things. It may be that he had previously been in league with Catiline—that he was in league with him till the time came for the great attempt. The evidence, as far as it goes, seems to show that it was so. Rome had been the prey of many conspiracies. The dominion of Marius and the dominion of Sulla had been effected by conspiracies. No doubt the opinion was strong with many that both Caesar and Crassus, the rich man, were concerned with Catiline. But Caesar was very far-seeing, and, if such connection existed, knew how to withdraw from it when the time was not found to be opportune. But from first to last he always was opposed to the oligarchy. The various steps from the Gracchi to him were as those which had to be made from the Girondists to Napoleon. Catiline, no doubt, was one of the steps, as were Danton and Robespierre steps. The continuation of steps in each case was at first occasioned by the bad government and greed of a few men in power. But as

Robespierre was vile and low, whereas Vergniaud was honest and Napoleon great, so was it with Catiline between the Gracchi and Caesar. There is, to my thinking, no excuse for Catiline in the fact that he was a natural step, not even though he were a necessary step, between the Gracchi and Caesar.

I regard as futile the attempts which are made to rewrite history on the base of moral convictions and philosophical conclusion. History very often has been, and no doubt often again will be, rewritten, with good effect and in the service of truth, on the finding of new facts. Records have been brought to light which have hitherto been buried, and testimonies are compared with testimonies which have not before been seen together. But to imagine that a man may have been good who has lain under the ban of all the historians, all the poets, and all the tellers of anecdotes, and then to declare such goodness simply in accordance with the dictates of a generous heart or a contradictory spirit, is to disturb rather than to assist history. Of Catiline we at least know that he headed a sedition in Rome in the year of Cicero's Consulship; that he left the city suddenly; that he was killed in the neighborhood of Pistoia fighting against the Generals of the Republic, and that he left certain accomplices in Rome who were put to death by an edict of the Senate. So much I think is certain to the most truculent doubter. From his contemporaries, Sallust and Cicero, we have a very strongly expressed opinion of his character. They have left to us denunciations of the man which have made him odious to all after-ages, so that modern poets have made him a stock character, and have dramatized him as a fiend. Voltaire has described him as calling upon his fellow-conspirators to murder Cicero and Cato, and to burn the city. Ben Jonson makes Catiline kill a slave and mix his blood, to be drained by his friends. "There cannot be a fitter drink to make this sanction in. " The friends of Catiline will say that this shows no evidence against the man. None, certainly; but it is a continued expression of the feeling that has prevailed since Catiline's time. In his own age Cicero and Sallust, who were opposed in all their political views, combined to speak ill of him. In the next, Virgil makes him as suffering his punishment in hell. [179] In the next, Velleius Paterculus speaks of him as the conspirator whom Cicero had banished. [180] Juvenal makes various allusions to him, but all in the same spirit. Juvenal cared nothing for history, but used the names of well-known persons as illustrations of the idea which he was presenting. [181] Valerius Maximus, who wrote commendable little essays about all the virtues and all the vices, which he illustrated with the names of all the vicious and all the virtuous people he knew, is very severe on Catiline. [182] Florus, who wrote two centuries and a half after the conspiracy, gives us of Catiline the same personal story as that told both by Sallust and Cicero: "Debauchery, in the first place; and then the poverty which that had produced; and then the opportunity of the time, because the Roman armies were in distant lands, induced Catiline to conspire for the destruction of his country. "[183] Mommsen, who was certainly biassed by no feeling in favor of Cicero, declares that Catiline in particular was "one of the most nefarious men in that nefarious age. His villanies belong to the criminal records, not to history. "[184] All this is no evidence. Cicero and Sallust may possibly have combined to lie about Catiline. Other Roman writers may have followed them, and modern poets and modern historians may have followed the Roman writers. It is possible that the world may have been wrong as to a period of Roman history with which it has thought itself to be well acquainted; but the world now has nothing to go by but the facts as they have come down to it. The writers of the ages since have combined to speak of Cicero with respect and admiration. They have combined, also, to speak of Catiline with abhorrence. They have agreed, also, to treat those other rebels, the Gracchi, after such a fashion that, in spite of their sedition, a sweet savor, as I have said, attaches itself to their names. For myself, I am contented to take the opinion of the world, and feel assured that I shall do no injustice in speaking of Catiline as all who have written about him hitherto have spoken of him I cannot consent to the building up of a noble patriot out of such materials as we have concerning him. [185]

Two strong points have been made for Catiline in Mr. Beesly's defence. His ancestors had been Consuls when the forefathers of patricians of a later date "were clapping their chapped hands and throwing up their sweaty nightcaps. " That scorn against the people should be expressed by the aristocrat Casca was well supposed by Shakspeare; but how did a liberal of the present day bring himself to do honor to his hero by such allusions? In truth, however, the glory of ancient blood and the disgrace attaching to the signs of labor are ideas seldom relinquished even by democratic minds. A Howard is nowhere lovelier than in America, or a sweaty nightcap less relished. We are then reminded how Catiline died fighting, with the wounds all in front; and are told that the "world has generally a generous word for the memory of a brave man dying for his cause, be that cause what it will; but for Catiline none! " I think there is a mistake in the sentiment expressed here. To die readily when death must come is but a little thing, and is done daily by the poorest of mankind. The Romans could generally do it, and so can the Chinese. A Zulu is quite equal to it, and people lower in civilization than Chinese or Zulus. To encounter death, or the danger of death, for the sake of duty—when the choice is there; but duty and death are preferred to ignominious security, or, better still, to security which shall bring with it self-abasement—that is grand. When I hear that a man "rushed into the field and, foremost fighting, fell, "if there have been no adequate occasion, I think him a fool. If it be that he has chosen to hurry on the necessary event, as was Catiline's case, I recognize him as having been endowed with certain physical attributes which are neither glorious nor disgraceful. That Catiline was constitutionally a brave man no one has denied. Rush, the murderer, was one of the bravest men of whom I remember to have heard. What credit is due to Rush is due to Catiline.

What we believe to be the story of Catiline's life is this: In Sulla's time he was engaged, as behooved a great nobleman of ancient blood, in carrying out the Dictator's proscriptions and in running through whatever means he had. There are fearful stories told of him as to murdering his own son and other relatives; as to which Mr. Beesly is no doubt right in saying that such tales were too lightly told in Rome to deserve implicit confidence. To serve a purpose any one would say anything of any enemy. Very marvellous qualities are attributed to him—as to having been at the same time steeped in luxury and yet able and willing to bear all bodily hardships. He probably had been engaged in murders—as how should a man not have been so who had served under Sulla during the Dictatorship? He had probably allured some young aristocrats into debauchery, when all young aristocrats were so allured. He had probably undergone some extremity of cold and hunger. In reading of these things the reader will know by instinct how much he may believe, and how much he should receive as mythic. That he was a fast young nobleman, brought up to know no scruples, to disregard blood, and to look upon his country as a milch cow from which a young nobleman might be fed with never-ending streams of rich cream in the shape of money to be borrowed, wealth to be snatched, and, above all, foreigners to be plundered, we may take, I think, as proved. In spite of his vices, or by aid of them, he rose in the service of his country. That such a one should become a Praetor and a Governor was natural. He went to Africa with proconsular authority, and of course fleeced the Africans. It was as natural as that a flock of sheep should lose their wool at shearing time. He came back intent, as was natural also, on being a Consul, and of carrying on the game of promotion and of plunder. But there came a spoke in his wheel—the not unusual spoke of an accusation from the province. While under accusation for provincial robbery he could not come forward as a candidate, and thus he was stopped in his career.

It is not possible now to unravel all the personal feuds of the time—the ins and outs of family quarrels. Clodius—the Clodius who was afterward Cicero's notorious enemy and the victim of Milo's fury—became the accuser of Catiline on behalf of the Africans. Though Clodius was much the younger, they were men of the same class. It may be possible that Clodius was appointed to the work—as it had been intended that Caecilius should be appointed at the prosecution of Verres—in order to assure not the conviction but the acquittal of the guilty man. The historians and biographers say that Clodius was at last bought by a bribe, and that he betrayed the Africans after that fashion. It may be that such bribery was arranged from the first. Our interest in that trial lies in the fact that Cicero no doubt intended, from political motives, to defend Catiline. It has been said that he did do so. As far as we know, he abandoned the intention. We have no trace of his speech, and no allusion in history to an occurrence which would certainly have been mentioned. [186] But there was *no* reason why he should not have done so. He defended Fonteius, and I am quite willing to own that he knew Fonteius to have been a robber. When I look at the practice of our own times, I find that thieves and rebels are defended by honorable advocates, who do not scruple to take their briefs in opposition to their own opinions. It suited Cicero to do the same. If I were detected in a plot for blowing up a Cabinet Council, I do not doubt but that I should get the late attorney-general to defend me. [187]

But Catiline, though he was acquitted, was balked in his candidature for the Consulship of the next year, B.C. 65. P. Sulla and Antronius were elected—that Sulla to whose subsequent defence I have just referred in this note—but were ejected on the score of bribery, and two others, Torquatus and Cotta, were elected in their place. In this way three men standing on high before their countrymen—one having been debarred from standing for the Consulship, and the other two having been robbed of their prize even when it was within their grasp—not unnaturally became traitors at heart. Almost as naturally they came together and conspired. Why should they have been selected as victims, having only done that which every aristocrat did as a matter of course in following out his recognized profession in living upon the subject nations? Their conduct had probably been the same as that of others, or if more glaring, only so much so as is always the case with vices as they become more common. However, the three men fell, and became the centre of a plot which is known as the first Catiline conspiracy.

The reader must bear in mind that I am now telling the story of Catiline, and going back to a period of two years before Cicero's Consulship, which was B. C. 63. How during that year Cicero successfully defended Murena when Cato endeavored to rob him of his coming Consulship, has been already told. It may be that Murena's hands were no cleaner than those of Sulla and Autronius, and that they lacked only the consular authority and forensic eloquence of the advocate who defended Murena. At this time, when the two appointed Consuls were rejected, Cicero had hardly as yet taken any part in public politics. He had been Quaestor, Aedile, and Praetor, filling those administrative offices to the best of his ability. He had, he says, hardly heard of the first conspiracy. [189] That what he says is true, is, I think, proved by the absence of all allusion to it in his early letters, or in the speeches or fragments of speeches that are extant. But that there was such a conspiracy we cannot doubt, nor that the three men named, Catiline, Sulla, and Autronius, were leaders in it. What would interest us, if only we could have the truth, is whether Caesar and Crassus were joined in it.

It is necessary again to consider the condition of the Republic. To us a conspiracy to subvert the government under which the conspirer lives seems either a very terrible remedy for great evils, or an attempt to do evil which all good men should oppose. We have the happy conspiracy in which Washington became the military leader, and the French Revolution, which, bloody as it was, succeeded in rescuing Frenchmen from the condition of serfdom. At home we have our own conspiracy against the Stuart royalty, which had also noble results. The Gracchi had attempted to effect something of the same kind at Rome; but the moral condition of the people had become so low that no real love of liberty remained. Conspiracy! oh yes. As long as there was anything to get, of course he who had not got it would conspire against him who had. There had been conspiracies for and against Marius, for and against Cinna, for and against Sulla. There was a grasping for plunder, a thirst for power which meant luxury, a greed for blood which grew from the hatred which such rivalry produced. These were the motive causes for conspiracies; not whether Romans should be free but whether a Sulla or a Cotta should be allowed to run riot in a province.

Caesar at this time had not done much in the Roman world except fall greatly into debt. Knowing, as we do know now, his immense intellectual capacity, we cannot doubt but at the age he had now reached, thirty-five, B.C. 65, he had considered deeply his prospects in life. There is no reason for supposing that he had conceived the idea of being a great soldier. That came to him by pure accident, some years afterward. To be Quaestor, Praetor, and Consul, and catch what was going, seems to have been the cause to him of having encountered extraordinary debt. That he would have been a Verres, or a Fonteius, or a Catiline, we certainly are not entitled to think. Over whatever people he might have come to reign, and in whatever way he might have procured his kingdom, he would have reigned with a far-seeing eye, fixed upon future results. At this period he was looking out for a way to advance himself. There were three men, all just six years his senior, who had risen or were rising into great repute; they were Pompey, Cicero, and Catiline. There were two who were noted for having clean hands in the midst of all the dirt around; and they were undoubtedly the first Romans of the day. Catiline was determined that he too would be among the first Romans of the day; but his hands had never been clean. Which was the better way for such a one as Caesar to go?

To have had Pompey under his feet, or Cicero, must have then seemed to Caesar to be impracticable, though the time came when he did, in different ways, have his feet on both. With Catiline the chance of success might be better. Crassus he had already compassed. Crassus was like M. Poirier in the play—a man who, having become rich, then allowed himself the luxury of an ambition. If Caesar joined the plot we can well understand that Crassus should have gone with him. We have all but sufficient authority for saying that it was so, but authority insufficient for declaring it. That Sallust, in his short account of the first conspiracy, should not have implicated Caesar was a matter of course, [190] as he wrote altogether in Caesar's interest. That Cicero should not have mentioned it is also quite intelligible. He did not wish to pull down upon his ears the whole house of the aristocracy. Throughout his career it was his object to maintain the tenor of the law with what smallest breach of it might be possible; but he was wise enough to know that when the laws were being broken on every side he could not catch in his nets all those who broke them. He had to pass over much; to make the best of the state of things as he found them. It is not to be supposed that a conspirator against the Republic would be horrible to him, as would be to us a traitor against the Crown: there were too many of them for horror. If Caesar and Crassus could be got to keep themselves quiet, he would be willing enough not to have to add them to his list of enemies. Livy is presumed to have told us that this conspiracy intended to restore the ejected Consuls, and to kill the Consuls who had been established in their place. But the book in which this was written is lost, and we have only the Epitome, or heading of the book, of which we know that it was not written by Livy. [191] Suetonius, who got his story not improbably from Livy, tells us that Caesar was suspected of having joined this conspiracy with Crassus; [192] and he goes on to say that Cicero, writing subsequently to one Axius, declared that "Caesar had attempted in his Consulship to accomplish the dominion which he had intended to grasp in his Aedile-ship" the year in question. There is, however, no such letter extant. Asconius, who, as I have said before, wrote in the time of Tiberius, declares that Cicero in his lost oration, "In toga candida, " accused Crassus of having been the author of the conspiracy. Such is the information we have; and if we elect to believe that Caesar was then joined with Catiline, we must be guided by our ideas of probability rather than by evidence. [193]

As I have said before, conspiracies had been very rife. To Caesar it was no doubt becoming manifest that the Republic, with its oligarchs, must fall. Subsequently it did fall, and he was—I will not say the conspirator, nor will I judge the question by saying that he was the traitor; but the man of power who, having the legions of the Republic in his hands, used them against the Republic. I can well understand that he should have joined such a conspiracy as this first of Catiline, and then have backed out of it when he found he could not trust those who were joined with him.

This conspiracy failed. One man omitted to give a signal at one time, and another at another. The Senate was to have been slaughtered; the two Consuls, Cotta and Torquatus, murdered, and the two ex-Consuls, Sulla and Autronius, replaced. Though all the details seem to have been known to the Consuls, Catiline was allowed to go free, nor were any steps taken for the punishment of the conspirators.

The second conspiracy was attempted in the Consulship of Cicero, B.C. 63, two years after the first. Catiline had struggled for the Consulship, and had failed. Again there would be no province, no plunder, no power. This interference, as it must have seemed to him, with his peculiar privileges, had all come from Cicero. Cicero was the busybody who was attempting to stop the order of things which had, to his thinking, been specially ordained by all the gods for the sustenance of one so well born, and at the same time so poor, as himself. There was a vulgar meddling about it—all coming from the violent virtue of a Consul whose father had been a nobody at Arpinum—which was well calculated to drive Catiline into madness. So he went to work and got together in Rome a body of men as discontented and almost as nobly born as himself, and in the country north of Rome an army of rebels, and began his operations with very little secrecy. In all the story the most remarkable feature is the openness with which many of the details of the conspiracy were carried on. The existence of the rebel army was known; it was known that Catiline was the leader; the causes of his disaffection were known; his comrades in guilt were known When any special act was intended, such as might be the murder of the Consul or the firing of the city, secret plots were concocted in abundance. But the grand fact of a wide-spread conspiracy could go naked in Rome, and not even a Cicero dare to meddle with it.

[Sidenote: B.C. 63, aetat. 44]

As to this second conspiracy, the conspiracy with which Sallust and Cicero have made us so well acquainted, there is no sufficient ground for asserting that Caesar was concerned in it. [194]

That he was greatly concerned in the treatment of the conspirators there is no doubt. He had probably learned to appreciate the rage, the madness, the impotence of Catiline at then propel worth. He too, I think, must have looked upon Cicero as a meddling, over-virtuous busybody; as did even Pompey when he returned from the East. What practical use could there be in such a man at such a time—in one who really believed in honesty, who thought of liberty and the Republic, and imagined that he could set the world right by talking? Such must have been the feeling of Caesar, who had both experience and foresight to tell him that Rome wanted and must have a master. He probably had patriotism enough to feel that he, if he could acquire the mastership, would do something beyond robbery— would not satisfy himself with cutting the throats of all his enemies, and feeding his supporters with the property of his opponents. But Cicero was impracticable—unless, indeed, he could be so flattered as to be made useful. It was thus, I think, that Caesar regarded Cicero, and thus that he induced Pompey to regard him. But now, in the year of his Consulship, Cicero had really talked himself into power, and for this year his virtue must be allowed to have its full way.

He did so much in this year, was so really efficacious in restraining for a time the greed and violence of the aristocracy, that it is not surprising that he was taught to believe in himself. There were, too, enough of others anxious for the Republic to bolster him up in his own belief. There was that Cornelius in whose defence Cicero made the two great speeches which have been unfortunately lost, and there was Cato, and up to this tune there was Pompey, as Cicero thought. Cicero, till he found himself candidate for the Consulship, had contented himself with undertaking separate cases, in which, no doubt, politics were concerned, but which were not exclusively political. He had advocated the employment of Pompey in the East, and had defended Cornelius. He was well acquainted with the history of the Republic; but he had probably never asked himself the question whether it was in mortal peril, and if so, whether it might possibly be saved. In his Consulship he did do so; and, seeing less of the Republic than we can see now, told himself that it was possible.

The stories told to us of Catiline's conspiracy by Sallust and by Cicero are so little conflicting that we can trust them both. Trusting them both, we are justified in believing that we know the truth. We are here concerned only with the part which Cicero took. Nothing, I think, which Cicero says is contradicted by Sallust, though of much that Cicero certainly did Sallust is silent. Sallust damns him, but only by faint praise. We may, therefore, take the account of the plot as given by Cicero himself as verified: indeed, I am not aware that any of Cicero's facts have been questioned.

Sallust declares that Catiline's attempt was popular in Rome generally. [195] This, I think, must be taken as showing simply that revolution and conspiracy were in themselves popular: that, as a condition of things around him such as existed in Rome, a plotter of state plots should be able to collect a body of followers, was a thing of course; that there were many citizens who would not work, and who expected to live in luxury on public or private plunder, is certain. When the conspiracy was first announced in the Senate, Catiline had an army collected; but we have no proof that the hearts of the inhabitants of Rome generally were with the conspirators. On the other hand, we have proof, in the unparalleled devotion shown by the citizens to Cicero after the conspiracy was quelled, that their hearts were with him. The populace, fond of change, liked a disturbance; but there is nothing to show that Catiline was ever beloved as had been the Gracchi, and other tribunes of the people who came after them.

Catiline, in the autumn of the year B. C. 63, had arranged the outside circumstances of his conspiracy, knowing that he would, for the third time, be unsuccessful in his canvass for the Consulship. That Cicero with other Senators should be murdered seems to have been their first object, and that then the Consulship should be seized by force. On the 21st of October Cicero made his first report to the Senate as to the conspiracy, and called upon Catiline for his answer. It was then that Catiline made his famous reply: "That the Republic had two bodies, of which one was weak and had a bad head"— meaning the aristocracy, with Cicero as its chief—"and the other strong, but without any head, " meaning the people; "but that as for himself, so well had the people deserved of him, that as long as he lived a head should be forth-coming. "[196] Then, at that sitting, the Senate decreed, in the usual formula, "That the Consuls were to take care that the Republic did not suffer. [197] On the 22d of October, the new Consuls, Silanus and Murena, were elected. On the 23d, Catiline was regularly accused of conspiracy by Paulus Lepidus, a young nobleman, in conformity with a law which had been enacted fifty-five years earlier, "de vi publica, " as to violence applied to the State. Two days afterward it was officially reported that Manlius—or Mallius, as he seems to have been generally called—Catiline's lieutenant, had openly taken up arms in Etruria. The 27th had been fixed by the conspirators for the murder of Cicero and the other Senators. That all this was to be, and was so arranged by Catiline, had been declared in the Senate by Cicero himself on that day when Catiline told them of the two bodies and the two heads. Cicero, with his intelligence, ingenuity, and industry, had learned every detail. There was one Curius among the conspirators, a fair specimen of the young Roman nobleman of the day, who told it all to his mistress Fulvia, and she carried the information to the Consul. It is all narrated with fair dramatic accuracy in Ben Jonson's dull play, though he has attributed to Caesar a share in the plot, for doing which he had no authority. Cicero, on that sitting in the Senate, had been specially anxious to make Catiline understand that he knew privately every circumstance of the plot. Throughout the whole conspiracy his object was not to take Catiline, but to drive him out of Rome. If the people could be stirred up to kill him in their wrath, that might be well; in that way there might be an end of all the trouble. But if that did not come to pass, then it would be best to make the city unbearable to the conspirators. If they could be driven out, they must either take themselves to foreign parts and be dispersed, or must else fight and assuredly be conquered. Cicero himself was never blood-thirsty, but the necessity was strong upon him of ridding the Republic from these blood-thirsty men.

The scheme for destroying Cicero and the Senators on the 27th of October had proved abortive. On the 6th of the next month a meeting was held in the house of one Marcus Porcius Laeca, at which a plot was arranged for the killing of Cicero the next day—for the killing of Cicero alone—he having been by this time found to be the one great obstacle in their path. Two knights were told off for the service, named Vargunteius and Cornelius. These, after the Roman fashion, were to make their way early on the following morning into the Consul's bedroom for the ostensible purpose of paying him their morning compliments, but, when there, they were to slay him. All this, however, was told to Cicero, and the two knights, when they came, were refused admittance. If Cicero had been a man given to fear, as has been said of him, he must have passed a wretched life at this period. As far as I can judge of his words and doings throughout his life, he was not harassed by constitutional timidity. He feared to disgrace his name, to lower his authority, to become small in the eyes of men, to make political mistakes, to do that which might turn against him. In much of this there was a falling off from that dignity which, if we do not often find it in a man, we can all of us imagine; but of personal dread as to his own skin, as to his own life, there was very little. At this time, when, as he knew well, many men with many weapons in their hands, men who were altogether unscrupulous, were in search for his blood he never seems to have trembled.

But all Rome trembled—even according to Sallust. I have already shown how he declares in one part of his narrative that the common people as a body were with Catiline, and have attempted to explain what was meant by that expression. In another, in an earlier chapter, he says "that the State, " meaning the city, "was disturbed by all this, and its appearance changed. [198] Instead of the joy and ease which had lately prevailed, the effect of the long peace, a sudden sadness fell upon every one. " I quote the passage because that other passage has been taken as proving the popularity of Catiline. There can, I think, be no doubt that the population of Rome was, as a body, afraid of Catiline. The city was to be burnt down, the Consuls and the Senate were to be murdered, debts were to be wiped out, slaves were probably to be encouraged against their masters. The "permota civitas" and the "cuncta plebes, " of which Sallust speaks, mean that all the "householders" were disturbed, and that all the "roughs" were eager with revolutionary hopes.

On the 8th of November, the day after that on which the Consul was to have been murdered in his own house, he called a special meeting of the Senate in the temple of Jupiter Stator. The Senate in Cicero's time was convened according to expedience, or perhaps as to the dignity of the occasion, in various temples. Of these none had a higher reputation than that of the special Jupiter who is held to have befriended Romulus in his fight with the Sabines. Here was launched that thunderbolt of eloquence which all English school-boys have known for its "Quousque tandem abutere, Catilina, patientia nostra. " Whether it be from the awe which has come down to me from my earliest years, mixed perhaps with something of dread for the great pedagogue who first made the words to sound grandly in my ears, or whether true critical judgment has since approved to me the real weight of the words, they certainly do contain for my intelligence an expression of almost divine indignation. Then there follows a string of questions, which to translate would be vain, which to quote, for those who read the language, is surely unnecessary. It is said to have been a fault with Cicero that in his speeches he runs too much into that vein of wrathful interrogation which undoubtedly palls upon us in English oratory when frequent resort is made to it. It seems to be too easy, and to contain too little of argument. It was this, probably, of which his contemporaries complained when they declared him to be florid, redundant, and Asiatic in his style. [199] This questioning runs through nearly the whole speech, but the reader cannot fail to acknowledge its efficacy in reference to the matter in hand. Catiline was sitting there himself in the Senate, and the questions were for the most part addressed to him. We can see him now, a man of large frame, with bold, glaring eyes, looking in his wrath as though he were hardly able to keep his hands from the Consul's throat, even there in the Senate. Though he knew that this attack was to be made on him, he had stalked into the temple and seated himself in a place of honor, among the benches intended for those who had been Consuls. When there, no one spoke to him, no one saluted him. The consular Senators shrunk away, leaving their places of privilege. Even his brother-conspirators, of whom many were present, did not dare to recognize him. Lentulus was no doubt there, and Cethegus, and two of the Sullan family, and Cassius Longinus, and Autronius, and Laeca, and Curins. All of them were or had been conspirators in the same cause. Caesar was there too, and Crassus. A fellow conspirator with Catiline would probably be a Senator. Cicero knew them all. We cannot say that in this matter Caesar was guilty, but Cicero, no doubt, felt that Caesar's heart was with Catiline. It was his present task so to thunder with his eloquence that he should turn these bitter enemies into seeming friends—to drive Catiline from out of the midst of them, so that it should seem that he had been expelled by those who were in truth his brother-conspirators; and this it was that he did.

He declared the nature of the plot, and boldly said that, such being the facts, Catiline deserved death. "If, " he says, "I should order you to be taken and killed, believe me I should be blamed rather for my delay in doing so than for my cruelty. "

He spoke throughout as though all the power were in his own hands, either to strike or to forbear. But it was his object to drive him out and not to kill him. "Go, " he said; "that camp of yours and Mallius, your lieutenant, are too long without you. Take your friends with you. Take them all. Cleanse the city of your presence. When its walls are between you and me then I shall feel myself secure. Among us here you may no longer stir yourself. I will not have it—I will not endure it. If I were to suffer you to be killed, your followers in the conspiracy would remain here; but if you go out, as I desire you, this cesspool of filth will drain itself off from out the city. Do you hesitate to do at my command that which you would fain do yourself? The Consul requires an enemy to depart from the city. Do you ask me whether you are to go into exile? I do not order it; but if you ask my counsel, I advise it. " Exile was the severest punishment known by the Roman law, as applicable to a citizen, and such a punishment it was in the power of no Consul or other officer of state to inflict. Though he had taken upon himself the duty of protecting the Republic, still he could not condemn a citizen. It was to the moral effect of his words that he must trust: "Non jubeo, sed si me consulis, suadeo. " Catiline heard him to the end, and then, muttering a curse, left the Senate, and went out of the city. Sallust tells us that he threatened to extinguish, in the midst of the general ruin he would create, the flames prepared for his own destruction. Sallust, however, was not present on the occasion, and the threat probably had been uttered at an earlier period of Catiline's career. Cicero tells us expressly, in one of his subsequent works, that Catiline was struck dumb. [200] Of this first Catiline oration Sallust says, that "Marcus Tullius the Consul, either fearing the presence of the man, or stirred to anger, made a brilliant speech, very useful to the Republic. "[201] This, coming from an enemy, is stronger testimony to the truth of the story told by Cicero, than would have been any vehement praise from the pen of a friend.

Catiline met some of his colleagues the same night. They were the very men who as Senators had been present at his confusion, and to them he declared his purpose of going. There was nothing to be done in the city by him. The Consul was not to be reached. Catiline himself was too closely watched for personal action. He would join the army at Faesulae and then return and burn the city. His friends, Lentulus, Cethegus, and the others, were to remain and be ready for fire and slaughter as soon as Catiline with his army should appear before the walls. He went, and Cicero had been so far successful.

But these men, Lentulus, Cethegus, and the other Senators, though they had not dared to sit near Catiline in the Senate, or to speak a word to him, went about their work zealously when evening had come. A report was spread among the people that the Consul had taken upon himself to drive a citizen into exile. Catiline, the ill-used Catiline—Catiline, the friend of the people, had, they said, gone to Marseilles in order that he might escape the fury of the tyrant Consul. In this we see the jealousy of Romans as to the infliction of any punishment by an individual officer on a citizen. It was with a full knowledge of what was likely to come that Cicero had ironically declared that he only advised the conspirator to go. The feeling was so strong that on the next morning he found himself compelled to address the people on the subject. Then was uttered the second Catiline oration, which was spoken in the open air to the citizens at large. Here too there are words, among those with which he began his speech, almost as familiar to us as the "Quousque tandem"—"Abiit; excessit; evasit; erupit! " This Catiline, says Cicero, this pest of his country, raging in his madness, I have turned out of the city. If you like it better, I have expelled him by my very words. "He has departed. He has fled. He has gone out from among us. He has broken away! " "I have made this conspiracy plain to you all, as I said I would, unless indeed there may be some one here who does not believe that the friends of Catiline will do the same as Catiline would have done. But there is no time now for soft measures. We have to be strong-handed. There is one thing I will do for these men. Let them too go out, so that Catiline shall not pine for them. I will show them the road. He has gone by the Via Aurelia. If they will hurry they may catch him before night. " He implies by this that the story about Marseilles was false. Then he speaks with irony of himself as that violent Consul who could drive citizens into exile by the very breath of his mouth. "Ego vehemens ille consul qui verbo cives in exsilium ejicio. " So he goes on, in truth defending himself, but leading them with him to take part in the accusation which he intends to bring against the chief conspirators who remain in the city. If they too will go, they may go unscathed; if they choose to remain, let them look to themselves.

Through it all we can see there is but one thing that he fears — that he shall be driven by the exigencies of the occasion to take some steps which shall afterward be judged not to have been strictly legal, and which shall put him into the power of his enemies when the day of his ascendency shall have passed away. It crops out repeatedly in these speeches. [202] He seems to be aware that some over-strong measure will be forced upon him for which he alone will be held responsible. If he can only avoid that, he will fear nothing else; if he cannot avoid it, he will encounter even that danger. His foresight was wonderfully accurate. The strong hand was used, and the punishment came upon him, not from his enemies but from his friends, almost to the bursting of his heart.

Though the Senate had decreed that the Consuls were to see that the Republic should take no harm, and though it was presumed that extraordinary power was thereby conferred, it is evident that no power was conferred of inflicting punishment. Antony, as Cicero's colleague, was nothing. The authority, the responsibility, the action were, and were intended, to remain with Cicero. He could not legally banish any one. It was only too evident that there must be much slaughter. There was the army of rebels with which it would be necessary to fight. Let them go, these rebels within the city, and either join the army and get themselves killed, or else disappear, whither they would, among the provinces. The object of this second Catiline oration, spoken to the people, was to convince the remaining conspirators that they had better go, and to teach the citizens generally that in giving such counsel he was "banishing" no one. As far as the citizens were concerned he was successful; but he did not induce the friends of Catiline to follow their chief. This took place on the 9th of November. After the oration the Senate met again, and declared Catiline and Mallius to be public enemies.

Twenty-four days elapsed before the third speech was spoken—twenty-four days during which Rome must have been in a state of very great fever. Cicero was actively engaged in unravelling the plots the details of which were still being carried on within the city; but nevertheless he made that speech for Murena before the judicial bench of which I gave an account in the last chapter, and also probably another for Piso, of which we have nothing left. We cannot but marvel that he should have been able at such a time to devote his mind to such subjects, and carefully to study all the details of legal cases. It was only on October 21st that Murena had been elected Consul; and yet on the 20th of November Cicero defended him with great skill on a charge of bribery. There is an ease, a playfulness, a softness, a drollery about this speech which appears to be almost incompatible with the stern, absorbing realities and great personal dangers in the midst of which he was placed; but the agility of his mind was such that there appears to have been no difficulty to him in these rapid changes.

On the same day, the 20th of November, when Cicero was defending Murena, the plot was being carried on at the house of a certain Roman lady named Sempronia. It was she of whom Sallust said that she danced better than became an honest woman. If we can believe Sallust, she was steeped in luxury and vice. At her house a most vile project was hatched for introducing into Rome Rome's bitterest foreign foes. There were in the city at this time certain delegates from a people called the Allobroges, who inhabited the lower part of Savoy. The Allobroges were of Gaulish race. They were warlike, angry, and at the present moment peculiarly discontented with Rome. There had been certain injuries, either real or presumed, respecting which these delegates had been sent to the city. There they had been delayed, and fobbed off with official replies which gave no satisfaction, and were supposed to be ready to do any evil possible to the Republic. What if they could be got to go back suddenly to their homes, and bring a legion of red-haired Gauls to assist the conspirators in burning down Rome? A deputation from the delegates came to Sempronia's house and there met the conspirators—Lentulus and others. They entered freely into the project; but having, as was usual with foreign embassies at Rome, a patron or peculiar friend of their own among the aristocracy, one Fabius Sanga by name, they thought it well to consult him. [203] Sanga, as a matter of course, told everything to our astute Consul.

Then the matter was arranged with more than all the craft of a modern inspector of police. The Allobroges were instructed to lend themselves to the device, stipulating, however, that they should have a written signed authority which they could show to their rulers at home. The written signed documents were given to them. With certain conspirators to help them out of the city they were sent upon their way. At a bridge over the Tiber they were stopped by Cicero's emissaries. There was a feigned fight, but no blood was shed; and the ambassadors with their letters were brought home to the Consul.

We are astonished at the marvellous folly of these conspirators, so that we could hardly have believed the story had it not been told alike by Cicero and by Sallust, and had not allusion to the details been common among later writers. [204] The ambassadors were taken at the Milvian bridge early on the morning of the 3d of December, and in the course of that day Cicero sent for the leaders of the conspiracy to come to him. Lentulus, who was then Praetor, Cethegus, Gabinius, and Statilius all obeyed the summons. They did not know what had occurred, and probably thought that their best hope of safety lay in compliance. Caeparius was also sent for, but he for the moment escaped—in vain; for before two days were over he had been taken and put to death with the others. Cicero again called the Senate together, and entered the meeting leading the guilty Praetor by the hand. Here the offenders were examined and practically acknowledged their guilt. The proofs against them were so convincing that they could not deny it. There were the signatures of some; arms were found hidden in the house of another. The Senate decreed that the men should be kept in durance till some decision as to their fate should have been pronounced. Each of them was then given in custody to some noble Roman of the day. Lentulus the Praetor was confided to the keeping of a Censor, Cethegus to Cornificius, Statilius to Caesar, Gabinius to Crassus, and Caeparius, who had not fled very far before he was taken, to one Terentius. We can imagine how willingly would Crassus and Caesar have let their men go, had they dared. But Cicero was in the ascendant. Caesar, whom we can imagine to have understood that the hour had not yet come for putting an end to the effete Republic, and to have perceived also that Catiline was no fit helpmate for him in such a work, must bide his time, and for the moment obey. That he was inclined to favor the conspirators there is no doubt; but at present he could befriend them only in accordance with the law. The Allobroges were rewarded. The Praetors in the city who had assisted Cicero were thanked. To Cicero himself a supplication was decreed. A supplication was, in its origin, a thanksgiving to the gods on account of a victory, but had come to be an honor shown to the General who had gained the victory.

In this case it was simply a means of adding glory to Cicero, and was peculiar, as hitherto the reward had only been conferred for military service. [205] Remembering that, we can understand what at the time must have been the feeling in Rome as to the benefits conferred by the activity and patriotism of the Consul.

On the evening of the same day, the 3d of December, Cicero again addressed the people, explaining to them what he had done, and what he had before explained in the Senate. This was the third Catiline speech, and for rapid narrative is perhaps surpassed by nothing that he ever spoke. He explains again the motives by which he had been actuated; and in doing so extols the courage, the sagacity, the activity of Catiline, while he ridicules the folly and the fury of the others. [206] Had Catiline remained, he says, we should have been forced to fight with him here in the city; but with Lentulus the sleepy, and Cassius the fat, and Cethegus the mad, it has been comparatively easy to deal. It was on this account that he had got rid of him, knowing that their presence would do no harm. Then he reminds the people of all that the gods have done for them, and addresses them in language which makes one feel that they did believe in their gods. It is one instance, one out of many which history and experience afford us, in which an honest and a good man has endeavored to use for salutary purposes a faith in which he has not himself participated. Does the bishop of to-day, when he calls upon his clergy to pray for fine weather, believe that the Almighty will change the ordained seasons, and cause his causes to be inoperative because farmers are anxious for their hay or for their wheat? But he feels that when men are in trouble it is well that they should hold communion with the powers of heaven. So much also Cicero believed, and therefore spoke as he did on this occasion. As to his own religious views, I shall say something in a future chapter.

Then in a passage most beautiful for its language, though it is hardly in accordance with our idea of the manner in which a man should speak of himself, he explains his own ambition: "For all which, my fellow-countrymen, I ask for no other recompense, no ornament or honor, no monument but that this day may live in your memories. It is within your breasts that I would garner and keep fresh my triumph, my glory, the trophies of my exploits. No silent, voiceless statue, nothing which can be bestowed upon the worthless, can give me delight. Only by your remembrance can my fortunes be nurtured—by your good words, by the records which you shall cause to be written, can they be strengthened and perpetuated. I do think that this day, the memory of which, I trust, may be eternal, will be famous in history because the city has been preserved, and because my Consulship has been glorious. "[207] He ends the paragraph by an allusion to Pompey, admitting Pompey to a brotherhood of patriotism and praise. We shall see how Pompey repaid him.

How many things must have been astir in his mind when he spoke those words of Pompey! In the next sentence he tells the people of his own danger. He has taken care of their safety; it is for them to take care of his. [208] But they, these Quirites, these Roman citizens, these masters of the world, by whom everything was supposed to be governed, could take care of no one; certainly not of themselves, as certainly not of another. They could only vote, now this way and now that, as somebody might tell them, or more probably as somebody might pay them. Pompey was coming home, and would soon be the favorite. Cicero must have felt that he had deserved much of Pompey, but was by no means sure that the debt of gratitude would be paid.

Now we come to the fourth or last Catiline oration, which was made to the Senate, convened on the 5th of December with the purpose of deciding the fate of the leading conspirators who were held in custody. We learn to what purport were three of the speeches made during this debate—those of Caesar and of Cato and of Cicero. The first two are given to us by Sallust, but we can hardly think that we have the exact words. The Caesarean spirit which induced Sallust to ignore altogether the words of Cicero would have induced him to give his own representation of the other two, even though we were to suppose that he had been able to have them taken down by short-hand writers—Cicero's words, we have no doubt, with such polishing as may have been added to the short-hand writers' notes by Tiro, his slave and secretary. The three are compatible each with the other, and we are entitled to believe that we know the line of argument used by the three orators.

Silanus, one of the Consuls elect, began the debate by counselling death. We may take it for granted that he had been persuaded by Cicero to make this proposition. During the discussion he trembled at the consequences, and declared himself for an adjournment of their decision till they should have dealt with Catiline. Murena, the other Consul elect, and Catulus, the Prince of the Senate, [209] spoke for death. Tiberius Nero, grandfather of Tiberius the Emperor, made that proposition for adjournment to which Silanus gave way. Then— or I should rather say in the course of the debate, for we do not know who else may have spoken—Caesar got up and made his proposition. His purpose was to save the victims, but he knew well that, with such a spirit abroad as that existing in the Senate and the city, he could only do so not by absolving but by condemning. Wicked as these men might be, abominably wicked it was, he said, for the Senate to think of their own dignity rather than of the enormity of the crime. As they could not, he suggested, invent any new punishment adequate to so abominable a crime, it would be better that they should leave the conspirators to be dealt with by the ordinary laws. It was thus that, cunningly, he threw out the idea that as Senators they had no power of death. He did not dare to tell them directly that any danger would menace them, but he exposed the danger skilfully before their eyes. "Their crimes, " he says again, "deserve worse than any torture you can inflict. But men generally recollect what comes last. When the punishment is severe, men will remember the severity rather than the crime. " He argues all this extremely well. The speech is one of great ingenuity, whether the words be the words of Sallust or of Caesar. We may doubt, indeed, whether the general assertion he made as to death had much weight with the Senators when he told them that death to the wicked was a relief, whereas life was a lasting punishment; but when he went on to remind them of the Lex Porcia, by which the power of punishing a Roman citizen, even under the laws, was limited to banishment, unless by a plebiscite of the people generally ordering death, then he was efficacious. He ended by proposing that the goods of the conspirators should be sold, and that the men should be condemned to imprisonment for life, each in some separate town. This would, I believe, have been quite as illegal as the death-sentence, but it would not have been irrevocable. The Senate, or the people, in the next year could have restored to the men their liberty, and compensated them for their property. Cicero was determined that the men should die. They had not obeyed him by leaving the city, and he was convinced that while they lived the conspiracy would live also. He fully understood the danger, and resolved to meet it. He replied to Caesar, and with infinite skill refrained from the expression of any strong opinion, while he led his hearers to the conviction that death was necessary. For himself he had been told of his danger; "but if a man be brave in his duty death cannot be disgraceful to him; to one who had reached the honors of the Consulship it could not be premature; to no wise man could it be a misery. " Though his brother, though his wife, though his little boy, and his daughter just married were warning him of his peril, not by all that would he be influenced. "Do you, " he says, "Conscript Fathers, look to the safety of the Republic. These are not the Gracchi, nor Saturninus, who are brought to you for judgment—men who broke the laws, indeed, and therefore suffered death, but who still were not unpatriotic. These men had sworn to burn the city, to slay the Senate, to force Catiline upon you as a ruler. The proofs of this are in your own hands. It was for me, as your Consul, to bring the facts before you. Now it is for you, at once, before night, to decide what shall be done. The conspirators are very many; it is not only with these few that you are dealing. On whatever you decide, decide quickly. Caesar tells you of the Sempronian law[210]—the law, namely, forbidding the death of a Roman citizen—but can he be regarded as a citizen who has been found in arms against the city? " Then there is a fling at Caesar's assumed clemency, showing us that Caesar had already endeavored to make capital out of that virtue which he diplayed afterward so signally at Alesia and Uxellodunum. Then again he speaks of himself in words so grand that it is impossible but to sympathize with him: "Let Scipio's name be glorious—he by whose wisdom and valor Hannibal was forced out of Italy. Let Africanus be praised loudly, who destroyed Carthage and Numantia, the two cities which were most hostile to Rome. Let Paulus be regarded as great—he whose triumph that great King Perses adorned. Let Marius be held in undying honor, who twice saved Italy from foreign yoke. Let Pompey be praised above all, whose noble deeds are as wide as the sun's course. Perhaps among them there may be a spot, too, for me; unless, indeed, to win provinces to which we may take ourselves in exile is more than to guard that city to which the conquerors of provinces may return in safety. " The last words of the orator also are fine: "Therefore, Conscript Fathers, decide wisely and without fear. Your own safety, and that of your wives and children, that of your hearths and altars, the temples of your gods, the homes contained in your city, your liberty, the welfare of Italy and of the whole Republic are at stake. It is for you to decide. In me you have a Consul who will obey your decrees, and will see that they be made to prevail while the breath of life remains to him. " Cato then spoke advocating death, and the Senate decreed that the men should die. Cicero himself led Lentulus down to the vaulted prison below, in which executioners were ready for the work, and the other four men were made to follow. A few minutes afterward, in the gleaming of the evening, when Cicero was being led home by the applauding multitude, he was asked after the fate of the conspirators. He answered them but by one word "Vixerunt"—there is said to have been a superstition with the Romans as to all mention of death— "They have lived their lives. "

As to what was being done outside Rome with the army of conspirators in Etruria, it is not necessary for the biographer of Cicero to say much. Catiline fought, and died fighting. The conspiracy was then over. On the 31st of December Cicero retired from his office, and Catiline fell at the battle of Pistoia on the 5th of January following, B.C. 62.

A Roman historian writing in the reign of Tiberius has thought it worth his while to remind us that a great glory was added to Cicero's consular year by the birth of Augustus—him who afterward became Augustus Caesar. [211] Had a Roman been living now, he might be excused for saying that it was an honor to Augustus to have been born in the year of Cicero's Consulship.

NOTES:

[177] Catiline, by Mr. Beesly. Fortnightly Review, 1865.

[178] Pro Murena, xxv. : "Quem omnino vivum illine exire non oportuerat. " I think we must conclude from this that Cicero had almost expected that his attack upon the conspirators, in his first Catiline oration, would have the effect of causing him to be killed.

[179] Aeneid, viii., 668:

"Te, Catalina, minaci
Pendentem scopulo. "

[180] Velleius Paterculus, lib. ii, xxxiv.

[181] Juvenal, Sat. ii., 27: "Catilina Cethegum! " Could such a one as Catiline answer such a one as Cethegus? Sat. viii., 232: "Arma tamen vos Nocturna et flammas domibus templisque parastis. " Catiline, in spite of his noble blood, had endeavored to burn the city. Sat. xiv., 41: "Catilinam quocunque in populo videas. " It is hard to find a

good man, but it is easy enough to put your hand anywhere on a Catiline.

[182] Val Maximus, lib. v., viii., 5; lib. ix., 1, 9; lib. ix., xi., 3.

[183] Florus, lib. iv.

[184] Mommsen's History of Rome, book v., chap v.

[185] I feel myself constrained here to allude to the treatment given to Catiline by Dean Merivale in his little work on the two Roman Triumvirates. The Dean's sympathies are very near akin to those of Mr. Beesly, but he values too highly his own historical judgment to allow it to run on all fours with Mr. Beesly's sympathies. "The real designs, " he says, "of the infamous Catiline and his associates must indeed always remain shrouded in mystery. — — Nevertheless, it is impossible to deny, and on the whole it would be unreasonable to doubt, that such a conspiracy there really was, and that the very existence of the commonwealth was for a moment seriously imperilled. " It would certainly be unreasonable to doubt it. But the Dean, though he calls Catiline infamous, and acknowledges the conspiracy, never- theless give us ample proof of his sympathy with the conspirators, or rather of his strong feeling against Cicero. Speaking of Catiline at a certain moment, he says that he "was not yet hunted down. " He speaks of the "upstart Cicero, " and plainly shows us that his heart is with the side which had been Caesar's. Whether conspiracy or no conspiracy, whether with or without wholesale murder and rapine, a single master with a strong hand was the one remedy needed for Rome! The reader must understand that Cicero's one object in public life was to resist that lesson.

[186] Asconius, "In to gacandida, " reports that Fenestella, a writer of the time of Augustus, had declared that Cicero had defended Catiline; but Asconius gives his reasons for disbelieving the story.

[187] Cicero, however, declares that he has made a difference between traitors to their country and other criminals. Pro P. Sulla, ca. iii. : "Verum etiam quaedam contagio scelens, si defendas eum, quem obstrictum esse patriae parricidio suspicere. " Further on in the same oration, ca. vi., he explains that he had refused to defend Autronius because he had known Autronius to be a conspirator against his country. I cannot admit the truth of the argument in

which Mr. Forsyth defends the practice of the English bar in this respect, and in doing so presses hard upon Cicero. "At Rome, " he says, "it was different. The advocate there was conceived to have a much wider discretion than we allow. " Neither in Rome nor in England has the advocate been held to be disgraced by undertaking the defence of bad men who have been notoriously guilty. What an English barrister may do, there was no reason that a Roman advocate should not do, in regard to simple criminality. Cicero himself has explained in the passage I have quoted how the Roman practice did differ from ours in regard to treason. He has stated also that he knew nothing of the first conspiracy when he offered to defend Catiline on the score of provincial peculations. No writer has been heavy on Hortensius for defending Verres, but only because he took bribes from Verres.

[188] Publius Cornelius Sulla, and Publius Autronius Poetus.

[189] Pro P. Sulla, iv. He declares that he had known nothing of the first conspiracy and gives the reason: "Quod nondum penitus in republic aver sabar, quod nondum ad propositum mihi finem honoris perveneram, quod mea me ambitio et forensis labor ab omni illa cogitatione abstrahebat. "

[190] Sallust, Catilinaria, xviii.

[191] Livy, Epitome, lib. ci.

[192] Suetonius, J. Caesar, ix.

[193] Mommsen, book v., ca. v., says of Caesar and Crassus as to this period, "that this notorious action corresponds with striking exactness to the secret action which this report ascribes to them. " By which he means to imply that they probably were concerned in the plot.

[194] Sallust tells us, Catilinaria, xlix., that Cicero was instigated by special enemies of Caesar to include Caesar in the accusation, but refused to mix himself up in so great a crime. Crassus also was accused, but probably wrongfully. Sallust declares that an attempt was made to murder Caesar as he left the Senate. There was probably some quarrel and hustling, but no more.

[195] Sallust, Catilinaria, xxxvii. : "Omnino cuneta plebes, novarum rerum studio, Catilinae incepta probabat. " By the words "novarum rerum studio—by a love of revolution—we can understand the kind of popularity which Sallust intended to express.

[196] Pro Murena, xxv.

[197] "Darent operam consules ne quid detrimenti respublica capiat"

[198] Catilinaria, xxxi.

[199] Quintilian, lib. xii, 10: "Quem tamen et suorum homines temporum incessere audebant, ut tumidiorem, et asianum, et redundantem. "

[200] Orator., xxxvii. : "A nobis homo audacissimus Catilina in senatu accusatus obmutuit. "

[201] 2 Catilinaria, xxxi.

[202] In the first of them to the Senate, chap. ix., he declares this to Catiline himself: "Si mea voce perterritus ire in exsilium animum induxeris, quanta tempestas invidiae nobis, si minus in praesens tempus, recenti memoria scelerum tuorum, at in posteritatem impendeat. " He goes on to declare that he will endure all that, if by so doing he can save the Republic "Sed est mihi tanti; dummodo ista privata sit calamitas, et a reipublicae periculis sejungatui"

[203] Sallust, Catilinaria, xli. : "Itaque Q. Fabio Sangae cujus patrocinio civitas plurimum utebatur rem omnem uti cognoverant aperiunt. "

[204] Horace, Epo. xvi., 6: "Novisque rebus infidelis Allobrox. " The unhappy Savoyard has from this line been known through ages as a conspirator, false even to his fellow-conspirators. Juvenal, vii., 214: "Rufum qui toties Ciceronem Allobroga dixit. " Some Rufus, acting as advocate, had thought to put down Cicero by calling him an Allobrogian.

[205] The words in which this honor was conferred he himself repeats: "Quod urbem incendiis, caede cives, Italiam bello

liberassem" — " because I had rescued the city from fire, the citizens from slaughter, and Italy from war. "

[206] It is necessary in all oratory to read something between the lines. It is allowed to the speaker to produce effect by diminishing and exaggeratng. I think we should detract something from the praises bestowed on Catiline's military virtues. The bigger Catiline could be made to appear, the greater would be the honor of having driven him out of the city.

[207] In Catilinam, iii., xi.

[208] In Catilinam, ibid., xii. : "Ne mihi noceant vestrum est providere. "

[209] "Prince of the Senate" was an honorary title, conferred on some man of mark as a dignity — at this period on some ex-Consul; it conferred no power. Cicero, the Consul who had convened the Senate, called on the speakers as he thought fit.

[210] Caesar, according to Sallust, had referred to the Lex Porcia. Cicero alludes, and makes Caesar allude, to the Lex Sempronia. The Porcian law, as we are told by Livy, was passed B. C. 299, and forbade that a Roman should be scourged or put to death. The Lex Sempronia was introduced by C. Gracchus, and enacted that the life of a citizen should not be taken without the voice of the citizens.

[211] Velleius Paterculus, xxxvi. : "Consulatui Ciceronis non mediocre adjecit decus natus eo anno Divus Augustus. "

CHAPTER X.

CICERO AFTER HIS CONSULSHIP.

The idea that the great Consul had done illegally in putting citizens to death was not allowed to lie dormant even for a day. It must be remembered that a decree of the Senate had no power as a law. The laws could be altered, or even a new law made, only by the people. Such was the constitution of the Republic. Further on, when Cicero will appeal as, in fact, on trial for the offence so alleged to have been committed, I shall have to discuss the matter; but the point was raised against him, even in the moment of his triumph, as he was leaving the Consulship. The reiteration of his self-praise had created for him many enemies. It had turned friends against him, and had driven men even of his own party to ask themselves whether all this virtue was to be endured. When a man assumes to be more just than his neighbors there will be many ways found of throwing in a shell against him. It was customary for a Consul when he vacated his office to make some valedictory speech. Cicero was probably expected to take full advantage of the opportunity. From other words which have come from him, on other occasions but on the same subject, it would not be difficult to compose such a speech as he might have spoken. But there were those who were already sick of hearing him say that Rome had been saved by his intelligence and courage. We can imagine what Caesar might have said among his friends of the expediency of putting down this self-laudatory Consul. As it was, Metellus Nepos, one of the Tribunes, forbade the retiring officer to do more than take the oath usual on leaving office, because he had illegally inflicted death upon Roman citizens. Metellus, as Tribune, had the power of stopping any official proceeding. We hear from Cicero himself that he was quite equal to the occasion. He swore, on the spur of the moment, a solemn oath, not in accordance with the form common to Consuls on leaving office, but to the effect that during his Consulship Rome had been saved by his work alone. [212] We have the story only as it is told by Cicero himself, who avers that the people accepted the oath as sworn with exceeding praise. [213] That it was so we may, I think, take as true. There can be no doubt as to Cicero's popularity at this moment, and hardly a doubt also as to the fact that Metellus was acting in agreement with Caesar, and also in accord with the understood feelings of Pompey, who was absent with his army in the East. This Tribune had been till lately an officer under Pompey, and went into office together with Caesar, who in that year became Praetor. This, probably, was the beginning of the party which two years afterward formed the first Triumvirate, B.C. 60. It was certainly now, in the year succeeding the Consulship of Cicero, that Caesar, as Praetor, began his great career.

[Sidenote: B.C. 62, aetat. 45.]

It becomes manifest to us, as we read the history of the time, that the Dictator of the future was gradually entertaining the idea that the old forms of the Republic were rotten, and that any man who intended to exercise power in Rome or within the Roman Empire must obtain it and keep it by illegal means. He had probably adhered to Catiline's first conspiracy, but only with such moderate adhesion as enabled him to withdraw when he found that his companions were not fit for the work. It is manifest that he sympathized with the later conspiracy, though it may be doubted whether he himself had ever been a party to it. "When the conspiracy had been crushed by Cicero, he had given his full assent to the crushing, of it. We have seen how loudly he condemned the wickedness of the conspirators in his endeavor to save their lives. But, through it all, there was a well-grounded conviction in his mind that Cicero, with all his virtues, was not practical. Not that Cicero was to him the same as Cato, who with his Stoic grandiloquence must, to his thinking, have been altogether useless. Cicero, though too virtuous for supreme rule, too virtuous to seize power and hold it, too virtuous to despise as effete the institutions of the Republic, was still a man so gifted, and capable in so many things, as to be very great as an assistant, if he would only condescend to assist. It is in this light that Caesar seems to have regarded Cicero as time went on; admiring him, liking him, willing to act with him if it might be possible, but not the less determined to put down all the attempts at patriotic republican virtue in which the orator delighted to indulge. Mr. Forsyth expresses an opinion that Caesar, till he crossed the Rubicon after his ten years' fighting in Gaul, had entertained no settled plan of overthrowing the Constitution. Probably not; nor even then. It may be doubted whether Caesar ever spoke to himself of overthrowing the Constitution. He came gradually to see that power and wealth were to be obtained by violent action, and only by violent action, He had before him the examples of Marius and Sulla, both of whom had enjoyed power and had died in their beds. There was the example, also, of others who, walking unwarily in those perilous times, had been banished as was Verres, or killed as was

Catiline. We can easily understand that he, with his great genius, should have acknowledged the need both of courage and caution. Both were exercised when he consented to be absent from Rome, and almost from Italy, during the ten years of the Gallic wars. But this, I think, is certain, that from the time in which his name appears prominent—from the period, namely, of the Catiline conspiracy—he had determined not to overthrow the Constitution, but so to carry himself, amid the great affairs of the day, as not to be overthrown himself.

Of what nature was the intercourse between him and Pompey when Pompey was still absent in the East we do not know; but we can hardly doubt that some understanding had begun to exist. Of this Cicero was probably aware. Pompey was the man whom Cicero chose to regard as his party-leader, not having himself been inured to the actual politics of Rome early enough in life to put himself forward as the leader of his party. It had been necessary for him, as a "novus homo, " to come forward and work as an advocate, and then as an administrative officer of the State, before he took up with politics. That this was so I have shown by quoting the opening words of his speech Pro Lege Manilia. Proud as he was of the doings of his Consulship, he was still too new to his work to think that thus he could claim to stand first. Nor did his ambition lead him in that direction. He desired personal praise rather than personal power. When in the last Catiline oration to the people he speaks of the great men of the Republic—of the two Scipios, and of Paulus Aemilius and of Marius—he adds the name of Pompey to these names; or gives, rather, to Pompey greater glory than to any of them; "Anteponatur omnibus Pompeius. " This was but a few days before Metellus as Tribune had stopped him in his speech—at the instigation, probably, of Caesar, and in furtherance of Pompey's views. Pompey and Caesar could agree, at any rate, in this—that they did not want such a one as Cicero to interfere with them.

All of which Cicero himself perceived. The specially rich, province of Macedonia, which would have been his had he chosen to take it on quitting the Consulship, he made over to Antony—no doubt as a bribe, as with us one statesman may resign a special office to another to keep that other from kicking over the traces. Then Gaul became his province, as allotted—Cisalpine Gaul, as northern Italy was then called; a province less rich in plunder and pay than Macedonia. But Cicero wanted no province, and had contrived that this should be confided to Metellus Celer, the brother of Nepos, who, having been

Praetor when he himself was Consul, was entitled to a government. This too was a political bribe. If courtesy to Caesar, if provinces given up here and there to Antonys and Metelluses, if flattery lavished on Pompey could avail anything, he could not afford to dispense with such aids. It all availed nothing. From this time forward, for the twenty years which were to run before his death, his life was one always of trouble and doubt, often of despair, and on many occasions of actual misery. The source of this was that Pompey whom, with divine attributes, he had extolled above all other Romans.

The first extant letter written by Cicero after his Consulship was addressed to Pompey. [214] Pompey was still in the East, but had completed his campaigns against Mithridates successfully. Cicero begins by congratulating him, as though to do so were the purpose of his letter. Then he tells the victorious General that there were some in Rome not so well pleased as he was at these victories. It is supposed that he alluded here to Caesar; but, if so, he probably misunderstood the alliance which was already being formed between Caesar and Pompey. After that comes the real object of the epistle. He had received letters from Pompey congratulating him in very cold language as to the glories of his Consulship. He had expected much more than that from the friend for whom he had done so much. Still, he thanks his friend, explaining that the satisfaction really necessary to him was the feeling that he had behaved well to his friend. If his friend were less friendly to him in return, then would the balance of friendship be on his side. If Pompey were not bound to him, Cicero, by personal gratitude, still would he be bound by necessary co-operation in the service of the Republic. But, lest Pompey should misunderstand him, he declares that he had expected warmer language in reference to his Consulship, which he believes to have been withheld by Pompey lest offence should be given to some third person. By this he means Caesar, and those who were now joining themselves to Caesar. Then he goes on to warn him as to the future: "Nevertheless, when you return, you will find that my actions have been of such a nature that, even though you may loom larger than Scipio, I shall be found worthy to be accepted as your Laelius. "[215] Infinite care had been given to the writing of this letter, and sharp had been the heart-burnings which dictated it. It was only by asserting that he, on his own part, was satisfied with his own fidelity as a friend, that Cicero could express his dissatisfaction at Pompey's coldness. It was only by continuing to lavish upon Pompey such flattery as was contained in the reference to Scipio, in which a touch of subtle irony is mixed with the flattery, that he could explain the nature of the praise which had, he thought, been due to himself. There is something that would have been abject in the nature of these expressions, had it not been Roman in the excess of the adulation. But there is courage in the letter, too, when he tells his correspondent what he believes to have been the cause of the coldness of which he complains: "Quod verere ne cujus animum offenderes" — "Because you fear lest you should give offence to some one. " But let me tell you, he goes on to say, that my Consulship has been of such a nature that you, Scipio, as you are, must admit me as your friend.

In these words we find a key to the whole of Cicero's connection with the man whom he recognizes as his political leader. He was always dissatisfied with Pompey; always accusing Pompey in his heart of ingratitude and insincerity; frequently speaking to Atticus with bitter truth of the man's selfishness and incapacity, even of his cruelty and want of patriotism; nicknaming him because of his absurdities; declaring of him that he was minded to be a second Sulla; but still clinging to him as the political friend and leader whom he was bound to follow. In their earlier years, when he could have known personally but little of Pompey, because Pompey was generally absent from Rome, he had taken it into his head to love the man. He had been called "Magnus; " he had been made Consul long before the proper time; he had been successful on behalf of the Republic, and so far patriotic. He had hitherto adhered to the fame of the Republic. At any rate, Cicero had accepted him, and could never afterward bring himself to be disloyal to the leader with whom he had professed to act. But the feeling evinced in this letter was carried on to the end. He had been, he was, he would be, true to his political connection with Pompey; but of Pompey's personal character to himself he had nothing but complaints to make.

[Sidenote: B.C. 62, aetat. 45.]

We have two other letters written by Cicero in this year, the first of which is in answer to one from Metellus Celer to him, also extant. Metellus wrote to complain of the ill-treatment which he thought he had received from Cicero in the Senate, and from the Senate generally. Cicero writes back at much greater length to defend himself, and to prove that he had behaved as a most obliging friend to his correspondent, though he had received a gross affront from his correspondent's brother Nepos. Nepos had prevented him in that matter of the speech. It is hardly necessary to go into the question of this quarrel, except in so far as it may show how the feeling which led to Cicero's exile was growing up among many of the aristocracy in Rome. There was a counterplot going on at the moment—a plot on the behalf of the aristocracy for bringing back Pompey to Rome, not only with glory but with power, probably originating in a feeling that Pompey would be a more congenial master than Cicero. It was suggested that as Pompey had been found good in all State emergencies—for putting down the pirates, for instance, and for conquering Mithridates—he would be the man to contend in arms with Catiline. Catiline was killed before the matter could be brought to an issue, but still the conspiracy went on, based on the jealousy which was felt in regard to Cicero. This man, who had declared so often that he had served his country, and who really had crushed the Catilinarians by his industry and readiness, might, after all, be coming forward as another Sulla, and looking to make himself master by dint of his virtues and his eloquence. The hopelessness of the condition of the Republic may be recognized in the increasing conspiracies which were hatched on every side. Metellus Nepos was sent home from Asia in aid of the conspiracy, and got himself made Tribune, and stopped Cicero's speech. In conjunction with Caesar, who was Praetor, he proposed his new law for the calling of Pompey to their aid. Then there was a fracas between him and Caesar on the one side and Cato on the other, in which Cato at last was so far victorious that both Caesar and Metellus were stopped in the performance of their official duties. Caesar was soon reinstated, but Metellus Nepos returned to Pompey in the East, and nothing came of the conspiracy. It is only noticed here as evidence of the feeling which existed as to Cicero in Rome, and as explaining the irritation on both sides indicated in the correspondence between Cicero and Metellus Celer, the brother of Nepos, [216] whom Cicero had procured the government of Gaul.

The third letter from Cicero in this year was to Sextius, who was then acting as Quaestor—or Proquaestor, as Cicero calls him—with Antony as Proconsul in Macedonia. It is specially interesting as telling us that the writer had just completed the purchase of a house in Rome from Crassus for a sum amounting to about £30,000 of our money. There was probably no private mansion in Rome of greater pretension. It had been owned by Livius Drusus, the Tribune—a man of colossal fortune, as we are told by Mommsen—who was murdered at the door of it thirty years before. It afterward passed into the hands of Crassus the rich, and now became the property of

Cicero. We shall hear how it was destroyed during his exile, and how fraudulently made over to the gods, and then how restored to Cicero, and how rebuilt at the public expense. The history of the house has been so well written that we know even the names of Cicero's two successors in it, Censorinus and Statilius. [217] It is interesting to know the sort of house which Cicero felt to be suitable to his circumstances, for by that we may guess what his circumstances were. In making this purchase he is supposed to have abandoned the family house in which his father had lived next door to the new mansion, and to have given it up to his brother. Hence we may argue that he had conceived himself to have risen in worldly circumstances. Nevertheless, we are informed by himself in this letter to Sextius that he had to borrow money for the occasion—so much so that, being a man now indebted, he might be supposed to be ripe for any conspiracy. Hence has come to us a story through Aulus Gellius, the compiler of anecdotes, to the effect that Cicero was fain to borrow this money from a client whose cause he undertook in requital for the favor so conferred. Aulus Gellius collected his stories two centuries afterward for the amusement of his children, and has never been regarded as an authority in matters for which confirmation has been wanting. There is no allusion to such borrowing from a client made by any contemporary. In this letter to Sextius, in which he speaks jokingly of his indebtedness, he declares that he has been able to borrow any amount he wanted at six per cent—twelve being the ordinary rate—and gives as a reason for this the position which he has achieved by his services to the State. Very much has been said of the story, as though the purchaser of the house had done something of which he ought to have been ashamed, but this seems to have sprung entirely from the idea that a man who, in the midst of such wealth as prevailed at Rome, had practised so widely and so successfully the invaluable profession of an advocate, must surely have taken money for his services. He himself has asserted that he took none, and all the evidence that we have goes to show that he spoke the truth. Had he taken money, even as a loan, we should have heard of it from nearer witnesses than Aulus Gellius, if, as Aulus Gellius tells us, it had become known at the time. But because he tells his friend that he has borrowed money for the purpose, he is supposed to have borrowed it in a disgraceful manner! It will be found that all the stones most injurious to Cicero's reputation have been produced in the same manner. His own words have been misinterpreted—either the purport of them, if spoken in earnest, or their bearing, if spoken in joke—and then accusations have been founded on them. [218]

Another charge of dishonest practice was about this time made against Cicero without a gram of evidence, though indeed the accusations so made, and insisted upon, apparently from a feeling that Cicero cannot surely have been altogether clean when all others were so dirty, are too numerous to receive from each reader's judgment that indignant denial to which each is entitled. The biographer cannot but fear that when so much mud has been thrown some will stick, and therefore almost hesitates to tell of the mud, believing that no stain of this kind has been in truth deserved.

It seems that Antony, Cicero's colleague in the Consulship, who became Proconsul in Macedonia, had undertaken to pay some money to Cicero. Why the money was to be paid we do not know, but there are allusions in Cicero's letters to Atticus to one Teucris (a Trojan woman), and it seems that Antony was designated by the nickname. Teucris is very slow at paying his money, and Cicero is in want of it. But perhaps it will be as well not to push the matter. He, Antony, is to be tried for provincial peculation, and Cicero declares that the case is so bad that he cannot defend his late colleague. Hence have arisen two different suspicions: one that Antony had agreed to make over to Cicero a share of the Macedonian plunder in requital of Cicero's courtesy in giving up the province which had been allotted to himself; the second, that Antony was to pay Cicero for defending him. As to the former, Cicero himself alludes to such a report as being common in Macedonia, and as having been used by Antony himself as an excuse for increased rapine. But this has been felt to be incredible, and has been allowed to fall to the ground because of the second accusation. But in support of that there is no word of evidence, [219] whereas the tenor of the story as told by Cicero himself is against it. Is it likely, would it be possible, that Cicero should have begun his letter to Atticus by complaining that he could not get from Antony money wanted for a peculiar purpose—it was wanted for his new house—and have gone on in the same letter to say that this might be as well, after all, as he did not intend to perform the service for which the money was to be paid? The reader will remember that the accusation is based solely on Cicero's own statement that Antony was negligent in paying to him money that had been promised. In all these accusations the evidence against Cicero, such as it is, is brought exclusively from Cicero's own words. Cicero did afterward defend this Antony, as we learn from his speech Pro Domo Suâ; but his change of purpose in that respect has nothing to do with the argument.

[Sidenote: B.C. 62, aetat. 45.]

We have two speeches extant made this year: one on behalf of P. Sulla, nephew to the Dictator; the other for Archias the Greek scholar and poet, who had been Cicero's tutor and now claimed to be a citizen of Rome. I have already given an extract from this letter, as showing the charm of words with which Cicero could recommend the pursuit of literature to his hearers. The whole oration is a beautiful morsel of Latinity, in which, however, strength of argument is lacking. Cicero declares of Archias that he was so eminent in literature that, if not a Roman citizen, he ought to be made one. The result is not known, but the literary world believes that the citizenship was accorded to him. [220]

The speech on behalf of Sulla was more important, but still not of much importance. This Sulla, as may be remembered, had been chosen as Consul with Autronius, two years before the Consulship of Cicero, and he had then after his election been deposed for bribery, as had also Autronius. L. Aurelius Cotta and L. Manlius Torquatus had been elected in their places. It has also been already explained that the two rejected Consuls had on this account joined Catiline in his first conspiracy.

There can be no doubt that whether as Consuls or as rejected Consuls, and on that account conspirators, their purpose was to use their position as aristocrats for robbing the State. They were of the number of those to whom no other purpose was any longer possible. Then there came Catiline's second conspiracy—the conspiracy which Cicero had crushed—and there naturally rose the question whether from time to time this or the other noble Roman should not be accused of having joined it. Many noble Romans had no doubt joined besides those who had fallen fighting, or who had been executed in the dungeons. Accusations became very rife. One Vettius accused Caesar, the Praetor; but Caesar, with that potentiality which was peculiar to him, caused Vettius to be put into prison instead of going to prison himself. Many were convicted and banished; among them Portius Leca, Vargunteius, Servius Sulla, the brother of him of whom we are now speaking, and Autronius his colleague. In the trial of these men Cicero took no part. He was specially invited by Autronius, who was an old school-fellow, to defend him, but he refused; indeed, he gave evidence against Autrionius at the trial. But this Publius Sulla he did defend, and defended successfully. He was joined in the case with Hortensius, and declared that as to the matter of the former conspiracy he left all that to his learned friend, who was concerned with political matters of that date. [221] He, Cicero, had known nothing about them. The part of the oration which most interests us is that in which he defends himself from the accusations somewhat unwisely made against himself personally by young Torquatus, the son of him who had been raised to the Consulship in the place of P. Sulla. Torquatus had called him a foreigner because he was a "novus homo, " and had come from the municipality of Arpinum, and had taunted him with being a king, because he had usurped authority over life and death in regard to Lentulus and the other conspirators. He answers this very finely, and does so without an ill-natured word to young Torquatus, whom, from respect to his father, he desires to spare. "Do not, " he says, "in future call me a foreigner, lest you be answered with severity, nor a king, lest you be laughed at—unless, indeed, you think it king-like so to live as to be a slave not only to no man but to no evil passion; unless you think it be king-like to despise all lusts, to thirst for neither gold nor silver nor goods, to express yourself freely in the Senate, to think more of services due to the people than of favors won from them, to yield to none, and to stand firm against many. If this be king-like, then I confess that I am a king. " Sulla was acquitted, but the impartial reader will not the less feel sure that he had been part and parcel with Catiline in the conspiracy. It is trusted that the impartial reader will also remember how many honest, loyal gentlemen have in our own days undertaken the causes of those whom they have known to be rebels, and have saved those rebels by their ingenuity and eloquence.

At the end of this year, B.C. 62, there occurred a fracas in Rome which was of itself but of little consequence to Rome, and would have been of none to Cicero but that circumstances grew out of it which created for him the bitterest enemy he had yet encountered, and led to his sorest trouble. This was the affair of Clodius and of the mysteries of the Bona Dea, and I should be disposed to say that it was the greatest misfortune of his life, were it not that the wretched results which sprung from it would have been made to spring from some other source had that source not sufficed. I shall have to tell how it came to pass that Cicero was sent into exile by means of the misconduct of Clodius; but I shall have to show also that the misconduct of Clodius was but the tool which was used by those who were desirous of ridding themselves of the presence of Cicero.

This Clodius, a young man of noble family and of debauched manners, as was usual with young men of noble families, dressed himself up as a woman, and made his way in among the ladies as they were performing certain religious rites in honor of the Bona Dea, or Goddess Cybele, a matron goddess so chaste in her manners that no male was admitted into her presence. It was specially understood that nothing appertaining to a man was to be seen on the occasion, not even the portrait of one; and it may possibly have been the case that Clodius effected his entrance among the worshipping matrons on this occasion simply because his doing so was an outrage, and therefore exciting. Another reason was alleged. The rites in question were annually held, now in the house of this matron and then of that, and during the occasion the very master of the house was excluded from his own premises. They were now being performed under the auspices of Pompeia, the wife of Julius Caesar, the daughter of one Quintus Pompeius, and it was alleged that Clodius came among the women worshippers for the sake of carrying on an intrigue with Caesar's wife. This was highly improbable, as Mr. Forsyth has pointed out to us, and the idea was possibly used simply as an excuse to Caesar for divorcing a wife of whom he was weary. At any rate, when the scandal got abroad, he did divorce Pompeia, alleging that it did not suit Caesar to have his wife suspected.

[Sidenote: B.C. 61, aetat. 46.]

The story became known through the city, and early in January Cicero wrote to Atticus, telling him the facts: "You have probably heard that Publius Clodius, the son of Appius, has been taken dressed in a woman's clothes in the house of Cains Caesar, where sacrifice was being made for the people, and that he escaped by the aid of a female slave. You will be sorry to hear that it has given rise to a great scandal. [222]

A few days afterward Cicero speaks of it again to Atticus at greater length, and we learn that the matter had been taken up by the magistrates with the view of punishing Clodius. Cicero writes without any strong feeling of his own, explaining to his friend that he had been at first a very Lycurgus in the affair, but that he is now tamed down. [223] Then there is a third letter in which Cicero is indignant because certain men of whom he disapproves, the Consul Piso among the number[224] are anxious to save this wicked young nobleman from the punishment due to him; whereas others of whom he approves Cato among the number, are desirous of seeing justice done. But it was no affair special to Cicero. Shortly afterward he writes again to Atticus as to the result of the trial—for a trial did take place—and explains to his friend how justice had failed. Atticus had asked him how it had come to pass that he, Cicero, had not exerted himself as he usually did. [225] This letter, though there is matter enough in it of a serious kind, yet jests with the Clodian affair so continually as to make us feel that he attributed no importance to it as regarded himself. He had exerted himself till Hortensius made a mistake as to the selection of the judges. After that he had himself given evidence. An attempt was made to prove an alibi, but Cicero came forward to swear that he had seen Clodius on the very day in question. There had, too, been an exchange of repartee in the Senate between himself and Clodius after the acquittal, of which he gives the details to his correspondent with considerable self-satisfaction. The passage does not enhance our idea of the dignity of the Senate, or of the power of Roman raillery. It was known that Clodius had been saved by the wholesale bribery of a large number of the judges. There had been twenty-five for condemning against thirty-one for acquittal. [226]

Cicero in the Catiline affair had used a phrase with frequency by which he boasted that he had "found out" this and "found out" that—"comperisse omnia. " Clodius, in the discussion before the trial, throws this in his teeth: "Comperisse omnia criminabatur. " This gave rise to ill-feeling, and hurt Cicero much worse than the dishonor done to the Bona Dea. As for that, we may say that he and the Senate and the judges cared personally very little, although there was no doubt a feeling that it was wise to awe men's minds by the preservation of religious respect. Cicero had cared but little about the trial; but as he had been able to give evidence he had appeared as a witness, and enmity sprung from the words which were spoken both on one side and on the other. Clodius was acquitted, which concerns us not at all, and concerns Rome very little; but things had so come to pass at the trial that Cicero had been very bitter, and that Clodius had become his enemy. When a man was wanted, three years afterward, to take the lead in persecuting Cicero, Clodius was ready for the occasion.

While the expediency of putting Clodius on his trial was being discussed, Pompey had returned from the East, and taken up his residence outside the city, because he was awaiting his triumph. The General, to whom it was given to march through the city with triumphal glory, was bound to make his first entrance after his victories with all his triumphal appendages, as though he was at that moment returning from the war with all his warlike spoils around him. The usage had obtained the strength of law, but the General was not on that account deburred from city employment during the interval. The city must be taken out to him instead of his coming into the city. Pompey was so great on his return from his Mithridatic victories that the Senate went out to sit with him in the suburbs, as he could not sit with it within the walls. We find him taking part in these Clodian discussions. Cicero at once writes of him to Athens with evident dissatisfaction. When questioned about Clodius, Pompey had answered with the grand air of aristocrat. Crassus on this occasion, between whom and Cicero there was never much friendship, took occasion to belaud the late great Consul on account of his Catiline successes. Pompey, we are told, did not bear this well. [227] Crassus had probably intended to produce some such effect. Then Cicero had spoken in answer to the remarks of Crassus, very glibly, no doubt, and had done his best to "show off" before Pompey, his new listener. [228]

More than six years had passed since Pompey could have heard him, and then Cicero's voice had not become potential in the Senate. Cicero had praised Pompey with all the eloquence in his power. "Anteponatur omnibus Pompeius, " he had said, in the last Catiline oration to the Senate; and Pompey, though he had not heard the words spoken, knew very well what had been said. Such oratory was never lost upon those whom it most concerned the orator to make acquainted with it. But in return for all this praise, for that Manilian oration which had helped to send him to the East, for continual loyalty, Pompey had replied to Cicero with coldness. He would now let Pompey know what was his standing in Rome. "If ever, " he says to Atticus, "I was strong with my grand rhythm, with my quick rhetorical passages, with enthusiasm, and with logic, I was so now. Oh, the noise that I made on the occasion! You know what my voice can do. I need say no more about it, as surely you must have heard me away there in Epirus. " The reader, I trust, will have already a sufficiently vivid idea of Cicero's character to understand the mingling of triumph and badinage, with a spark of disappointment, which is here expressed. "This Pompey, though I have so true to him, has not thought much of me—of me, the great Consul who saved Rome! He has now heard what even Crassus has been forced to say about me. He shall hear me too, me myself, and perhaps he will then know better. " It was thus that Cicero's mind was at work while he was turning his loud periods. Pompey was sitting next to him listening, by no means admiring his admirer as that admirer expected to be admired. Cicero had probably said to himself that they two together, Pompey and Cicero, might suffice to preserve the Republic. Pompey, not thinking much of the Republic, was probably telling himself that he wanted no brother near the throne. When of two men the first thinks himself equal to the second, the second will generally feel himself to be superior to the first. Pompey would have liked Cicero better if his periods had not been so round nor his voice so powerful. Not that Pompey was distinctly desirous of any throne. His position at the moment was peculiar. He had brought back his victorious army from the East to Brundisium, and had then disbanded his legions. I will quote here the opening words from one of Mommsen's chapters: [229] "When Pompeius, after having transacted the affairs committed to his charge, again turned his eyes toward home, he found, for the second time, the diadem at his feet. " He says farther on, explaining why Pompey did not lift the diadem: "The very peculiar temperament of Pompeius naturally turned once more the scale. He was one of those men who are capable, it may be, of a crime, but not of insubordination. " And again: "While in the capital all was preparation for receiving the new monarch, news came that Pompeius, when barely landed at Brundisium, had broken up his legions, and with a small escort had entered his journey to the capital. If it is a piece of good-fortune to gain a crown without trouble, fortune never did more for mortal than it did for Pompeius; but on those who lack courage the gods lavish every favor and every gift in vain. " I must say here that, while I acknowledge the German historian's research and knowledge without any reserve, I cannot accept his deductions as to character. I do not believe that Pompey found any diadem at his feet, or thought of any diadem, nor, according to my reading of Roman history, had Marius or had Sulla; nor did Caesar. The first who thought of that perpetual rule—a rule to be perpetuated during the ruler's life, and to be handed down to his successors—was Augustus. Marius, violent, self-seeking, and uncontrollable, had tumbled into supreme power; and, had he not died, would have held it as long as he could, because it pleased his ambition for the moment. Sulla, with a purpose, had seized it, yet seems never to have got beyond the old Roman idea of a temporary Dictatorship. The old Roman horror of a king was present to these Romans, even after they had become kings. Pompey, no doubt, liked to be first, and when he came back from the East thought that by his deeds he was first, easily first. Whether Consul year after year, as Marius had been, or Dictator, as Sulla had been, or Imperator, with a running command over all the Romans, it was his idea still to adhere to the forms of the Republic. Mommsen, foreseeing—if an historian can be said to foresee the future from his standing-point in the past—that a master was to come for the Roman Empire, and giving all his sympathies to the Caesarean idea, despises Pompey because Pompey would not pick up the diadem. No such idea ever entered Pompey's head. After a while he "Sullaturized"—was desirous of copying Sulla—to use an excellent word which Cicero coined. When he was successfully opposed by those whom he had thought inferior to himself, when he found that Caesar had got the better of him, and that a stronger body of Romans went with Caesar than with him, then proscriptions, murder, confiscations, and the seizing of dictatorial power presented themselves to his angry mind, but of permanent despotic power there was, I think, no thought, nor, as far as I can read the records, had such an idea been fixed in Caesar's bosom. To carry on the old trade of Praetor, Consul, Proconsul, and Imperator, so as to get what he could of power and wealth and dignity in the scramble, was, I think, Caesar's purpose. The rest grew upon him. As Shakspeare, sitting down to write a play that might serve his theatre, composed some Lear or Tempest—that has lived and will live forever, because of the genius which was unknown to himself—so did Caesar, by his genius, find his way to a power which he had not premeditated. A much longer time is necessary for eradicating an idea from men's minds than a fact from their practice. This should be proved to us by our own loyalty to the word "monarch, " when nothing can be farther removed from a monarchy than our own commonwealth. From those first breaches in republican practice which the historian Florus dates back to the siege of Numantia, [230] B. C. 133, down far into the reign of Augustus, it took a century and a quarter to make the people understand that there was no longer a republican form of government, and to produce a leader who could himself see that there was room for a despot.

Pompey had his triumph; but the same aristocratic airs which had annoyed Cicero had offended others. He was shorn of his honors. Only two days were allowed for his processions. He was irritated, jealous, and no doubt desirous of making his power felt; but he thought of no diadem. Caesar saw it all; and he thought of that conspiracy which we have since called the First Triumvirate.

[Sidenote: B.C. 62, 61. aetat. 45,46.]

The two years to which this chapter has been given were uneventful in Cicero's life, and produced but little of that stock of literature by which he has been made one of mankind's prime favorites. Two discourses were written and published, and probably spoken, which are now lost—that, namely, to the people against Metellus, in which, no doubt, he put forth all that he had intended to say when Metellus stopped him from speaking at the expiration of his Consulship; the second, against Clodius and Curio, in the Senate, in reference to the discreditable Clodian affair. The fragments which we have of this contain those asperities which he retailed afterward in his letter to Atticus, and are not either instructive or amusing. But we learn from these fragments that Clodius was already preparing that scheme for entering the Tribunate by an illegal repudiation of his own family rank, which he afterward carried out, to the great detriment of Cicero's happiness. Of the speeches extant on behalf of Archias and P. Sulla I have spoken already. We know of no others made during this period. We have one letter besides this to Atticus, addressed to Antony, his former colleague, which, like many of his letters, was written solely for the sake of popularity.

During these years he lived no doubt splendidly as one of the great men of the greatest city in the world. He had his magnificent new mansion in Rome, and his various villas, which were already becoming noted for their elegance and charms of upholstery and scenic beauty. Not only had he climbed to the top of official life himself, but had succeeded in taking his brother Quintus up with him. In the second of the two years, B.C. 61, Quintus had been sent out as Governor or Propraetor to Asia, having then nothing higher to reach than the Consulship, which, however, he never attained. This step in the life of Quintus has become famous by a letter which the elder brother wrote to him in the second year of his office, to which reference will be made in the next chapter.

So far all things seemed to have gone well with Cicero. He was high in esteem and authority, powerful, rich, and with many people popular. But the student of his life now begins to see that troubles are enveloping him. He had risen too high not to encounter envy, and had been too loud in his own praise not to make those who envied him very bitter in their malice.

NOTES:

[212] In Pisonem, iii. : "Sine ulla dubitatione juravi rempublicam atque hanc urbem mea unius opera esse salvam. "

[213] Dio Cassius tells the same story, lib. xxxvii., ca. 38, but he adds that Cicero was more hated than ever because of the oath he took: [Greek: Kai ho men ek touton poly mallon emisaethae.]

[214] It is the only letter given in the collection as having been addressed direct to Pompey. In two letters written some years later to Atticus, B.C. 49, lib. viii., 11, and lib. viii., 12, he sends copies of a correspondence between himself and Pompey and two of the Pompeian generals.

[215] Lib. v., 7. It is hardly necessary to explain that the younger Scipio and Laelius were as famous for their friendship as Pylades and Orestes. The "Virtus Scipiadae et mitis sapientia Laeli" have been made famous to us all by Horace.

[216] These two brothers, neither of whom was remarkable for great qualities, though they were both to be Consuls, were the last known of the great family of the Metelli, a branch of the "Gens Caecilia. " Among them had been many who had achieved great names for themselves in Roman history, on account of the territories added to the springing Roman Empire by their victories. There had been a Macedonicus, a Numidicus, a Balearicus, and a Creticus. It is of the first that Velleius Paterculus sings the glory—lib. i., ca. xi., and the elder Pliny repeats the story, Hist. Nat., vii., 44—that of his having been carried to the grave by four sons, of whom at the time of his death three had been Consuls, one had been a Praetor, two had enjoyed triumphal honors, and one had been Censor. In looking through the consular list of Cicero's lifetime, I find that there were no less than seven taken from the family of the Metelli. These two brothers, Metellus Nepos and Celer, again became friends to Cicero; Nepos, who had stopped his speech and assisted in forcing him into exile, having assisted as Consul in obtaining his recall from exile. It is very difficult to follow the twistings and turnings of Roman friendships at this period.

[217] Velleius Paterculus, lib. ii., ca. xiv. Paterculus tells us how, when the architect offered to build the house so as to hide its interior

from the gaze of the world, Drusus desired the man so to construct it that all the world might see what he was doing.

[218] It may be worth while to give a translation of the anecdote as told by Aulus Gellius, and to point out that the authors intention was to show what a clever fellow Cicero was. Cicero did defend P. Sulla this year; but whence came the story of the money borrowed from Sulla we do not know. "It is a trick of rhetoric craftily to confess charges made, so as not to come within the reach of the law. So that, if any- thing base be alleged which cannot be denied, you may turn it aside with a joke, and make it a matter of laughter rather than of disgrace, as it is written that Cicero did when, with a drolling word, he made little of a charge which he could not deny. For when he was anxious to buy a house on the Palatine Hill, and had not the ready money, he quietly borrowed from P. Sulla—who was then about to stand his trial, 'sestertium viciens'—twenty million sesterces. When that became known, before the purchase was made, and it was objected to him that he had borrowed the money from a client, then Cicero, instigated by the unexpected charge, denied the loan, and denied also that he was going to buy the house. But when he had bought it and the fib was thrown in his teeth, he laughed heartily, and asked whether men had so lost their senses as not to be aware that a prudent father of a family would deny an intended purchase rather than raise the price of the article against himself"—Noctes Atticae, xii., 12. Aulus Gellius though he tells us that the story was written, does not tell us where he read it.

[219] I must say this, "pace" Mr. Tyrrell, who, in his note on the letter to Atticus, lib. i, 12, attempts to show that some bargain for such professional fee had been made. Regarding Mr. Tyrrell as a critic always fair, and almost always satisfactory, I am sorry to have to differ from him; but it seems to me that he, too, has been carried away by the feeling that in defending a man's character it is best to give up some point.

[220] I have been amused at finding a discourse, eloquent and most enthusiastic, in praise of Cicero and especially of this oration, spoken by M. Gueroult at the College of France in June, 1815. The worst literary faults laid to the charge of Cicero, if committed by him—which M. Gueroult thinks to be doubtful—had been committed even by Voltaire and Racine! The learned Frenchman, with whom I altogether sympathize, rises to an ecstasy of violent admiration, and this at the very moment in which Waterloo was being fought. But in

truth the great doings of the world do not much affect individual life. We should play our whist at the clubs though the battle of Dorking were being fought.

[221] Pro P. Sulla, iv. : "Scis me——illorum expertem temporum et sermonum fuisse; credo, quod nondum penitus in republica versabar, quod nondum ad propositum mihi finem honoris perveneram. ——Quis ergo intererat vestris consiliis? Omnes hi, quos vides huic adesse et in primis Q. Hortensius. "

[222] Ad Att., lib. i., 12.

[223] Ad Att., lib. i., 13.

[224] Ibid., i., 14.

[225]Ibid., i., 16: "Vis scire quomodo minus quam soleam praeliatus sum. "

[226] "You have bought a fine house, " said Clodius. "There would be more in what you say if you could accuse me of buying judges, " replied Cicero. "The judges would not trust you on your oath, " said Clodius, referring to the alibi by which he had escaped in opposition to Cicero's oath. "Yes, " replied Cicero, "twenty-five trusted me; but not one of the thirty-one would trust you without having his bribe paid beforehand. "

[227] Ad Att., i., 14: "Proxime Pompeium sedebam. Intellexi hominem moveri. "

[228] Ibid. : "Quo modo [Greek: eneperpereusamaen], novo auditori Pompeio. "

[229] Mommsen, book v., chap.vi. This probably has been taken from the statement of Paterculus, lib. ii., 40: "Quippe plerique non sine exercitu venturum in urbem adfirmabant, et libertati publicae statuturum arbitrio suo modum. Quo magis hoc homines timuerant, eo gratior civilis tanti imperatoris reditus fuit. " No doubt there was a dread among many of Pompey coming back as Sulla had come: not from indications to be found in the character of Pompey, but because Sulla had done so.

[230] Florus, lib. ii., xix. Having described to us the siege of Numantia, he goes on "Ilactenus populus Romanus pulcher, egregius, pius, sanctusarque magnificus. Reliqua seculi, ut grandia aeque, ita vel magis turbida et foeda".

CHAPTER XI.

THE TRIUMVIRATE.

[Sidenote: BC. 60, aetat. 47.]

I know of no great fact in history so impalpable, so shadowy, so unreal, as the First Triumvirate. Every school-boy, almost every school-girl, knows that there was a First Triumvirate, and that it was a political combination made by three great Romans of the day, Julius Caesar, Pompey the Great, and Crassus the Rich, for managing Rome among them. Beyond this they know little, because there is little to know. That it was a conspiracy against the ordained government of the day, as much so as that of Catiline, or Guy Faux, or Napoleon III., they do not know generally, because Caesar, who, though the youngest of the three, was the mainspring of it, rose by means of it to such a galaxy of glory that all the steps by which he rose to it have been supposed to be magnificent and heroic. But of the method in which this Triumvirate was constructed, who has an idea? How was it first suggested, where, and by whom? What was it that the conspirators combined to do? There was no purpose of wholesale murder like that of Catiline for destroying the Senate, and of Guy Faux for blowing up the House of Lords. There was no plot arranged for silencing a body of legislators like that of Napoleon. In these scrambles that are going on every year for place and power, for provinces and plunder, let us help each other. If we can manage to stick fast by each other, we can get all the power and nearly all the plunder. That, said with a wink by one of the Triumvirate—Caesar, let us say—and assented to with a nod by Pompey and Crassus, was sufficient for the construction of such a conspiracy as that which I presume to have been hatched when the First Triumvirate was formed. [231]

Mommsen, who never speaks of a Triumvirate under that name, except in his index, [232] where he has permitted the word to appear for the guidance of persons less well instructed than himself, connects the transaction which we call the First Triumvirate with a former coalition, which he describes as having been made in (B. C. 71) the year before the Consulship of Pompey and Crassus. With that we need not concern ourselves as we are dealing with the life of Cicero rather than with Roman history, except to say that Caesar. who was the motive power of the second coalition, could have had no personal hand in that of 71. Though he had spent his early years in "harassing the aristocracy, " as Dean Merivale tells us, he had not been of sufficient standing in men's minds to be put on a par with Pompey and Crassus. When this First Triumvirate was formed, as the modern world generally calls it, or the second coalition between the democracy and the great military leaders, as Mommsen with greater, but not with perfect, accuracy describes it, Caesar no doubt had at his fingers' ends the history of past years. "The idea naturally occurred, " says Mommsen, "whether — — an alliance firmly based on mutual advantage might not be established between the democrats, with their ally, Crassus, on the one side, and Pompeius and the great capitalists on the other. For Pompeius such a coalition was certainly a political suicide. "[233] The democracy here means Caesar. Caesar during his whole life had been learning that no good could come to any one from an effete Senate, or from republican forms which had lost all their salt. Democracy was in vogue with him; not, as I think, from any philanthropic desire for equality; not from any far-seeing view of fraternal citizenship under one great paternal lord—the study of politics had never then reached to that height—but because it was necessary that some one, or perhaps some two or three, should prevail in the coming struggle, and because he felt himself to be more worthy than others. He had no conscience in the matter. Money was to him nothing. Another man's money was the same as his own—or better, if he could get hold of it. That doctrine taught by Cicero that men are "ad justitiam natos" must have been to him simply absurd. Blood was to him nothing. A friend was better than a foe, and a live man than a dead. Blood-thirstiness was a passion unknown to him; but that tenderness which with us creates a horror of blood was equally unknown. Pleasure was sweet to him; but he was man enough to feel that a life of pleasure was contemptible. To pillage a city, to pilfer his all from a rich man, to debauch a friend's wife, to give over a multitude of women and children to slaughter, was as easy to him as to forgive an enemy. But nothing rankled with him, and he could forgive an enemy. Of courage he had that better sort which can appreciate and calculate danger, and then act as though there were none. Nothing was wrong to him but what was injudicious. He could flatter, cajole, lie, deceive, and rob; nay, would think it folly not to do so if to do so were expedient. [234] In this coalition he appears as supporting and supported by the people. Therefore Mommsen speaks of him as "the democrat. " Crassus is called the ally of the democrats. It will be enough for us here to know that Crassus had achieved his position in the Senate by his enormous wealth, and that it was because of his wealth, which was essential to Caesar, that he was admitted into the league. By means of his wealth he had risen to power and had conquered and killed Spartacus, of the honor and glory of which Pompey robbed him. Then he had been made Consul. When Caesar had gone as Propraetor to Spain, Crassus had found the money. Now Caesar had come back, and was hand and glove with Crassus. When the division of the spoil came, some years afterward—the spoil won by the Triumvirate—when Caesar had half perfected his grand achievements in Gaul, and Crassus had as yet been only a second time Consul, he got himself to be sent into Syria, that by conquering the Parthians he might make himself equal to Caesar. We know how he and his son perished there, each of them probably avoiding the last extremity of misery to a Roman—that of falling into the hands of a barbarian enemy—by destroying himself. Than the life of Crassus nothing could be more contemptible; than the death nothing more pitiable. "For Pompeius, " says Mommsen, "such a coalition was certainly a political suicide. " As events turned out it became so, because Caesar was the stronger man of the two; but it is intelligible that at that time Pompey should have felt that he could not lord it over the Senate, as he wished to do, without aid from the democratic party. He had no well-defined views, but he wished to be the first man in Rome. He regarded himself as still greatly superior to Caesar, who as yet had been no more than Praetor, and at this time was being balked of his triumph because he could not at one and the same moment be in the city, as candidate for the Consulship, and out of the city waiting for his triumph. Pompey had triumphed three times, had been Consul at an unnaturally early age with abnormal honors, had been victorious east and west, and was called "Magnus. " He did not as yet fear to be overshadowed by Ceasar. [235]

Cicero was his bugbear.

Mommsen I believe to be right in eschewing the word "Triumvirate. " I know no mention of it by any Roman writer as applied to this conspiracy, though Tacitus, Suetonius, and Florus call by that name the later coalition of Octavius, Antony, and Lepidus. The Langhornes, in translating Plutarch's life of Crassus, speak of the Triumvirate; but Plutarch himself says that Caesar combined "an impregnable stronghold" by joining the three men. [236]

Paterculus and Suetonius[237] explain very clearly the nature of the compact, but do not use the term. There was nothing in the conspiracy entitling it to any official appellation, though, as there were three leading conspirators, that which has been used has been so far appropriate.

[Sidenote: B.C. 60, aetat. 47.]

Cicero was the bugbear to them all. That he might have been one of them, if ready to share the plunder and the power, no reader of the history of the time can doubt. Had he so chosen he might again have been a "real power in the State; " but to become so in the way proposed to him it was necessary that he should join others in a conspiracy against the Republic.

I do not wish it to be supposed that Cicero received the overtures made to him with horror. Conspiracies were too common for horror; and these conspirators were all our Cicero's friends in one sense, though in another they might be his opponents. We may imagine that at first Crassus had nothing to do with the matter, and that Pompey would fain have stood aloof in his jealousy. But Caesar knew that it was well to have Cicero, if Cicero was to be had. It was not only his eloquence which was marvellously powerful, or his energy which had been shown to be indomitable: there was his character, surpassed by that of no Roman living; if only, in giving them the use of his character, he could be got to disregard the honor and the justice and the patriotism on which his character had been founded. How valuable may character be made, if it can be employed under such conditions! To be believed because of your truth, and yet to lie; to be trusted for your honesty, and yet to cheat; to have credit for patriotism, and yet to sell your country! The temptations to do this are rarely put before a man plainly, in all their naked ugliness. They certainly were not so presented to Cicero by Caesar and his associates. The bait was held out to him, as it is daily to others, in a form not repellent, with words fitted to deceive and powerful almost to persuade. Give us the advantage of your character, and then by your means we shall be able to save our country. Though our line of action may not be strictly constitutional, if you will look into it you will see that it is expedient. What other course is there? How else shall any wreck of the Republic be preserved? Would you be another Cato, useless and impractical? Join us, and save Rome to some purpose. We can understand that in such way was the lure held out to Cicero, as it has been to many a politician since. But when the politician takes the office offered to him—and the pay, though it be but that of a Lord of the Treasury—he must vote with his party.

That Cicero doubted much whether he would or would not at this time throw in his lot with Caesar and Pompey is certain. To be of real use—not to be impractical, as was Cato—to save his country and rise honestly in power and glory—not to be too straitlaced, not over-scrupulous—giving and taking a little, so that he might work to good purpose with others in harness—that was his idea of duty as a Roman. To serve in accord with Pompey was the first dream of his political life, and now Pompey was in accord with Caesar. It was natural that he should doubt—natural that he should express his doubts. Who should receive them but Atticus, that "alter ego? " Cicero doubted whether he should cling to Pompey—as he did in every phase of his political life, till Pompey had perished at the mouth of the Nile. But at last he saw his way clear to honesty, as I think he always did. He tells his friend that Caesar had sent his confidential messenger, Balbus, to sound him. The present question is whether he shall resist a certain agrarian law of which he does not approve, but which is supported by both Pompey and Caesar, or retire from the contest and enjoy himself at his country villas, or boldly stay at Rome and oppose the law. Caesar assures him that if he will come over to them, Caesar will be always true to him and Pompey, and will do his best to bring Crassus into the same frame of mind. Then he reckons up all the good things which would accrue to him: "Closest friendship with Pompey—with Caesar also, should he wish it; the making up of all quarrels with his enemies; popularity with the people; ease for his old age, which was coming on him. But that conclusion moves me to which I came in my third book. "[238] Then he repeats the lines given in the note below, which he had written, probably this very year, in a poem composed in honor of his own Consulship. The lines are not in themselves grand, but the spirit of them is magnificent: "Stick to the good cause which in your early youth you chose for yourself, and be true to the party you have made your own. " "Should I doubt when the muse herself has so written, " he says, alluding to the name of Calliope, given to this third book of his. Then he adds a line of Homer, very excellent for the occasion: "No augury for the future can be better for you than that which bids you serve your country. " "But, " he says, "we will talk of all that when you come to me for the holidays. Your bath shall be ready for you: your sister and mother shall be of the party. " And so the doubts are settled.

Now came on the question of the Tribuneship of Clodius, in reference to which I will quote a passage out of Middleton, because the phrase which he uses exactly explains the purposes of Caesar and Pompey.

[Sidenote: B.C. 60, aetat. 47.]

"Clodius, who had been contriving all this while how to revenge himself on Cicero, began now to give an opening to the scheme which he had formed for that purpose. His project was to get himself chosen Tribune, and in that office to drive him out of the city, by the publication of a law which, by some stratagem or other, he hoped to obtrude on the people. But as all Patricians were incapable of the Tribunate, by its original institution so his first step was to make himself a Plebeian by the pretence of an adoption into a Plebeian house, which could not yet be done without the suffrage of the people. This case was wholly new, and contrary to all the forms — wanting every condition, and serving none of the ends which were required in regular adoptions — so that, on the first proposal, it seemed too extravagant to be treated seriously, and would soon have been hissed off with scorn, had it not been concerted and privately supported by persons of much more weight than Clodius. Caesar was at the bottom of it, and Pompey secretly favored it — not that they intended to ruin Cicero, but to keep him only under the lash — and if they could not draw him into their measures, to make him at least sit quiet, and let Clodius loose upon him. "[239]

This, no doubt, was the intention of the political leaders in Rome at this conjunction of affairs. It had been found impossible to draw Cicero gently into the net, so that he should become one of them. If he would live quietly at his Antian or Tusculan villa, amid his books and writings, he should be treated with all respect; he should be borne with, even though he talked so much of his own Consulate. But if he would interfere with the politics of the day, and would not come into the net, then he must be dealt with. Caesar seems to have respected Cicero always, and even to have liked him; but he was not minded to put up with a "friend" in Rome who from day to day abused all his projects. In defending Antony, the Macedonian Proconsul who was condemned, Cicero made some unpleasant remarks on the then condition of things. Caesar, we are told, when he heard of this, on the very spur of the moment, caused Clodius to be accepted as a Plebeian.

In all this we are reminded of the absolute truth of Mommsen's verdict on Rome, which I have already quoted more than once: "On the Roman oligarchy of this period no judgment can be passed, save one of inexorable and remorseless condemnation. " How had it come to pass that Caesar had the power of suddenly causing an edict to become law, whether for good or for evil? Cicero's description of what took place is as follows: [240]

"About the sixth hour of the day, when I was defending my colleague Antony in court, I took occasion to complain of certain things which were being done in the Republic, and which I thought to be injurious to my poor client. Some dishonest persons carried my words to men in power"—meaning Caesar and Pompey—"not, indeed, my own words, but words very different from mine. At the ninth hour on that very same day, you, Clodius, were accepted as a Plebeian. " Caesar, having been given to understand that Cicero had been making himself disagreeable, was determined not to put up with it. Suetonius tells the same story with admirable simplicity. Of Suetonius it must be said that, if he had no sympathy for a patriot such as Cicero, neither had he any desire to represent in rosy colors the despotism of a Caesar. He tells his stories simply as he has heard them. "Cicero, " says Suetonius, [241] "having at some trial complained of the state of the times, Caesar, on the very same day, at the ninth hour, passed Clodius over from the Patrician to the Plebeian rank, in accordance with his own desire. " How did it come to pass that Caesar, who, though Consul at the time, had no recognized power of that nature, was efficacious for any such work as this? Because the Republic had come to the condition which the German historian has described. The conspiracy between Caesar and his subordinates had not been made for nothing. The reader will require to know why Clodius should have desired degradation, and how it came to pass that this degradation should have been fatal to Cicero. The story has been partly told in the passage from Middleton. A Patrician, in accordance with the constitution, could not be a Tribune of the people. From the commencement of the Tribunate, that office had been reserved for the Plebeians. But a Tribune had a power of introducing laws which exceeded that of any Senator or any other official. "They had acquired the right, " we are told in Smith's Dictionary of Greek and Roman Antiquities, "of proposing to the comitia tributa, or to the Senate, measures on nearly all the important affairs of the State; " and as matters stood at this time, no one Tribune could "veto" or put an arbitrary stop to a proposition from another. When such proposition was made, it was simply for the people to decide by their votes whether it should or should not be law. The present object was to have a proposition made and carried suddenly, in reference to Cicero, which should have, at any rate, the effect of stopping his mouth. This could be best done by a Tribune of the people. No other adequate Tribune could be found—no Plebeian so incensed against Cicero as to be willing to do this, possessing at the same time power enough to be elected. Therefore it was that Clodius was so anxious to be degraded.

No Patrician could become a Tribune of the people; but a Patrician might be adopted by a Plebeian, and the adopted child would take the rank of his father—would, in fact, for all legal purposes, be the same as a son. For doing this in any case a law had to be passed—or, in other words, the assent of the people must be obtained and registered. But many conditions were necessary. The father intending to adopt must have no living son of his own, and must be past the time of life at which he might naturally hope to have one; and the adopted son must be of a fitting age to personate a son—at any rate, must be younger than the father; nothing must be done injurious to either family; there must be no trick in it, no looking after other result than that plainly intended. All these conditions were broken. The pretended father, Fonteius, had a family of his own, and was younger than Clodius. The great Claudian family was desecrated, and there was no one so ignorant as not to know that the purpose intended was that of entering the Tribunate by a fraud. It was required by the general law that the Sacred College should report as to the proper observances of the prescribed regulations, but no priest was ever consulted. Yet Clodius was adopted, made a Plebeian, and in the course of the year elected as Tribune.

In reading all this, the reader is mainly struck by the wonderful admixture of lawlessness and law-abiding steadfastness. If Caesar, who was already becoming a tyrant in his Consulship, chose to make use of this means of silencing Cicero, why not force Clodius into the Tribunate without so false and degrading a ceremony? But if, as was no doubt the case, he was not yet strong enough to ignore the old popular feelings on the subject, how was it that he was able to laugh in his sleeve at the laws, and to come forth at a moment's notice and cause the people to vote, legally or illegally, just as he pleased? It requires no conjurer to tell us the reason. The outside hulls and husks remain when the rich fruit has gone. It was in seeing this, and yet not quite believing that it must be so, that the agony of Cicero's life consisted. There could have been no hope for freedom, no hope for the Republic, when Rome had been governed as it was during the Consulship of Caesar; but Cicero could still hope, though faintly, and still buoy himself up with remembrances of his own year of office.

In carrying on the story of the newly-adopted child to his election as Tribune, I have gone beyond the time of my narration, so that the reader may understand the cause and nature and effect of the anger which Clodius entertained for Cicero. This originated in the bitter words spoken as to the profanation of the Bona Dea, and led to the means for achieving Cicero's exile and other untoward passages of his life. In the year 60 B. C., when Metellus Celer and Afranius were Consuls, Clodius was tried for insulting the Bona Dea, and the since so-called Triumvirate was instituted. It has already been shown that Cicero, not without many doubts, rejected the first offers which were made to him to join the forces that were so united. He seems to have passed the greater portion of this year in Rome. One letter only was written from the country, to Atticus, from his Tusculan villa, and that is of no special moment. He spent his time in the city, still engaged in the politics of the day; as to which, though he dreaded the coming together of Caesar and Pompey and Crassus—those "graves principum amicitias" which were to become so detrimental to all who were concerned in them—he foresaw as yet but little of the evil which was to fall upon his own head. He was by no means idle as to literature, though we have but little of what he wrote, and do not regret what we have lost. He composed a memoir of his Consulate in Greek, which he sent to Atticus with an allusion to his own use of the foreign language intended to show that he is quite at ease in that matter. Atticus had sent him a memoir, also written in Greek, on the same subject, and the two packets had crossed each other on the road. He candidly tells Atticus that his attempt seems to be "horridula atque incompta, " rough and unpolished; whereas Posidonius, the great Greek critic of Rhodes who had been invited by him, Cicero, to read the memoir, and then himself to treat the same subject, had replied that he was altogether debarred from such an attempt by the excellence of his correspondent's performance. [242] He also wrote three books of a poem on his Consulate, and sent them to Atticus; of which we have a fragment of seventy-five lines quoted by himself, [243] and four or five other lines including that unfortunate verse handed down by Quintilian, "O fortunatum natam me consule Romam"—unless, indeed, it be spurious, as is suggested by that excellent critic and whole- hearted friend of the orator's, M. Gueroult. Previous to these he had produced in hexameters, also, a translation of the Prognostics of Aratus. This is the second part of a poem on the heavenly bodies, the first part, the Phaenomena, having been turned into Latin verse by him when he was eighteen. Of the Prognostics we have only a few lines preserved by Priscian, and a passage repeated by the author, also in his De Divinatione. I think that Cicero was capable of producing a poem quite worthy of preservation; but in the work of this year the subjects chosen were not alluring.

[Sidenote: B.C. 60, aetat. 47.]

Among his epistles of the year there is one which might of itself have sufficed to bring down his name to posterity. This is a long letter, full of advice, to his brother Quintus, who had gone out in the previous year to govern the province of Asia as Propraetor. We may say that good advice could never have been more wanted, and that better advice could not have been given. It has been suggested that it was written as a companion to that treatise on the duties of a candidate which Quintus composed for his brother's service when standing for his Consulship. But I cannot admit the analogy. The composition attributed to Quintus contained lessons of advice equally suitable to any candidate, sprung from the people, striving to rise to high honors in the State. This letter is adapted not only to the special position of Quintus, but to the peculiarities of his character, and its strength lies in this: that while the one brother praises the other justly praises him, as I believe, for many virtues, so as to make the receipt of it acceptable, it points out faults—faults which will become fatal, if not amended—in language which is not only strong but unanswerable.

The style of this letter is undoubtedly very different from that of Cicero's letters generally—so as to suggest to the reader that it must have been composed expressly for publication whereas the daily correspondence is written "currente calamo, " with no other than the immediate idea of amusing, instructing, or perhaps comforting the correspondent. Hence has come the comparison between this and the treatise De Petitione Consulatus. I think that the gravity of the occasion, rather than any regard for posterity, produced the change of style. Cicero found it to be essential to induce his brother to remain at his post, not to throw up his government in disgust, and so to bear himself that he should not make himself absolutely odious to his own staff and to other Romans around him; for Quintus Cicero, though he had been proud and arrogant and ill tempered, had not made himself notorious by the ordinary Roman propensity to plunder his province "What is it that is required of you as a governor? "[244] asks Cicero. "That men should not be frightened by your journeys hither and thither—that they should not be eaten up by your extravagance—that they should not be disturbed by your coming among them—that there should be joy at your approach; when each city should think that its guardian angel, not a cruel master, had come upon it—when each house should feel that it entertained not a robber but a friend. Practice has made you perfect in this. But it is not enough that you should exercise those good offices yourself, but that you should take care that every one of those who come with you should seem to do his best for the inhabitants of the province, for the citizen of Rome, and for the Republic. " I wish that I could give the letter entire—both in English, that all readers might know how grand are the precepts taught, and in Latin, that they who understand the language might appreciate the beauty of the words—but I do not dare to fill my pages at such length. A little farther on he gives his idea of the duty of all those who have power over others—even over the dumb animals. [245] "To me it seems that the duty of those in authority over others consists in making those who are under them as happy as the nature of things will allow. Every one knows that you have acted on this principle since you first went to Asia. " This, I fear, must be taken as flattery, intended to gild the pill which comes afterward "This is not only his duty who has under him allies and citizens, but is also that of the man who has slaves under his control, and even dumb cattle, that he should study the welfare of all over whom he stands in the position of master! " Let the reader look into this, and ask himself what precepts of Christianity have ever surpassed it.

Then he points out that which he describes as the one great difficulty in the career of a Roman Provincial Governor. [246] The collectors of taxes, or "publicani, " were of the equestrian order. This business of farming the taxes had been their rich privilege for at any rate more than a century, and as Cicero says, farther on in his letter, it was impossible not to know with what hardship the Greek allies would be treated by them when so many stories were current of their cruelty even in Italy. Were Quintus to take a part against these tax-gatherers, he would make them hostile not only to the Republic but to himself also, and also to his brother Marcus; for they were of the equestrian order, and specially connected with these "publicani" by family ties. He implies, as he goes on, that it will be easier to teach the Greeks to be submissive than the tax-gatherers to be moderate.

After all, where would the Greeks of Asia be if they had no Roman master to afford them protection? He leaves the matter in the hands of his brother, with advice that he should do the best he can on one side and on the other. If possible, let the greed of the "publicani" be restrained; but let the ally be taught to understand that there may be usage in the world worse even than Roman taxation. It would be hardly worth our while to allude to this part of Cicero's advice, did it not give an insight into the mode in which Rome taxed her subject people.

After this he commences that portion of the letter for the sake of which we cannot but believe that the whole was written. "There is one thing, " he says, "which I will never cease to din into your ears, because I could not endure to think that, amid the praises which are lavished on you, there should be any matter in which you should be found wanting. All who come to us here"—all who come to Rome from Asia, that is—"when they tell us of your honesty and goodness of heart, tell us also that you fail in temper. It is a vice which, in the daily affairs of private life, betokens a weak and unmanly spirit; but there can be nothing so poor as the exhibition of the littleness of nature in those who have risen to the dignity of command. " He will not, he goes on to say, trouble his brother with repeating all that the wise men have said on the subject of anger; he is sure that Quintus is well acquainted with all that. But is it not a pity, when all men say that nothing could be pleasanter than Quintus Cicero when in a good-humor, the same Quintus should allow himself to be so provoked that his want of kindly manners should be regretted by all around him? "I cannot assert, " he goes on to say, "that when nature has produced a certain condition of mind, and that years as they run on have strengthened it, a man can change all that and pluck out from his very self the habits that have grown within him; yet I must tell you that if you cannot eschew this evil altogether—if you cannot protect yourself against the feeling of anger, yet you should prepare yourself to be ready for it when it comes, so that, when your very soul within you is hot with it, your tongue, at any rate, may be restrained. " Then toward the end of the letter there is a fraternal exhortation which is surely very fine: "Since chance has thrown into my way the duties of official life in Rome, and into yours that of administrating provincial government, if I, in the performance of my work, have been second to none, do you see that you in yours may be equally efficient. " How grand, from an elder brother to a younger! "And remember this, that you and I have not to strive after some excellence still unattained, but have to be on our watch to guard that which has been already won. If I should find myself in anything divided from you, I should desire no further advance in life. Unless your deeds and your words go on all-fours with mine, I should feel that I had achieved nothing by all the work and all the dangers which you and I have encountered together. " The brother at last was found to be a poor, envious, ill-conditioned creature—intellectually gifted, and capable of borrowing something from his brother's nobler nature; but when struggles came, and political feuds, and the need of looking about to see on which side safety lay, ready to sacrifice his brother for the sake of safety. But up to this time Marcus was prepared to believe all good of Quintus; and having made for himself and for the family a great name, was desirous of sharing it with his brother, and, as we shall afterward see, with his brother's son, and with his own. In this he failed. He lived to know that he had failed as regarded his brother and his nephew. It was not, however, added to his misery to live to learn how little his son was to do to maintain the honor of his family.

I find a note scribbled by myself some years ago in a volume in which I had read this epistle, "Probably the most beautiful letter ever written. " Reading it again subsequently, I added another note, "The language altogether different from that of his ordinary letters. " I do not dissent now either from the enthusiastic praise or the more careful criticism. The letter was from the man's heart—true, affectionate, and full of anxious, brotherly duty—but written in studied language, befitting, as Cicero thought, the need and the dignity of the occasion.

[Sidenote: B C 59, aetat. 48.]

The year following was that of Caesar's first Consulship, which he held in conjunction with Bibulus, a man who was altogether opposed to him in thought, in character, and in action. So hostile were these two great officers to each other that the one attempted to undo whatever the other did. Bibulus was elected by bribery, on behalf of the Senate, in order that he might be a counterpoise to Caesar. But Caesar now was not only Caesar: he was Caesar, Pompey, and Crassus united, with all their dependents, all their clients, all their greedy hangers-on. To give this compact something of the strength of family union, Pompey, who was now nearly fifty years of age, took in marriage Caesar's daughter Julia, who was a quarter of a century his junior. But Pompey was a man who could endear himself to women, and the opinion seems to be general that had not Julia died in childbirth the friendship between the men would have been more lasting. But for Caesar's purposes the duration of this year and the next was enough. Bibulus was a laughing-stock, the mere shadow of a Consul, when opposed to such an enemy. He tried to use all the old forms of the Republic with the object of stopping Caesar in his career; but Caesar only ridiculed him; and Pompey, though we can imagine that he did not laugh much, did as Caesar would have him. Bibulus was an augur, and observed the heavens when political manoeuvres were going on which he wished to stop. This was the old Roman system for using religion as a drag upon progressive movements. No work of state could be carried on if the heavens were declared to be unpropitious; and an augur could always say that the heavens were unpropitious if he pleased. This was the recognized constitutional mode of obstruction, and was quite in accord with the feelings of the people. Pompey alone, or Crassus with him, would certainly have submitted to an augur; but Caesar was above augurs. Whatever he chose to have carried he carried, with what approach he could to constitutional usage, but with whatever departure from constitutional usage he found to be necessary.

What was the condition of the people of Rome at the time it is difficult to learn from the conflicting statements of historians. That Cicero had till lately been popular we know. We are told that Bibulus was popular when he opposed Caesar. Of personal popularity up to this time I doubt whether Caesar had achieved much. Yet we learn that, when Bibulus with Cato and Lucullus endeavored to carry out their constitutional threats, they were dragged and knocked about, and one of them nearly killed. Of the illegality of Caesar's proceedings there can be no doubt. "The tribunitian veto was interposed; Caesar contented himself with disregarding it. "[247] This is quoted from the German historian, who intends to leave an impression that Caesar was great and wise in all that he did; and who tells us also of the "obstinate, weak creature Bibulus, " and of "the dogmatical fool Cato. " I doubt whether there was anything of true popular ferment, or that there was any commotion except that which was made by the "roughs" who had attached themselves for pay to Caesar or to Pompey, or to Crassus, or, as it might be, to Bibulus and the other leaders. The violence did not amount to more than "nearly" killing this man or the other. Some Roman street fights were no doubt more bloody—as for instance that in which, seven years afterward, Clodius was slaughtered by Milo—but the blood was made to flow, not by the people, but by hired bravoes. The Roman citizens of the day were, I think, very quiescent. Neither pride nor misery stirred them much. Caesar, perceiving this, was aware that he might disregard Bibulus and his auguries so long as he had a band of ruffians around him sufficient for the purposes of the hour. It was in order that he might thus prevail that the coalition had been made with Pompey and Crassus. His colleague Bibulus, seeing how matters were going, retired to his own house, and there went through a farce of consular enactments. Caesar carried all his purposes, and the people were content to laugh, dividing him into two personages, and talking of Julius and Caesar as the two Consuls of the year. It was in this way that he procured to be allotted to him by the people his irregular command in Gaul. He was to be Proconsul, not for one year, with perhaps a prolongation for two or three, but for an established period of five. He was to have the great province of Cisalpine Gaul — that is to say, the whole of what we now call Italy, from the foot of the Alps down to a line running from sea to sea just north of Florence. To this Transalpine Gaul was afterward added. The province so named, possessed at the time by the Romans, was called "Narbonensis", a country comparatively insignificant, running from the Alps to the Pyrenees along the Mediterranean. The Gaul or Gallia of which Caesar speaks when, in the opening words of his Commentary, he tells us that it was divided into three parts, was altogether beyond the Roman province which was assigned to him. Caesar, when he undertook his government, can hardly have dreamed of subjecting to Roman rule the vast territories which were then known as Gallia, beyond the frontiers of the Empire, and which we now call France.

But he caused himself to be supported by an enormous army. There were stationed three legions on the Italian side of the Alps, and one on the other. These were all to be under his command for five years certain, and amounted to a force of not less than thirty thousand men. "As no troops could constitutionally be stationed in Italy proper, the commander of the legions of Northern Italy and Gaul, " says Mommsen, "dominated at the same time Italy and Rome for the next five years; and he who was master for five years was master for life. "[248]

[Sidenote: B.C. 59, aetat. 48.]

Such was the condition of Rome during the second year of the Triumvirate, in which Caesar was Consul and prepared the way for the powers which he afterward exercised. Cicero would not come to his call; and therefore, as we are told, Clodius was let loose upon him. As he would not come to Caesar's call, it was necessary that he should he suppressed, and Clodius, notwithstanding all constitutional difficulties—nay, impossibilities—was made Tribune of the people. Things had now so far advanced with a Caesar that a Cicero who would not come to his call must be disposed of after some fashion.

Till we have thought much of it, often of it, till we have looked thoroughly into it, we find ourselves tempted to marvel at Cicero's blindness. Surely a man so gifted must have known enough of the state of Rome to have been aware that there was no room left for one honest, patriotic, constitutional politician. Was it not plain to him that if, "natus ad justitiam, " he could not bring himself to serve with those who were intent on discarding the Republic, he had better retire among his books, his busts, and his literary luxuries, and leave the government of the country to those who understood its people? And we are the more prone to say and to think all this because the man himself continually said it, and continually thought it. In one of the letters written early in the year[249] to Atticus from his villa at Antium he declares very plainly how it is with him; and this, too, in a letter written in good-humor, not in a despondent frame of mind, in which he is able pleasantly to ridicule his enemy Clodius, who it seems had expressed a wish to go on an embassy to Tigranes, King of Armenia. "Do not think, " he says, "that I am complaining of all this because I myself am desirous of being engaged in public affairs. Even while it was mine to sit at the helm I was tired of the work; but now, when I am in truth driven out of the ship, when the rudder has not been thrown down but seized out of my hands, how should I take a pleasure in looking from the shore at the wrecks which these other pilots have made? " But the study of human nature tells us, and all experience, that men are unable to fathom their own desires, and fail to govern themselves by the wisdom which is at their fingers' ends. The retiring Prime-minister cannot but hanker after the seals and the ribbons and the titles of office, even though his soul be able to rise above considerations of emolument, and there will creep into a man's mind an idea that, though reform of abuses from other sources may be impossible, if he were there once more the evil could at least be mitigated, might possibly be cured. So it was during this period of his life with Cicero. He did believe that political justice exercised by himself, with such assistance as his eloquence would obtain for it, might be efficacious for preserving the Republic, in spite of Caesar, and of Pompey, and of Crassus. He did not yet believe that these men would consent to such an outrage as his banishment. It must have been incredible to him that Pompey should assent to it. When the blow came, it crushed him for the time. But he retricked his beams and struggled on to the end, as we shall see if we follow his life to the close.

Such was the intended purpose of the degradation of Clodius. This, however, was not at once declared. It was said that Clodius as Tribune intended rather to oppose Caesar than to assist him. He at any rate chose that Cicero should so believe and sent Curio, a young man to whom Cicero was attached to visit the orator at his villa at Antium and to declare these friendly purposes. According to the story told by Cicero, [250] Clodius was prepared to oppose the Triumvirate; and the other young men of Rome, the *jeunesse dorée*, of which both Curio and Clodius were members, were said to be equally hostile to Caesar, Pompey, and Crassus, whose doings in opposition to the constitution were already evident enough; so that it suited Cicero to believe that the rising aristocracy of Rome would oppose them. But the aristocracy of Rome, whether old or young, cared for nothing but its fish-ponds and its amusements.

Cicero spent the earlier part of the year out of Rome, among his various villas—at Tusculanum, at Antium, and at Formiae. The purport of all his letters at this period is the same—to complain of the condition of the Republic, and especially of the treachery of his friend Pompey. Though there be much of despondency in his tone, there is enough also of high spirit to make us feel that his literary aspirations are not out of place, though mingled with his political wailing. The time will soon come when his trust even in literature will fail him for a while.

Early in the year he declares that he would like to accept a mission to Egypt, offered to him by Caesar and Pompey, partly in order that he might for a while be quit of Rome, and partly that Romans might feel how ill they could do without him. He then uses for the first time, as far as I am aware, a line from the Iliad, [251] which is repeated by him again and again, in part or in whole, to signify the restraint which is placed on him by his own high character among his fellow-citizens. "I would go to Egypt on this pleasant excursion, but that I fear what the men of Troy, and the Trojan women, with their wide-sweeping robes, would say of me. " And what, he asks, would the men of our party, "the optimates, " say? and what would Cato say, whose opinion is more to me than that of them all? And how would history tell the story in future ages? But he would like to go to Egypt, and he will wait and see. Then, after various questions to Atticus, comes that great one as to the augurship, of which so much has been made by Cicero's enemies, "quo quidem uno ego ab istis capi possim. " A few lines above he had been speaking of another lure, that of the mission to Egypt. He discusses that with his friend, and then goes on in his half-joking phrase, "but this would have been the real thing to catch me. " Nothing caught him. He was steadfast all through, accepting no offer of place from the conspirators by which his integrity or his honor could be soiled. That it was so was well known to history in the time of Quintilian, whose testimony as to the "repudiatus vigintiviratus"—his refusal of a place among the twenty commissioners—has been already quoted. [252] And yet biographers have written of him as of one willing to sell his honor, his opinions, and the commonwealth, for a "pitiful bribe; " not that he did do so, not that he attempted to do it, but because in a half-joking letter to the friend of his bosom he tells his friend which way his tastes lay! [253]

He had been thinking of writing a book on geography, and consulted Atticus on the subject; but in one of his letters he tells his friend that he had abandoned the idea. The subject was too dull; and if he took one side in a dispute that was existing, he would be sure to fall under the lash of the critics on the other. He is enjoying his leisure at Antium, and thinks it a much better place than Rome. If the weather will not let him catch fish, at any late he can count the waves. In all these letters Cicero asks questions about his money and his private affairs; about the mending of a wall, perhaps, and adds something about his wife or daughter or son. He is going from Antium to Formiae, but must return to Antium by a certain date because Tullia wants to see the games.

Then again he alludes to Clodius. Pompey had made a compact with Clodius—so at least Cicero had heard—that he, Clodius, if elected for the Tribunate, would do nothing to injure Cicero. The assurance of such a compact had no doubt been spread about for the quieting of Cicero; but no such compact had been intended to be kept, unless Cicero would be amenable, would take some of the good things offered to him, or at any rate hold his peace. But Cicero affects to hope that no such agreement may be kept. He is always nicknaming Pompey, who during his Eastern campaign had taken Jerusalem, and who now parodies the Africanus, the Asiaticus, and the

Macedonicus of the Scipios and Metelluses. "If that Hierosolymarian candidate for popularity does not keep his word with me, I shall be delighted. If that be his return for my speeches on his behalf"—the Anteponatur omnibus Pompeius, for instance—"I will play him such a turn of another kind that he shall remember it"[254]

He begins to know what the "Triumvirate" is doing with the Republic, but has not yet brought himself to suspect the blow that is to fall on himself. "They are going along very gayly, " he says, "and do not make as much noise as one would have expected. "[255] If Cato had been more on the alert, things would not have gone so quickly; but the dishonesty of others, who have allowed all the laws to be ignored, has been worse than Cato. If we used to feel that the Senate took too much on itself, what shall we say when that power has been transferred, not to the people, but to three utterly unscrupulous men? "They can make whom they will Consuls, whom they will Tribunes—so that they may hide the very goitre of Vatinius under a priest's robe. " For himself, Cicero says, he will be contented to remain with his books, if only Cledius will allow him; if not, he will defend himself. [256] As for his country, he has done more for his country than has even been desired of him; and he thinks it to be better to leave the helm in the hands of pilots, however incompetent, than himself to steer when passengers are so thankless. Then we find that he robs poor Tullia of her promised pleasure at the games, because it will be beneath his dignity to appear at them. He is always very anxious for his friend's letters, depending on them for news and for amusement. "My messenger will return at once, " he says, in one; "therefore, though you are coming yourself very soon, send me a heavy letter, full not only of news but of your own ideas. "[257] In another: "Cicero the Little sends greeting, " he says, in Greek, "to Titus the Athenian"—that is, to Titus Pomponius Atticus. The Greek letters were probably traced by the child at his father's knee as Cicero held the pen or the stylus. In another letter he declares that there, at Formiae, Pompey's name of Magnus is no more esteemed than that of Dives belonging to Crassus. In the next he calls Pompey Sampsiceramus. We learn from Josephus that there was a lady afterward in the East in the time of Vitellius, who was daughter of Sampsigeramus, King of the Emesi. It might probably be a royal family name. [258]

In choosing the absurd title, he is again laughing at his party leader. Pompey had probably boasted of his doings with the Sampsiceramus of the day and the priests of Jerusalem. "When this Sampsiceramus of ours finds how ill he is spoken of, he will rush headlong into revolution. " He complains that he can do nothing at Formiae because of the visitors. No English poet was ever so interviewed by American admirers. They came at all hours, in numbers sufficient to fill a temple, let alone a gentleman's house. How can he write anything requiring leisure in such a condition as this? Nevertheless he will attempt something. He goes on criticising all that is done in Rome, especially what is done by Pompey, who no doubt was vacillating sadly between Caesar, to whom he was bound, and Bibulus, the other Consul, to whom he ought to have been bound, as being naturally on the aristocratic side. He cannot for a moment keep his pen from public matters; nor, on the other hand, can he refrain from declaring that he will apply himself wholly, undividedly, to his literature. "Therefore, oh my Titus, let me settle down to these glorious occupations, and return to that which, if I had been wise, I never should have left. "[259] A day or two afterward, writing from the same place, he asks what Arabarches is saying of him. Arabarches is another name for Pompey—this Arabian chieftain.

In the early summer of this year Cicero returned to Rome, probably in time to see Atticus, who was then about to leave the city for his estates in Epirus. We have a letter written by him to his friend on the journey, telling us that Caesar had made him two distinct offers, evidently with the view of getting rid of him, but in such a manner as would be gratifying to Cicero himself. [260] Caesar asks him to go with him to Gaul as his lieutenant, or, if that will not suit him, to accept a "free legation for the sake of paying a vow. " This latter was a kind of job by which Roman Senators got themselves sent forth on their private travels with all the appanages of a Senator travelling on public business. We have his argument as to both. Elsewhere he objects to a "libera legatio" as being a job. [261]

Here he only points out that, though it enforce his absence from Rome at a time disagreeable to him—just when his brother Quintus would return—it would not give him the protection which he needs. Though he were travelling about the world as a Senator on some pretended embassy, he would still be open to the attacks of Clodius. He would necessarily be absent, or he would not be in enjoyment of his privilege, but by his very absence he would find his position weakened; whereas, as Caesar's appointed lieutenant, he need not leave the city at once, and in that position he would be quite safe against all that Clodius or other enemies could do to him. [262]

No indictment could be made against a Roman while he was in the employment of the State. It must be remembered, too, on judging of these overtures, that both the one and the other—and indeed all the offers then made to him—were deemed to be highly honorable, as Rome then existed. "The free legation"—the "libera legatio voti causa"—had no reference to parties. It was a job, no doubt, and, in the hands of the ordinary Roman aristocrat, likely to be very onerous to the provincials among whom the privileged Senator might travel; but it entailed no party adhesion. In this case it was intended only to guarantee the absence of a man who might be troublesome in Rome. The other was the offer of genuine work in which politics were not at all concerned. Such a position was accepted by Quintus, our Cicero's brother, and in performance of the duties which fell to him he incurred terrible danger, having been nearly destroyed by the Gauls in his winter quarters among the Nervii. Labienus, who was Caesar's right-hand man in Gaul, was of the same politics as Cicero—so much so that when Caesar rebelled against the Republic, Labienus, true to the Republic, would no longer fight on Caesar's side. It was open to Cicero, without disloyalty, to accept the offer made to him; but with an insight into what was coming, of which he himself was hardly conscious, he could not bring himself to accept offers which in themselves were alluring, but which would seem in future times to have implied on his part an assent to the breaking up of the Republic. [Greek: Aideomai Troas kai Troadas elkesipeplous.] What will be said of me in history by my citizens if I now do simply that which may best suit my own happiness? Had he done so, Pliny and the others would not have spoken of him as they have spoken, and it would not have been worth the while of modern lovers of Caesarism to write books against the one patriot of his age.

During the remainder of this year, B.C. 59, Cicero was at Rome, and seems gradually to have become aware that a personal attack was to be made upon him. At the close of a long and remarkable letter written to his brother Quintus in November, he explains the state of his own mind, showing us, who have now before us the future which was hidden from him, how greatly mistaken he was as to the results which were to be expected. He had been telling his brother how nearly Cato had been murdered for calling Pompey, in public, a Dictator. Then he goes on to describe his own condition. [263] "You may see from this what is the state of the Republic. As far as I am concerned, it seems that friends will not be wanting to defend me. They offer themselves in a wonderful way, and promise assistance. I feel great hope and still greater spirit—hope, which tells me that we shall be victors in the struggle; spirit, which bids me fear no casualty in the present state of public affairs. "[264]

But the matter stands in this way: "If he" —that is, Clodius—"should indict me in court, all Italy would come to my defence, so that I should be acquitted with honor. Should he attack me with open violence, I should have, I think, not only my own party but the world at large to stand by me. All men promise me their friends, their clients, their freedmen, their slaves, and even their money. Our old body of aristocrats" —Cato, Bibulus, and the makers of fish-ponds generally—"are wonderfully warm in my cause. If any of these have heretofore been remiss, now they join our party from sheer hatred of these kings" —the Triumvirs. "Pompey promises everything, and so does Caesar, whom I only trust so far as I can see them. " Even the Triumvirs promise him that he will be safe; but his belief in Pompey's honesty is all but gone. "The coming Tribunes are my friends. The Consuls of next year promise well. " He was wofully mistaken. "We have excellent Praetors, citizens alive to their duty. Domitius, Nigidius, Memmius, and Lentulus are specially trustworthy. The others are good men. You may therefore pluck up your courage and be confident. " From this we perceive that he had already formed the idea that he might perhaps be required to fight for his position as a Roman citizen; and it seems also that he understood the cause of the coming conflict. The intention was that he should be driven out of Rome by personal enmity. Nothing is said in any of these letters of the excuse to be used, though he knew well what that excuse was to be. He was to be charged by the Patrician Tribune with having put Roman citizens to death in opposition to the law. But there arises at this time no question whether he had or had not been justified in what he, as Consul, had done to Lentulus and the others. Would Clodius be able to rouse a mob against him? and, if so, would Caesar assist Clodius? or would Pompey who still loomed to his eyes as the larger of the two men? He had ever been the friend of Pompey, and Pompey had promised him all manner of assistance; but he knew already that Pompey would turn upon him. That Rome should turn upon him—Rome which he had preserved from the torches of Catiline's conspirators—that he could not bring himself to believe!

We must not pass over this long letter to Quintus without observing that through it all the evil condition of the younger brother's mind becomes apparent. The severity of his administration had given offence. His punishments had been cruel. His letters had been rash, and his language violent. In short, we gather from the brother's testimony that Quintus Cicero was very ill-fitted to be the civil governor of a province.

The only work which we have from Cicero belonging to this year, except his letters, is the speech, or part of the speech, he made for Lucius Valerius Flaccus. Flaccus had been Praetor when Cicero was Consul, and had done good service, in the eyes of his superior officers, in the matter of the Catiline conspiracy. He had then gone to Asia as governor, and, after the Roman manner, had fleeced the province. That this was so there is no doubt. After his return he was accused, was defended by Cicero, and was acquitted. Macrobius tells us that Cicero, by the happiness of a bon-mot, brought the accused off safely, though he was manifestly guilty. He adds also that Cicero took care not to allow the joke to appear in the published edition of his speech. [265] There are parts of the speech which have been preserved, and are sufficiently amusing even to us. He is very hard upon the Greeks of Asia, the class from which the witnesses against Flaccus were taken. We know here in England that a spaniel, a wife, and a walnut-tree may be beaten with advantage. Cicero says that in Asia there is a proverb that a Phrygian may be improved in the same way. "Fiat experimentum in corpore vili. " It is declared through Asia that you should take a Carian for your experiment. The "last of the Mysians" is the well-known Asiatic term for the lowest type of humanity. Look through all the comedies, you will find the leading slave is a Lydian. Then he turns to these poor Asiatics, and asks them whether any one can be expected to think well of them, when such is their own testimony of themselves! He attacks the Jew, and speaks of the Jewish religion as a superstition worthy in itself of no consideration. Pompey had spared the gold in the Temple of Jerusalem, because he thought it wise to respect the religious prejudices of the people; but the gods themselves had shown, by subjecting the Jews to the Romans, how little the gods had regarded these idolatrous worshippers! Such were the arguments used; and they prevailed with the judges—or jury, we should rather call them—to whom they were addressed.

NOTES:

[231] We have not Pollio's poem on the conspiracy, but we have Horace's record of Pollio's poem:

Motum ex Metello consule civicum,

Bellique causas et vitia, et modos,
  Ludumque Fortunae, gravesque
  Principum amicitias, et arma
Nondum expiatis uncta cruoribus,
Periculosae plenum opus aleae,
  Tractas, et incedis per ignes
    Suppositos cineri doloso—Odes, lib. ii., 1.

[232] The German index appeared—very much after the original work—as late as 1875.

[233] Mommsen, lib. v., chap. vi. I cannot admit that Mommsen is strictly accurate, as Caesar had no real idea of democracy. He desired to be the Head of the Oligarchs, and, as such, to ingratiate himself with the people.

[234] For the character of Caesar generally I would refer readers to Suetonius, whose life of the great man is, to my thinking, more graphic than any that has been written since. For his anecdotes there is little or no evidence. His facts are not all historical. His knowledge was very much less accurate than that of modern writers who have had the benefit of research and comparison. But there was enough of history, of biography, and of tradition to enable him to form a true idea of the man. He himself as a narrator was neither specially friendly nor specially hostile. He has told what was believed at the time, and he has drawn a character that agrees perfectly with all that we have learned since.

[235] By no one has the character and object of the Triumvirate been so well described as by Lucan, who, bombastic as he is, still manages to bring home to the reader the ideas as to persons and events which he wishes to convey. I have ventured to give in an Appendix, E, the passages referred to, with such a translation in prose as I have been able to produce. It will be found at the end of this volume.

[236] Plutarch—Crassus: [Greek: kai synestaesen ek ton tron ischyn amachon.]

[237] Velleius Paterculus, lib ii., 44 "Hoc igitur consule, inter eum et Cn Pompeium et M. Crassum inita potentiae societas, quae urbi orbique terrarum, nec minus diverso quoque tempore ipsis exitiabilis fuit. " Suetonius, Julius Caesar, xix., "Societatem cum utroque iniit. "

Officers called Triumviri were quite common, as were Quinqueviri and Decemviri. Livy speaks of a "Triumviratus"—or rather two such offices exercised by one man—ix., 46. We remember, too, that wretch whom Horace gibbeted, Epod. iv. : "Sectus flagellis hic triumviralibus. " But the word, though in common use, was not applied to this conspiracy.

[238] Ad Att, lib. ii., 3: "Is affirmabat, illum omnibus in rebus meo et Pompeii consilio usurum, daturumque operam, ut cum Pompeio Crassum conjungeret. Hic sunt haec. Conjunctio mihi summa cum Pompeio; si placet etiam cum Caesare; reditus in gratiam cum inimicis, pax cum multitudine; senectulis otium. Sed me [Greek: katakleis] mea illa commovet, quae est in libro iii.

> "Interea cursus, quos prima a parte juventae
> Quosque adeo consul virtute, animoque petisti,
> Hos retine, atque, auge famam laudesque bonorum."

Homer, Iliad, lib. xii., 243: [Greek: Eis oionos aristos amunesthai peri patraes.]

[239] Middleton's Life of Cicero, vol. i., p. 291.

[240] Pro Domo Sua, xvi. This was an oration, as the reader will soon learn more at length, in which the orator pleaded for the restoration of his town mansion after his return from exile. It has, however, been doubted whether the speech as we have it was ever made by Cicero.

[241] Suetonius, Julius Caesar, xx.

[242] Ad. Att., lib. ii., 1: "Quid quaeris? " says Cicero. "Conturbavi Graecam nationem"—"I have put all Greece into a flutter. "

[243] De Divinatione, lib. i.

[244] Ad Quin. Fratrem, lib. i., 1: "Non itineribus tuis perterreri homines? non sumptu exhauriri? non adventu commoveri? Esse, quocumque veneris, et publice et privatim maximam laetitiam; quum urbs custodem non tyrannum; domus hospitem non expilatorem, recipisse videatur? His autem in rebus jam te usus ipse profecto crudivit nequaquam satis esse, ipsum hasce habere virtutis, sed esse circumspiciendum diligentur, ut in hac custodia provinciae

non te unum, sed omnes ministros imperii tui, sociis, et civibus, et reipublicae praestare vidcare. "

[245] Ad Quin. Fratrem, lib. i., 1: "Ae mihi quidem videntur huc omnia esse referenda iis qui praesunt aliis; ut ii, qui erunt eorum in imperio sint quam beatissimi, quod tibi et esse antiquissimum et ab initio fuisse, ut primum Asiam attigisti, constante fama atque omnium sermone celebratum est. Est autem non modo ejus, qui sociis et civibus, sed etiam ejus qui servis, qui mutis pecudibus praesit, eorum quibus praesit commodis utilitatique servire. "

[246] "Haec est una in toto imperio tuo difficultas. "

[247] Mommsen, book v., ca. 6.

[248] Mommsen, vol. v., ca.vi.

[249] Ad Att., lib. ii., 7: "Atque haec, sin velim existimes, non me abs te [Greek: *kata to praktikon*] quaerere, quod gestiat animus aliquid agere in republica. Jam pridem gubernare me taedebat, etiam quum licebat. "

[250] Ad Att., lib. ii., 8: "Seito Curionem adolescentem venisse ad me salutatum. Valde ejus sermo de Publio cum tuis litteris congruebat, ipse vero mirandum in modum Reges odisse superbos. Peraeque narrabat incensam esse juventutem, neque ferre haec posse. " The "reges superbos" were Caesar and Pompey.

[251] Ad Att., lib. ii., 5: [Greek: Aideomai Troas kai Troadase lkesipeplous]. —Il., vi., 442. "I fear what Mrs. Grundy would say of me, " is Mr. Tyrrell's homely version. Cicero's mind soared, I think, higher when he brought the words of Hector to his service than does the ordinary reference to our old familiar critic.

[252] Quint., xii., 1.

[253] Enc. Britannica on Cicero.

[254] Ad Att., lib. ii., 9.

[255] Ibid. : "Festive, mihi crede, et minore sonitu, quam putaram, orbis hic in republica est conversus. " "Orbis hic, " this round body of three is the Triumvirate.

[256] We cannot but think of the threat Horace made, Sat., lib. ii., 1:

> "At ille
> Qui me commorit, melius non tangere! clamo,
> Flebit, et insignis tota cantabitur urbe."

[257] Ad Att., lib. ii., 11: "Da ponderosam aliquam epistolam. "

[258] Josephus, lib. xviii., ca. 5.

[259] Ad Att., lib. ii., 16.

[260] Ad Att., lib. ii., 18: "A Caesare valde liberaliter invitor in legationem illam, sibi ut sim legatua; atque etiam libera legatio voti causa datur. "

[261] De Legibus, lib. iii., ca. viii. : "Jam illud apertum prefecto est nihil esse turpius, quam quenquam legari nisi republica causa. "

[262] It may be seen from this how anxious Caesar was to secure his silence, and yet how determined not to screen him unless he could secure his silence.

[263] Ad Quintum, lib. i., 2.

[264] Of this last sentence I have taken a translation given by Mr. Tyrrell, who has introduced a special reading of the original which the sense seems to justify.

[265] Macrobius, Saturnalia, lib. ii., ca. i.: We are told that Cicero had been called the consular buffoon. "And I, " says Macrobius, "if it would not be too long, could relate how by his jokes he has brought off the most guilty criminals. " Then he tells the story of Lucius Flaccus.

CHAPTER XII.

HIS EXILE.

We now come to that period of Cicero's life in which, by common consent of all who have hitherto written of him, he is supposed to have shown himself as least worthy of his high name. Middleton, who certainly loved his hero's memory and was always anxious to do him justice, condemns him. "It cannot be denied that in this calamity of his exile he did not behave himself with that firmness which might reasonably be expected from one who had borne so glorious a part in the Republic. " Morabin, the French biographer, speaks of the wailings of his grief, of its injustice and its follies. "Cicéron était trop plein de son malheur pour donner entrée à de nouvelles espérances, " he says. "Il avait supporté ce malheur avec peu de courage, " says another Frenchman, M. Du Rozoir, in introducing us to the speeches which Cicero made on his return. Dean Merivale declares that "he marred the grace of the concession in the eyes of posterity"—alluding to the concession made to popular feeling by his voluntary departure from Rome, as will hereafter be described—"by the unmanly lamentations with which he accompanied it. " Mommsen, with a want of insight into character wonderful in an author who has so closely studied the history of the period, speaks of his exile as a punishment inflicted on a "man notoriously timid, and belonging to the class of political weather-cocks. " "We now come, " says Mr. Forsyth, "to the most melancholy period of Cicero's life, melancholy not so much from its nature and the extent of the misfortunes which overtook him, as from the abject prostration of mind into which he was thrown. " Mr. Froude, as might be expected, uses language stronger than that of others, and tells us that "he retired to Macedonia to pour out his sorrows and his resentments in lamentations unworthy of a woman. " We have to admit that modern historians and biographers have been united in accusing Cicero of want of manliness during his exile. I propose — not, indeed, to wash the blackamoor white—but to show, if I can, that he was as white as others might be expected to have been in similar circumstances.

We are, I think, somewhat proud of the courage shown by public men of our country who have suffered either justly or unjustly under the laws. Our annals are bloody, and many such have had to meet their death. They have done so generally with becoming manliness.

Even though they may have been rebels against the powers of the day, their memories have been made green because they have fallen like brave men. Sir Thomas More, who was no rebel, died well, and crowned a good life by his manner of leaving it. Thomas Cromwell submitted to the axe without a complaint. Lady Jane Grey, when on the scaffold, yielded nothing in manliness to the others. Cranmer and the martyr bishops perished nobly. The Earl of Essex, and Raleigh, and Strafford, and Strafford's master showed no fear when the fatal moment came. In reading the fate of each, we sympathize with the victim because of a certain dignity at the moment of death. But there is, I think, no crisis of life in which it is so easy for a man to carry himself honorably as that in which he has to leave it. "Venit summa dies et ineluctabile tempus. " No doubting now can be of avail. No moment is left for the display of conduct beyond this, which requires only decorum and a free use of the pulses to become in some degree glorious. The wretch from the lowest dregs of the people can achieve it with a halter round his neck. Cicero had that moment also to face; and when it came he was as brave as the best Englishman of them all.

But of those I have named no one had an Atticus to whom it had been the privilege of his life to open his very soul, in language so charming as to make it worth posterity's while to read it, to study it, to sift it, and to criticise it. Wolsey made many plaints in his misery, but they have reached us in such forms of grace that they do not disparage him; but then he too had no Atticus. Shaftesbury and Bolingbroke were dismissed ministers and doomed to live in exile, the latter for many years, and felt, no doubt, strongly their removal from the glare of public life to obscurity. We hear no complaint from them which can justify some future critic in saying that their wails were unworthy of a woman; but neither of them was capable of telling an Atticus the thoughts of his mind as they rose. What other public man ever had an Atticus to whom, in the sorrows which the ingratitude of friends had brought upon him, he could disclose every throb of his heart?

I think that we are often at a loss, in our efforts at appreciation of character, and in the expressions of our opinion respecting it, to realize the meaning of courage and manliness. That sententious Swedish Queen, one of whose foolish maxims I have quoted, has said that Cicero, though a coward, was capable of great actions, because she did not know what a coward was. To doubt—to tremble with anxiety—to vacillate hither and thither between this course and the other as to which may be the better—to complain within one's own breast that this or that thing has been an injustice—to hesitate within one's self, not quite knowing which way honor may require us to go—to be indignant even at fancied wrongs—to rise in wrath against another, and then, before the hour has passed, to turn that wrath against one's self—that is not to be a coward. To know what duty requires, and then to be deterred by fear of results—that is to be a coward; but the man of many scruples may be the greatest hero of them all. Let the law of things be declared clearly so that the doubting mind shall no longer doubt, so that scruples may be laid at rest, so that the sense of justice may be satisfied—and he of whom I speak shall be ready to meet the world in arms against him. There are men, very useful in their way, who shall never doubt at all, but shall be ready, as the bull is ready, to encounter any obstacles that there may be before them. I will not say but that for the coarse purposes of the world they may not be the most efficacious, but I will not admit that they are therefore the bravest. The bull, who has no imagination to tell him what the obstacle may do to him, is not brave. He is brave who, fully understanding the potentiality of the obstacle, shall, for a sufficient purpose, move against it.

This Cicero always did. He braved the murderous anger of Sulla when, as a young man, he thought it well to stop the greed of Sulla's minions. He trusted himself amid the dangers prepared for him, when it was necessary that with extraordinary speed he should get together the evidence needed for the prosecution of Verres. He was firm against all that Catiline attempted for his destruction, and had courage enough for the responsibility when he thought it expedient to doom the friends of Catiline to death. In defending Milo, whether the cause were good or bad, he did not blench. [266] He joined the Republican army in Macedonia though he distrusted Pompey and his companions. When he thought that there was a hope for the Republic, he sprung at Antony with all the courage of a tigress protecting her young; and when all had failed and was rotten around him, when the Republic had so fallen that he knew it to be gone—then he was able to give his neck to the swordsman with all the apparent indifference of life which was displayed by those countrymen of our own whom I have named.

But why did he write so piteously when he was driven into exile? Why, at any rate, did he turn upon his chosen friend and scold him, as though that friend had not done enough for friendship? Why did he talk of suicide as though by that he might find the easiest way of escape? I hold it to be natural that a man should wail to himself under a sense, not simply of misfortune, but of misfortune coming to him from the injustice of others, and specially from the ingratitude of friends. Afflictions which come to us from natural causes, such as sickness and physical pain, or from some chance such as the loss of our money by the breaking of a bank, an heroic man will bear without even inward complainings. But a sense of wrong done to him by friends will stir him, not by the misery inflicted, but because of the injustice; and that which he says to himself he will say to his wife, if his wife be to him a second self, or to his friend, if he have one so dear to him. The testimony by which the writers I have named have been led to treat Cicero so severely has been found in the letters which he wrote during his exile; and of these letters all but one were addressed either to Atticus or to his wife or to his brother. [267] Twenty-seven of them were to Atticus. Before he accepted a voluntary exile, as the best solution of the difficulty in which he was placed—for it was voluntary at first, as will be seen—he applied to the Consul Piso for aid, and for the same purpose visited Pompey. So far he was a suppliant, but this he did in conformity with Roman usage. In asking favor of a man in power there was held to be no disgrace, even though the favor asked were one improper to be granted, which was not the case with Cicero. And he went about the Forum in mourning—"sordidatus"—as was the custom with men on their trial. We cannot doubt that in each of these cases he acted with the advice of his friends. His conduct and his words after his return from exile betray exultation rather than despondency.

It is from the letters which he wrote to Atticus that he has been judged—from words boiling with indignation that such a one as he should have been surrendered by the Rome that he had saved, by those friends to whom he had been so true to be trampled on by such a one as Clodius! When a man has written words intended for the public ear, it is fair that he should bear the brunt of them, be it what it may. He has intended them for public effect, and if they are used against him he should not complain. But here the secret murmurings of the man's soul were sent forth to his choicest friend, with no idea that from them would he be judged by the "historians to come in 600 years, "[268] of whose good word he thought so much. "Quid vero historiae de nobis ad annos DC praedicarint! " he says, to Atticus. How is it that from them, after 2000 years, the Merivales, Mommsens, and Froudes condemn their great brother in letters whose lightest utterances have been found worthy of so long a life! Is there not an injustice in falling upon a man's private words, words when written intended only for privacy, and making them the basis of an accusation in which an illustrious man shall be arraigned forever as a coward? It is said that he was unjust even to Atticus, accusing even Atticus of lukewarmness. What if he did so—for an hour? Is that an affair of ours? Did Atticus quarrel with him? Let any leader of these words who has lived long enough to have an old friend, ask himself whether there has never been a moment of anger in his heart—of anger of which he has soon learned to recognize the injustice? He may not have written his angel, but then, perhaps, he has not had the pen of a Cicero. Let those who rebuke the unmanliness of Cicero's wailings remember what were his sufferings. The story has yet to be told, but I may in rough words describe their nature. Everything was to be taken from him: all that he had—his houses, his books, his pleasant gardens, his busts and pictures, his wide retinue of slaves, and possessions lordly as are those of our dukes and earls. He was driven out from Italy and so driven that no place of delight could be open to him. Sicily, where he had friends, Athens, where he might have lived, were closed against him. He had to look where to live, and did live for a while on money borrowed from his friends. All the cherished occupations of his life were over for him—the law courts, the Forum, the Senate, and the crowded meetings of Roman citizens hanging on his words. The circumstances of his exile separated him from his wife and children, so that he was alone. All this was assured to him for life, as far as Roman law could assure it. Let us think of the condition of some great and serviceable Englishman in similar circumstances. Let us suppose that Sir Robert Peel had been impeached, and forced by some iniquitous sentence to live beyond the pale of civilization: that the houses at Whitehall Gardens and at Drayton had been confiscated, dismantled, and levelled to the ground, and his rents and revenues made over to his enemies; that everything should have been done to destroy him by the country he had served, except the act of taking away that life which would thus have been made a burden to him. Would not his case have been more piteous, a source of more righteous indignation, than that even of the Mores or Raleighs? He suffered under invectives in the House of Commons, and we sympathized with him; but if some Clodius of the day could have done this to him, should we have thought the worse of him had he opened his wounds to his wife, or to his brother, or to his friend of friends?

Had Cicero put an end to his life in his exile, as he thought of doing, he would have been a second Cato to admiring posterity, and some

Lucan with rolling verses would have told us narratives of his valor. The judges of today look back to his half-formed purposes in this direction as being an added evidence of the weakness of the man; but had he let himself blood and have perished in his bath, he would have been thought to have escaped from life as honorably as did Junius Brutus It is because he dared to live on that we are taught to think so little of him? because he had antedated Christianity so far as to feel when the moment came that such an escape was, in truth, unmanly. He doubted, and when the deed had not been done he expressed regret that he had allowed himself to live. But he did not do it? as Cato would have done, or Brutus.

It may be as well here to combat, in as few words as possible, the assertions which have been made that Cicero, having begun life as a democrat, discarded his colors as soon as he had received from the people those honors for which he had sought popularity. They who have said so have taken their idea from the fact that, in much of his early forensic work, he spoke against the aristocratic party. He attacked Sulla, through his favorite Chrysogonus, in his defence of Roscius Amerinus. He afterward defended a woman of Arretium in the spirit of antagonism to Sulla. His accusation of Verres was made on the same side in politics, and was carried on in opposition to Hortensius and the oligarchs. He defended the Tribune Caius Cornelius. Then, when he became Consul, he devoted himself to the destruction of Catiline, who was joined with many, perhaps with Caesar's sympathy, in the conspiracy for the overthrow of the Republic. Caesar soon became the leader of the democracy? became rather what Mommsen describes as "Democracy" itself; and as Cicero had defended the Senate from Catiline, and had refused to attach himself to Caesar, he is supposed to have turned from the political ideas of his youth, and to have become a Conservative when Conservative ideas suited his ambition.

I will not accept the excuse put forward on his behalf, that the early speeches were made on the side of democracy because the exigencies of the occasion required him to so devote his energies as an advocate. No doubt he was an advocate, as are our barristers of to-day, and, as an advocate, supported this side or that; but we shall be wrong if we suppose that the Roman "patronus" supplied his services under such inducements. With us a man goes into the profession of the law with the intention of making money, and takes the cases right and left, unless there be special circumstances which may debar him from doing so with honor. It is a point of etiquette with him to give his assis- tance, in turn, as he may be called on; so much so, that leading men are not unfrequently employed on one side simply that they may not be employed on the other side. It should not be urged on the part of Cicero that, so actuated, he defended Amerinus, a case in which he took part against the aristocrats, or defended Publius Sulla, in doing which he appeared on the side of the aristocracy. Such a defence of his conduct would be misleading, and might be confuted. It would be confuted by those who suppose him to have been "notoriously a political trimmer, " as Mommsen has[269] called him; or a "deserter, " as he was described by Dio Cassius and by the Pseudo-Sallust, [270] by showing that in fact he took up causes under the influence of strong personal motives such as rarely govern an English barrister. These motives were in many cases partly political; but they operated in such a manner as to give no guide to his political views. In defending Sulla's nephew he was moved, as far as we know, solely by private motives. In defending Amerinus he may be said to have attacked Sulla. His object was to stamp out the still burning embers of Sulla's cruelty; but not the less was he wedded to Sulla's general views as to the restoration of the authority of the Senate. In his early speeches, especially in that spoken against Verres, he denounces the corruption of the senatorial judges; but at that very period of his life he again and again expresses his own belief in the glory and majesty of the Senate. In accusing Verres he accused the general corruption of Rome's provincial governors; and as they were always past-Consuls or past-Praetors, and had been the elite of the aristocracy, he may be said so far to have taken the part of a democrat; but he had done so only so far as he had found himself bound by a sense of duty to put a stop to corruption. The venality of the judges and the rapacity of governors had been fit objects for his eloquence; but I deny that he can be fairly charged with having tampered with democracy because he had thus used his eloquence on behalf of the people.

He was no doubt stirred by other political motives less praiseworthy, though submitted to in accordance with the practice and the known usages of Rome. He had undertaken to speak for Catiline when Catiline was accused of corruption on his return from Africa, knowing that Catiline had been guilty. He did not do so; but the intention, for our present purpose, is the same as the doing. To have defended Catiline would have assisted him in his operations as a candidate for the Consulship. Catiline was a bad subject for a defence—as was Fonteius, whom he certainly did defend—and

Catiline was a democrat. But Cicero, had he defended Catiline, would not have done so as holding out his hand to democracy. Cicero, when, in the Pro Lege Manilia, he for the first time addressed the people, certainly spoke in opposition to the wishes of the Senate in proposing that Pompey should have the command of the Mithridatic war; but his views were not democratic. It has been said that this was done because Pompey could help him to the Consulship. To me it seems that he had already declared to himself that among leading men in Rome Pompey was the one to whom the Republic would look with the most security as a bulwark, and that on that account he had resolved to bind himself to Pompey in some political marriage. Be that as it may, there was no tampering with democracy in the speech Pro Lege Manilia. Of all the extant orations made by him before his Consulship, the attentive reader will sympathize the least with that of Fonteius. After his scathing onslaught on Verres for provincial plunder, he defended the plunderer of the Gauls, and held up the suffering allies of Rome to ridicule as being hardly entitled to good government. This he did simply as an advocate, without political motive of any kind—in the days in which he was supposed to be currying favor with democracy—governed by private friendship, looking forward, probably, to some friendly office in return, as was customary. It was thus that afterward he defended Antony, his colleague in the Consulship, whom he knew to have been a corrupt governor. Autronius had been a party to Catiline's conspiracy, and Autronius had been Cicero's school-fellow; but Cicero, for some reserved reason with which we are not acquainted, refused to plead for Autronius. There is, I maintain, no ground for suggesting that Cicero had shown by his speeches before his Consulship any party adherence. The declaration which he made after his Consulship, in the speech for Sulla, that up to the time of Catiline's first conspiracy forensic duties had not allowed him to devote himself to party politics, is entitled to belief: we know, indeed, that it was so. As Quaestor, as Aedile, and as Praetor, he did not interfere in the political questions of Rome, except in demanding justice from judges and purity from governors. When he became Consul then he became a politician, and after that there was certainly no vacillation in his views. Critics say that he surrendered himself to Caesar when Caesar became master. We shall come to that hereafter; but the accusation with which I am dealing now is that which charges him with having abandoned the democratic memories of his youth as soon as he had enveloped himself with the consular purple. There had been no democratic promises, and there was no change when he became

Consul. In truth, Cicero's political convictions were the same from the beginning to the end of his career, with a consistency which is by no means usual in politicians; for though, before his Consulship, he had not taken up politics as a business he had entertained certain political views, as do all men who live in public. From the first to the last we may best describe him by the word we have now in use, as a conservative. The government of Rome had been an oligarchy for many years, though much had been done by the citizens to reduce the thraldom which an oligarchy is sure to exact. To that oligarchy Cicero was bound by all the convictions, by all the practices, and by all the prejudices of his life. When he speaks of a Republic he speaks of a people and of an Empire governed by an oligarchy; he speaks of a power to be kept in the hands of a few—for the benefit of the few, and of the many if it might be—but at any rate in the hands of a few. That those few should be so select as to admit of no new-comers among them, would probably have been a portion of his political creed, had he not been himself a "novus homo. " As he was the first of his family to storm the barrier of the fortress, he had been forced to depend much on popular opinion; but not on that account had there been any dealings between him and democracy. That the Empire should be governed according to the old oligarchical forms which had been in use for more than four centuries, and had created the power of Rome—that was his political creed. That Consuls, Censors, and Senators might go on to the end of time with no diminution of their dignity, but with great increase of justice and honor and truth among them—that was his political aspiration. They had made Rome what it was, and he knew and could imagine nothing better; and, odious as an oligarchy is seen to be under the strong light of experience to which prolonged ages has subjected it, the aspiration on his part was noble. He has been wrongly accused of deserting "that democracy with which he had flirted in his youth. " There had been no democracy in his youth, though there had existed such a condition in the time of the Gracchi. There was none in his youth and none in his age. That which has been wrongly called democracy was conspiracy—not a conspiracy of democrats such as led to our Commonwealth, or to the American Independence, or to the French Revolution; but conspiracy of a few nobles for the better assurance of the plunder, and the power, and the high places of the Empire. Of any tendency toward democracy no man has been less justly accused than Cicero, unless it might be Caesar. To Caesar we must accord the ment of having seen that a continuation of the old oligarchical forms was impracticable This Cicero did not see. He thought that the wounds inflicted by the degeneracy and profligacy of individuals were curable. It is attributed to Caesar that he conceived the grand idea of establishing general liberty under the sole dominion of one great, and therefore beneficent, ruler. I think he saw no farther than that he, by strategy, management, and courage might become this ruler, whether beneficent or the reverse. But here I think that it becomes the writer, whether he be historian, biographer, or fill whatever meaner position he may in literature, to declare that no beneficence can accompany such a form of government. For all temporary sleekness, for metropolitan comfort and fatness, the bill has to be paid sooner or later in ignorance, poverty, and oppression. With an oligarchy there will be other, perhaps graver, faults; but with an oligarchy there will be salt, though it be among a few. There will be a Cicero now and again—or at least a Cato. From the dead, stagnant level of personal despotism there can be no rising to life till corruption paralyzes the hands of power, and the fabric falls by its own decay Of this no proof can be found in the world's history so manifest as that taught by the Roman Empire.

I think it is made clear by a study of Cicero's life and works, up to the period of his exile, that an adhesion to the old forms of the Roman Government was his guiding principle. I am sure that they who follow me to the close of his career will acknowledge that after his exile he lived for this principle, and that he died for it. "Respublica, " the Republic, was the one word which to his ear contained a political charm. It was the shibboleth by which men were to be conjured into well-being. The word constitution is nearly as potent with us. But it is essential that the reader of Roman history and Roman biography should understand that the appellation had in it, for all Roman ears, a thoroughly conservative meaning. Among those who at Cicero's period dealt with politics in Rome—all of whom, no doubt, spoke of the Republic as the vessel of State which was to be defended by all persons—there were four classes. These were they who simply desired the plunder of the State—the Catilines, the Sullas of the day, and the Antonys; men such as Verres had been, and Fonteius, and Autronius. The other three can be best typified each by one man. There was Caesar, who knew that the Republic was gone, past all hope. There was Cato—"the dogmatical fool Cato" as Mommsen calls him, perhaps with some lack of the historian's dignity—who was true to the Republic, who could not bend an inch, and was thus as detrimental to any hope of reconstruction as a Catiline or a Caesar. Cicero was of the fourth class, believing in the Republic, intent on saving it, imbued amid all his doubts with a conviction that if the "optimates" or "boni"—the leading men of the party—would be true to themselves, Consuls, Censors, and Senate would still suffice to rule the world; but prepared to give and take with those who were opposed to him. It was his idea that political integrity should keep its own hands clean, but should wink at much dirt in the world at large. Nothing, he saw, could be done by Catonic rigor. We can see now that Ciceronic compromises were, and must have been, equally ineffective. The patient was past cure. But in seeking the truth as to Cicero, we have to perceive that amid all his doubts, frequently in despondency, sometimes overwhelmed by the misery and hopelessness of his condition, he did hold fast by this idea to the end. The frequent expressions made to Atticus in opposition to this belief are to be taken as the murmurs of his mind at the moment; as you shall hear a man swear that all is gone, and see him tear his hair, and shall yet know that there is a deep fund of hope within his bosom. It was the ingratitude of his political friends, his "boni" and his "optimates, " of Pompey as their head, which tried him the sorest; but he was always forgiving them, forgiving Pompey as the head of them, because he knew that, were he to be severed from them, then the political world must be closed to him altogether.

Of Cicero's strength or Cicero's weakness Pompey seems to have known nothing. He was no judge of men. Caesar measured him with a great approach to accuracy. Caesar knew him to be the best Roman of his day; one who, if he could be brought over to serve in Caesarean ranks, would be invaluable—because of his honesty, his eloquence, and his capability; but he knew him as one who must be silenced if he were not brought to serve on the Caesarean side. Such a man, however, might be silenced for a while—taught to perceive that his efforts were vain—and then brought into favor by further overtures, and made of use. Personally he was pleasant to Caesar, who had taste enough to know that he was a man worthy of all personal dignity. But Caesar was not, I think, quite accurate in his estimation, having allowed himself to believe at the last that Cicero's energy on behalf of the Republic had been quelled.

[Sidenote: B. C. 58, aetat. 49]

Now we will go back to the story of Cicero's exile. Gradually during the preceding year he had learned that Clodius was preparing to attack him, and to doubt whether he could expect protection from the Triumvirate. That he could be made safe by the justice either of the people or by that of any court before which he could be tried, seems never to have occurred to him. He knew the people and he knew the courts too well. Pompey no doubt might have warded off the coming evil; such at least was Cicero's idea. To him Pompey was the greatest political power as yet extant in Rome; but he was beginning to believe that Pompey would be untrue to him. When he had sent to Pompey a long account of the grand doings of his Consulship, Pompey had replied with faintest praises. He had rejected the overtures of the Triumvirate. In the last letter to Atticus in the year before, written in August, [271] he had declared that the Republic was ruined; that they who had brought things to this pass—meaning the Triumvirate—were hostile; but, for himself, he was confident in saying that he was quite safe in the good will of men around him. There is a letter to his brother written in November, the next letter in the collection, in which he says that Pompey and Caesar promise him everything. With the exception of two letters of introduction, we have nothing from him till he writes to Atticus from the first scene of his exile.

When the new year commenced, Clodius was Tribune of the people, and immediately was active. Piso and Gabinius were Consuls. Piso was kinsman to Piso Frugi, who had married Cicero's daughter, [272]and was expected to befriend Cicero at this crisis. But Clodius procured the allotment of Syria and Macedonia to the two Consuls by the popular vote. They were provinces rich in plunder; and it was matter of importance for a Consul to know that the prey which should come to him as Proconsul should be worthy of his grasp. They were, therefore, ready to support the Tribune in what he proposed to do. It was necessary to Cicero's enemies that there should be some law by which Cicero might be condemned. It would not be within the power of Clodius, even with the Triumvirate at his back, to drive the man out of Rome and out of Italy, without an alleged cause. Though justice had been tabooed, law was still in vogue. Now there was a matter as to which Cicero was open to attack. As Consul he had caused certain Roman citizens to be executed as conspirators, in the teeth of a law which enacted that no Roman citizen should be condemned to die except by a direct vote of the people. It had certainly become a maxim of the constitution of the Republic that a citizen should not be made to suffer death except by the voice of the people. The Valerian, the Porcian, and the Sempronian laws had all been passed to that effect. Now there had been no popular vote as to the execution of Lentulus and the other conspirators, who had been taken red-handed in Rome in the affair of Catiline. Their death had been decreed by the Senate, and the decree of the Senate had been carried out by Cicero; but no decree of the Senate had the power of a law. In spite of that decree the old law was in force; and no appeal to the people had been allowed to Lentulus. But there had grown up in the constitution a practice which had been supposed to override the Valerian and Porcian laws. In certain emergencies the Senate would call upon the Consuls to see that the Republic should suffer no injury, and it had been held that at such moments the Consuls were invested with an authority above all law. Cicero had been thus strengthened when, as Consul, he had struggled with Catiline; but it was an open question, as Cicero himself very well knew. In the year of his Consulship — the very year in which Lentulus and the others had been strangled — he had defended Rabirius, who was then accused of having killed a citizen thirty years before. Rabirius was charged with having slaughtered the Tribune Saturninus by consular authority, the Consuls of the day having been ordered to defend the Republic, as Cicero had been ordered. Rabirius probably had not killed Saturninus, nor did any one now care whether he had done so or not. The trial had been brought about notoriously by the agency of Caesar, who caused himself to be selected by the Praetor as one of the two judges for the occasion; [273] and Caesar's object as notoriously was to lessen the authority of the Senate, and to support the democratic interest. Both Cicero and Hortensius defended Rabirius, but he was condemned by Caesar, and, as we are told, himself only escaped by using that appeal to the people in support of which he had himself been brought to trial. In this, as in so many of the forensic actions of the day, there had been an admixture of violence and law. We must, I think, acknowledge that there was the same leaven of illegality in the proceedings against Lentulus. It had no doubt been the intention of the constitution that a Consul, in the heat of an emergency, should use his personal authority for the protection of the Commonwealth, but it cannot be alleged that there was such an emergency, when the full Senate had had time to debate on the fate of the Catiline criminals. Both from Caesar's words as reported by Sallust, and from Cicero's as given to us by himself, we are aware that an idea of the illegality of the proceeding was present in the minds of Senators at the moment. But, though law was loved at Rome, all forensic and legislative proceedings were at this time carried on with monstrous illegality. Consuls consulted the heavens falsely; Tribunes used their veto violently; judges accepted bribes openly; the votes of the people were manipulated fraudulently. In the trial and escape of Rabirius, the laws were despised by those who pretended to vindicate them.

Clodius had now become a Tribune by the means of certain legal provision, but yet in opposition to all law. In the conduct of the affair against Catiline Cicero seems to have been actuated by pure patriotism, and to have been supported by a fine courage; but he knew that in destroying Lentulus and Cethegus he subjected himself to certain dangers. He had willingly faced these dangers for the sake of the object in view. As long as he might remain the darling of the people, as he was at that moment, he would no doubt be safe; but it was not given to any one to be for long the darling of the Roman people. Cicero bad become so by using an eloquence to which the Romans were peculiarly susceptible; but though they loved sweet tongues, long purses went farther with them. Since Cicero's Consulship he had done nothing to offend the people, except to remain occasionally out of their sight; but he had lost the brilliancy of his popularity, and he was aware that it was so.

In discussing popularity in Rome we have to remember of what elements it was formed. We hear that this or that man was potent at some special time by the assistance coming to him from the popular voice. There was in Rome a vast population of idle men, who had been trained by their city life to look to the fact of their citizenship for their support, and who did, in truth, live on their citizenship. Of "panem et circenses" we have all heard, and know that eleemosynary bread and the public amusements of the day supplied the material and aesthetic wants of many Romans. But men so fed and so amused were sure to need further occupations. They became attached to certain friends, to certain patrons, and to certain parties, and soon learned that a return was expected for the food and for the excitement supplied to them. This they gave by holding themselves in readiness for whatever violence was needed from them, till it became notorious in Rome that a great party man might best attain his political object by fighting for it in the streets. This was the meaning of that saying of Crassus, that a man could not be considered rich till he could keep an army in his own pay. A popular vote obtained and declared by a faction fight in the forum was still a popular vote, and if supported by sufficient violence would be valid. There had been street fighting of the kind when Cicero had defended Cains Cornelius, in the year after his Praetorship; there had been fighting of the kind when Rabirius had been condemned in his Consulship. We shall learn by-and-by to what extent such fighting prevailed when Clodius was killed by Milo's body-guard. At the period of which we are now writing, when Clodius was intent on pursuing Cicero to his ruin, it was a question with Cicero himself whether he would not trust to a certain faction in Rome to fight for him, and so to protect him. Though his popularity was on the wane—that general popularity which, we may presume, had been produced by the tone of his voice and the grace of his language—there still remained to him that other popularity which consisted, in truth, of the trained bands employed by the "boni" and the "optimates, " and which might be used, if need were, in opposition to trained bands on the other side.

The bill first proposed by Clodius to the people with the object of destroying Cicero did not mention Cicero, nor, in truth, refer to him. It purported to enact that he who had caused to be executed any Roman citizen not duly condemned to death, should himself be deprived of the privilege of water or fire. [274] This condemned no suggested malefactor to death; but, in accordance with Roman law, made it impossible that any Roman so condemned should live within whatever bounds might be named for this withholding of fire and water. The penalty intended was banishment; but by this enactment no individual would be banished. Cicero, however, at once took the suggestion to himself, and put himself into mourning, as a man accused and about to be brought to his trial. He went about the streets accompanied by crowds armed for his protection; and Clodius also caused himself to be so accompanied. There came thus to be a question which might prevail should there be a general fight. The Senate was, as a body, on Cicero's side, but was quite unable to cope with the Triumvirate. Caesar no doubt had resolved that Cicero should be made to go, and Caesar was lord of the Triumvirate. On behalf of Cicero there was a large body of the conservative or oligarchical party who were still true to him; and they, too, all went into the usual public mourning, evincing their desire that the accused man should be rescued from his accusers.

The bitterness of Clodius would be surprising did we not know how bitter had been Cicero's tongue. When the affair of the Bona Dea had taken place there was no special enmity between this debauched young man and the great Consul. Cicero, though his own life had ever been clean and well ordered, rather affected the company of fast young men when he found them to be witty as well as clever. This very Clodius had been in his good books till the affair of the Bona Dea. But now the Tribune's hatred was internecine. I have hitherto said nothing, and need say but little, of a certain disreputable lady named Clodia. She was the sister of Clodius and the wife of Metellus Celer. She was accused by public voice in Rome of living in incest with her brother, and of poisoning her husband. Cicero calls her afterward, in his defence of Caelius, "amica omnium. " She had the nickname of Quadran- taria[275] given to her, because she frequented the public baths, at which the charge was a farthing. It must be said also of her, either in praise or in dispraise, that she was the Lesbia who inspired the muse of Catullus. It was rumored in Rome that she had endeavored to set her cap at Cicero. Cicero in his raillery had not spared the lady. To speak publicly the grossest evil of women was not opposed to any idea of gallantry current among the Romans. Our sense of chivalry, as well as decency, is disgusted by the language used by Horace to women who once to him were young and pretty, but have become old and ugly. The venom of Cicero's abuse of Clodia annoys us, and we have to remember that the gentle ideas which we have taken in with our mother's milk had not grown into use with the Romans. It is necessary that this woman's name should be mentioned, and it may appear here as she was one of the causes of that hatred which burnt between Clodius and Cicero, till Clodius was killed in a street row.

It has been presumed that Cicero was badly advised in presuming publicly that the new law was intended against himself, and in taking upon himself the outward signs of a man under affliction. "The resolution, " says Middleton, "of changing his gown was too hasty and inconsiderate, and helped to precipitate his ruin. " He was sensible of his error when too late, and oft reproaches Atticus that, being a stander-by, and less heated with the game than himself, he would suffer him to make such blunders. And he quotes the words written to Atticus: "Here my judgment first failed me, or, indeed, brought me into trouble. We were blind, blind I say, in changing our raiment and in appealing to the populace. — —I handed myself and all belonging to me over to my enemies, while you were looking on, while you were holding your peace; yes, you, who, if your wit in the matter was no better than mine, were impeded by no personal fears. "[276] But the reader should study the entire letter, and study it in the original, for no translator can give its true purport. This the reader must do before he can understand Cicero's state of mind when writing it, or his relation to Atticus; or the thoughts which distracted him when, in accordance with the advice of Atticus, he resolved, while yet uncondemned, to retire into banishment. The censure to which Atticus is subjected throughout this letter is that which a thoughtful, hesitating, scrupulous man is so often disposed to address to himself. After reminding Atticus of the sort of advice which should have been given—the want of which in the first moment of his exile he regrets—and doing this in words of which it is very difficult now to catch the exact flavor, he begs to be pardoned for his reproaches. "You will forgive me this, " he says. "I blame myself more than I do you; but I look to you as a second self, and I make you a sharer with me of my own folly. " I take this letter out of its course, and speak of it as connected with that terrible period of doubt to which it refers, in which he had to decide whether he would remain in Rome and fight it out, or run before his enemies. But in writing the letter afterward his mind was as much disturbed as when he did fly. I am inclined, therefore, to think that Middleton and others may have been wrong in blaming his flight, which they have done, because in his subsequent vacillating moods he blamed himself. How the battle might have gone had he remained, we have no evidence to show; but we do know that though he fled, he returned soon with renewed glory, and altogether overcame the attempt which had been made to destroy him.

In this time of his distress a strong effort was made by the Senate to rescue him. It was proposed to them that they all as a body should go into mourning on his behalf; indeed, the Senate passed a vote to this effect, but were prevented by the two Consuls from carrying it out. As to what he had best do he and his friends were divided. Some recommended that he should remain where he was, and defend himself by street-fighting should it be necessary. In doing this he would acknowledge that law no longer prevailed in Rome—a condition of things to which many had given in their adherence, but with which Cicero would surely have been the last to comply. He himself, in his despair, thought for a time that the old Roman mode of escape would be preferable, and that he might with decorum end his life and his troubles by suicide. Atticus and others dissuaded him from this, and recommended him to fly. Among these Cato and Hortensius have both been named. To this advice he at last yielded, and it may be doubted whether any better could have been given. Lawlessness, which had been rampant in Rome before, had, under the Triumvirate, become almost lawful. It was Caesar's intention to carry out his will with such compliance with the forms of the Republic as might suit him, but in utter disregard to all such forms when they did not suit him. The banishment of Cicero was one of the last steps taken by Caesar before he left Rome for his campaigns in Gaul. He was already in command of the legions, and was just without the city. He had endeavored to buy Cicero, but had failed. Having failed, he had determined to be rid of him. Clodius was but his tool, as were Pompey and the two Consuls. Had Cicero endeavored to support himself by violence in Rome, his contest would, in fact have been with Caesar.

Cicero, before he went, applied for protection personally to Piso the Consul, and to Pompey. Gabinius, the other Consul, had already declared his purpose to the Senate, but Piso was bound to him by family ties. He himself relates to us in his oration, spoken after his return, against this Piso, the manner of the meeting between him and Rome's chief officer. Piso told him—so at least Cicero declared in the Senate, and we have heard of no contradiction—that Gabinius was so driven by debts as to be unable to hold up his head without a rich province; that he himself, Piso, could only hope to get a province by taking part with Gabinius; that any application to the Consuls was useless, and that every one must look after himself. [277] Concerning his appeal to Pompey two stories have been given to us, neither of which appears to be true. Plutarch says that when Cicero had travelled out from Rome to Pompey's Alban villa, Pompey ran out of the back-door to avoid meeting him. Plutarch cared more for a good story than for accuracy, and is not worthy of much credit as to details unless when corroborated. The other account is based on Cicero's assertion that he did see Pompey on this occasion. Nine or ten years after the meeting he refers to it in a letter to Atticus, which leaves no doubt as to the fact. The story founded on that letter declares that Cicero threw himself bodily at his old friend's feet, and that Pompey did not lend a hand to raise him, but told him simply that everything was in Caesar's hands. This narrative is, I think, due to a misinterpretation of Cicero's words, though it is given by a close translation of them. He is describing Pompey when Caesar after his Gallic wars had crossed the Rubicon, and the two late Triumvirates—the third having perished miserably in the East—were in arms against each other. "Alter ardet furore et scelere" he says. [278] Caesar is pressing on unscrupulous in his passion. "Alter is qui nos sibi quondam ad pedes stratos ne sublevabat quidem, qui se nihil contra hujus voluntatem aiebat facere posse. " "That other one, " he continues—meaning Pompey, and pursuing his picture of the present contrast—"who in days gone by would not even lift me when I lay at his feet, and told me that he could do nothing but as Caesar wished it. " This little supposed detail of biography has been given, no doubt, from an accurate reading of the words; but in it the spirit of the writer's mind as he wrote it has surely been missed. The prostration of which he spoke, from which Pompey would not raise him, the memory of which was still so bitter to him, was not a prostration of the body. I hold it to have been impossible that Cicero should have assumed such an attitude before Pompey, or that he would so have written to Atticus had he done so. It would have been neither Roman nor Ciceronian, as displayed by Cicero to Pompey. He had gone to his old ally and told him of his trouble, and had no doubt reminded him of those promises of assistance which Pompey had so often made. Then Pompey had refused to help him, and had assured him, with too much truth, that Caesar's will was everything. Again, we have to remember that in judging of the meaning of words between two such correspondents as Cicero and Atticus, we must read between the lines, and interpret the words by creating for ourselves something of the spirit in which they were written and in which they were received. I cannot imagine that, in describing to Atticus what had occurred at that interview nine years after it had taken place, Cicero had intended it to be understood that he had really grovelled in the dust.

Toward the end of March he started from Rome, intending to take refuge among his friends in Sicily. On the same day Clodius brought in a bill directed against Cicero by name and caused it to be carried by the people, "Ut Marco Tullio aqua et igni interdictum sit" — that it should be illegal to supply Cicero with fire and water. The law when passed forbade any one to harbor the criminal within four hundred miles of Rome, and declared the doing so to be a capital offence. It is evident, from the action of those who obeyed the law, and of those who did not, that legal results were not feared so much as the ill-will of those who had driven Cicero to his exile. They who refused him succor did do so not because to give it him would be illegal, but lest Caesar and Pompey would be offended. It did not last long, and during the short period of his exile he found perhaps more of friendship than of enmity; but he directed his steps in accordance with the bearing of party-spirit. We are told that he was afraid to go to Athens, because at Athens lived that Autronius whom he had refused to defend. Autronius had been convicted of conspiracy and banished, and, having been a Catilinarian conspirator, had been in truth on Caesar's side. Nor were geographical facts sufficiently established to tell Cicero what places were and what were not without the forbidden circle. He sojourned first at Vibo, in the extreme south of Italy, intending to pass from thence into Sicily. It was there that he learned that a certain distance had been prescribed; but it seems that he had already heard that the Proconsular Governor of the island would not receive him, fearing Caesar. Then he came north from Vibo to Brundisium, that being the port by which travellers generally went from Italy to the East. He had determined to leave his family in Rome, feeling, probably, that it would be easier for him to find a temporary home for himself than for him and them together. And there were money difficulties in which Atticus helped him. [279] Atticus, always wealthy, had now become a very rich man by the death of an uncle. We do not know of what nature were the money arrangements made by Cicero at the time, but there can be no doubt that the losses by his exile were very great. There was a thorough disruption of his property, for which the subsequent generosity of his country was unable altogether to atone. But this sat lightly on Cicero's heart. Pecuniary losses never weighed heavily with him.

As he journeyed back from Vibo to Brundisium friends were very kind to him, in spite of the law. Toward the end of the speech which he made five years afterward on behalf of his friend C. Plancius he explains the debt of gratitude which he owed to his client, whose kindness to him in his exile had been very great. He commences his story of the goodness of Plancius by describing the generosity of the towns on the road to Brundisium, and the hospitality of his friend Flavius, who had received him at his house in the neighborhood of that town, and had placed him safely on board a ship when at last he resolved to cross over to Dyrrachium. There were many schemes running in his head at this time. At one period he had resolved to pass through Macedonia into Asia, and to remain for a while at Cyzicum. This idea he expresses in a letter to his wife written from Brundisium. Then he goes, wailing no doubt, but in words which to me seem very natural as coming from a husband in such a condition: "O me perditum, O me afflictum; "[280] exclamations which it is impossible to translate, as they refer to his wife's separation from himself rather than to his own personal sufferings. "How am I to ask you to come to me? " he says; "you a woman, ill in health worn out in body and in spirit. I cannot ask you! Must I then live without you? It must be so, I think. If there be any hope of my return, it is you must look to it, you that must strengthen it; but if, as I fear, the thing is done, then come to me. If I can have you I shall not be altogether destroyed. " No doubt these are wailings; but is a man unmanly because he so wails to the wife of his bosom? Other humans have written prettily about women: it was common for Romans to do so. Catullus desires from Lesbia as many kisses as are the stars of night or the sands of Libya. Horace swears that he would perish for Chloe if Chloe might be left alive. "When I am dying, " says Tibullus to Delia, "may I be gazing at you; may my last grasp hold your hand. " Propertius tells Cynthia that she stands to him in lieu of home and parents, and all the joys of life. "Whether he be sad with his friends or happy, Cynthia does it all. " The language in each case is perfect; but what other Roman was there of whom we have evidence that he spoke to his wife like this? Ovid in his letters from his banishment says much of his love for his wife; but there is no passion expressed in anything that Ovid wrote. Clodius, as soon as the enactment against Cicero became law, caused it be carried into effect with all its possible cruelties. The criminal's property was confiscated. The house on the Palatine Hill was destroyed, and the goods were put up to auction, with, as we arc told, a great lack of buyers. His choicest treasures were carried away by the Consuls themselves. Piso, who had lived near him in Rome, got for himself and for his father-in-law the rich booty from the town house. The country villas were also destroyed, and Gabinius, who had a country house close by Cicero's Tusculan retreat, took even the very shrubs out of the garden. He tells the story of the greed and enmity of the Consuls in the speech he made after his return, Pro Domo Sua, [281] pleading for the restitution of his household property. "My house on the Palatine was burnt, " he says, "not by any accident, but by arson. In the mean time the Consuls were feasting, and were congratulating themselves among the conspirators, when one boasted that he had been Catiline's friend, the other that Cethegus had been his cousin. " By this he implies that the conspiracy which during his Consulship had been so odious to Rome was now, in these days of the Triumvirate, again in favor among Roman aristocrats.

He went across from Brundisium to Dyrrachium, and from thence to Thessalonica, where he was treated with most loving-kindness by Plancius, who was Quaestor in these parts, and who came down to Dyrrachium to meet him, clad in mourning for the occasion. This was the Plancius whom he afterward defended, and indeed he was bound to do so. Plancius seems to have had but little dread of the law, though he was a Roman officer employed in the very province to the government of which the present Consul Piso had already been appointed. Thessalonica was within four hundred miles, and yet Cicero lived there with Plancius for some months.

The letters from Cicero during his exile are to me very touching, though I have been told so often that in having written them he lacked the fortitude of a Roman. Perhaps I am more capable of appreciating natural humanity than Roman fortitude. We remember the story of the Spartan boy who allowed the fox to bite him beneath his frock without crying. I think we may imagine that he refrained from tears in public, before some herd of school-fellows, or a bench of masters, or amid the sternness of parental authority; but that he told his sister afterward how he had been tortured, or his mother as he lay against her bosom, or perhaps his chosen chum. Such reticences are made dignified by the occasion, when something has to be won by controlling the expression to which nature uncontrolled would give utterance, but are not in themselves evidence either of sagacity or of courage. Roman fortitude was but a suit of armor to be worn on state occasions. If we come across a warrior with his crested helmet and his sword and his spear, we see, no doubt, an impressive object. If we could find him in his night-shirt, the same man would be there, but those who do not look deeply into things would be apt to despise him because his grand trappings were absent. Chance has given us Cicero in his night-shirt. The linen is of such fine texture that we are delighted with it, but we despise the man because he wore a garment—such as we wear ourselves indeed, though when we wear it nobody is then brought in to look at us.

There is one most touching letter written from Thessalonica to his brother, by whom, after thoughts vacillating this way and that, he was unwilling to be visited, thinking that a meeting would bring more of pain than of service. "Mi frater, mi frater, mi frater! " he begins. The words in English would hardly give all the pathos. "Did you think that I did not write because I am angry, or that I did not wish to see you? I angry with you! But I could not endure to be seen by you. You would not have seen your brother; not him whom you had left; not him whom you had known; not him whom, weeping as you went away, you had dismissed, weeping himself as he strove to follow you. "[282] Then he heaps blame on his own head, bitterly accusing himself because he had brought his brother to such a pass of sorrow. In this letter he throws great blame upon Hortensius, whom together with Pompey he accuses of betraying him. What truth there may have been in this accusation as to Hortensius we have no means of saying. He couples Pompey in the same charge, and as to Pompey's treatment of him there can be no doubt. Pompey had been untrue to his promises because of his bond with Caesar. It is probable that Hortensius had failed to put himself forward on Cicero's behalf with that alacrity which the one advocate had expected from the other. Cicero and Hortensius were friends afterward, but so were Cicero and Pompey. Cicero was forgiving by nature, and also by self-training. It did not suit his purposes to retain his enmities. Had there been a possibility of reconciling Antony to the cause of the "optimates" after the Philippies, he would have availed himself of it.

Cicero at one time intended to go to Buthrotum in Epirus, where Atticus possessed a house and property; but he changed his purpose. He remained at Thessalonica till November, and then returned to Dyrrachium, having all through his exile been kept alive by tidings of steps taken for his recall. There seems very soon to have grown up a feeling in Rome that the city had disgraced itself by banishing such a man; and Caesar had gone to his provinces. We can well imagine that when he had once left Rome, with all his purposes achieved, having so far quieted the tongue of the strong speaker who might have disturbed them, he would take no further steps to perpetuate the orator's banishment. Then Pompey and Clodius soon quarrelled. Pompey, without Caesar to direct him, found the arrogance of the Patrician Tribune insupportable. We hear of wheels within wheels, and stories within stories, in the drama of Roman history as it was played at this time. Together with Cicero, it had been necessary to Caesar's projects that Cato also should be got out of Rome; and this had been managed by means of Clodius, who had a bill passed for the honorable employment of Cato on state purposes in Cyprus. Cato had found himself obliged to go. It was as though our Prime-minister had got parliamentary authority for sending a noisy member of the Opposition to Asiatic Turkey for six months There was an attempt, or an alleged attempt, of Clodius to have Pompey murdered; and there was street-fighting, so that Pompey was besieged, or pretended to be besieged, in his own house. "We might as well seek to set a charivari to music as to write the history of this political witches' revel, " says Mommsen, speaking of the state of Rome when Caesar was gone, Cicero banished, and Pompey supposed to be in the ascendant. [283] There was, at any rate, quarrelling between Clodius and Pompey, in the course of which Pompey was induced to consent to Cicero's return. Then Clodius took upon himself, in revenge, to turn against the Triumvirate altogether, and to repudiate even Caesar himself. But it was all a vain hurly-burly, as to which Caesar, when he heard the details in Gaul, could only have felt how little was to be gained by maintaining his alliance with Pompey. He had achieved his purpose, which he could not have done without the assistance of Crassus, whose wealth, and of Pompey, whose authority, stood highest in Rome; and now, having had his legions voted to him, and his provinces, and his prolonged term of years, he cared nothing for either of them.

There is a little story which must be repeated, as against Cicero, in reference to this period of his exile, because it has been told in all records of his life. Were I to omit the little story, it would seem as though I shunned the records which have been repeated as opposed to his credit. He had written, some time back, a squib in which he had been severe upon the elder Curio; so it is supposed; but it matters little who was the object or what the subject. This had got wind in Rome, as such matters do sometimes, and he now feared that it would do him a mischief with the Curios and the friends of the Curios. The authorship was only matter of gossip. Could it not be denied? "As it is written, " says Cicero, "in a style inferior to that which is usual to me, can it not be shown not to have been mine? "[284] Had Cicero possessed all the Christian virtues, as we hope that prelates and pastors possess them in this happy land, he would not have been betrayed into, at any rate, the expression of such a wish. As it is, the enemies of Cicero must make the most of it. His friends, I think, will look upon it leniently.

Continued efforts were made among Cicero's friends at Rome to bring him back, with which he was not altogether contented. He argues the matter repeatedly with Atticus, not always in the best temper. His friends at Rome were, he thought, doing the matter amiss: they would fail, and he would still have to finish his days abroad. Atticus, in his way to Epirus, visits him at Dyrrachium, and he is sure that Atticus would not have left Rome but that the affair was hopeless. The reader of the correspondence is certainly led to the belief that Atticus must have been the most patient of friends; but he feels, at the same time, that Atticus would not have been patient had not Cicero been affectionate and true. The Consuls for the new year were Lentulus and Metellus Nepos. The former was Cicero's declared friend, and the other had already abandoned his enmity. Clodius was no longer Tribune, and Pompey had been brought to yield. The Senate were all but unanimous. But there was still life in Clodius and his party; and day dragged itself after day, and month after month, while Cicero still lingered at Dyrrachium, waiting till a bill should have been passed by the people. Pompey, who was never whole-hearted in anything, had declared that a bill voted by the people would be necessary. The bill at last was voted, on the 14th of August, and Cicero, who knew well what was being done at Rome, passed over from Dyrrachium to Brundisium on the same day, having been a year and four months absent from Rome. During the year B. C. 57, up to the time of his return, he wrote but three letters that have come to us—two very short notes to Atticus, in the first of which he declares that he will come over on the authority of a decree of the Senate, without waiting for a law. In the second he falls again into despair, declaring that everything is over. In the third he asks Metellus for his aid, telling the Consul that unless it be given soon the man for whom it is asked will no longer be living to receive it. Metellus did give the aid very cordially.

It has been remarked that Cicero did nothing for literature during his banishment, either by writing essays or preparing speeches; and it has been implied that the prostration of mind arising from his misfortunes must have been indeed complete, when a man whose general life was made marvellous by its fecundity had been repressed into silence. It should, however, be borne in mind that there could be no inducement for the writing of speeches when there was no opportunity of delivering them. As to his essays, including what we call his Philosophy and his Rhetoric, they who are familiar with his works will remember how apt he was, in all that he produced, to refer to the writings of others. He translates and he quotes, and he makes constant use of the arguments and illustrations of those who have gone before him. He was a man who rarely worked without the use of a library. When I think how impossible it would be for me to repeat this oft-told tale of Cicero's life without a crowd of books within reach of my hand, I can easily understand why Cicero was silent at Thessalonica and Dyrrachium. It has been remarked also by a modern critic that we find "in the letters from exile a carelessness and inaccuracy of expression which contrasts strongly with the style of his happier days". I will not for a moment put my judgment in such a matter in opposition to that of Mr. Tyrrell—but I should myself have been inclined rather to say that the style of Cicero's letters varies constantly, being very different when used to Atticus, or to his brother, or to lighter friends such as Poetus and Trebatius; and very different again when business of state was in hand, as are his letters to Decimus Brutus, Cassius Brutus, and Plancus. To be correct in familiar letters is not to charm. A studied negligence is needed to make such work live to posterity—a grace of loose expression which may indeed have been made easy by use, but which is far from easy to the idle and unpractised writer. His sorrow, perhaps, required a style of its own. I have not felt my own untutored perception of the language to be offended by unfitting slovenliness in the expression of his grief.

NOTES:

[266] See the evidence of Asconius on this point, as to which Cicero's conduct has been much mistaken. We shall come to Milo's trial before long.

[267] The statement is made by Mr. Tyrrell in his biographical introduction to the Epistles.

[268] The 600 years, or anni DC., is used to signify unlimited futurity.

[269] Mommsen's History, book v., ca. v.

[270] [Greek: *Automalos onomazeto*] is the phrase of Dio Cassius. "Levissume transfuga" is the translation made by the author of the "Declamatio in Ciceronem". If I might venture on a slang phrase, I should say that [Greek: *automalos*] was a man who "went off on his own hook. " But no man was ever more loyal as a political adherent than Cicero.

[271] Ad Att., ii., 25.

[272] We do not know when the marriage took place, or any of the circumstances; but we are aware that when Tullia came, in the following year, B.C. 57, to meet her father at Brundisium, she was a widow.

[273] Suetonius, Julius Caesar, xii. : "Subornavit etiam qui C. Rabirio perduellionis diem diceret. "

[274] "Qui civem Romanum indemnatum perimisset, ei aqua at igni interdiceretur. "

[275]Plutarch tells us of this sobriquet, but gives another reason for it, equally injurious to the lady's reputation.

[276] Ad Att., lib. iii., 15.

[277] In Pisonem, vi.

[278] Ad Att., lib. x., 4.

[279] We are told by Cornelius Nepos, in his life of Atticus, that when Cicero fled from his country Atticus advanced to him two hundred and fifty sesterces, or about £2000. I doubt, however, whether the flight here referred to was not that early visit to Athens which Cicero was supposed to have made in his fear of Sulla.

[280] Ad Fam., lib. xiv., iv. : "Tullius to his Terentia, and to his young Tullia, and to his Cicero, " meaning his boy.

[281] Pro Domo Sua, xxiv.

[282] Ad Quin. Fra., 1, 3.

[283] The reader who wishes to understand with what anarchy the largest city in the world might still exist, should turn to chapter viii. of book v. of Mommsen's History.

[284] Ad Att., lib. iii, 12.

APPENDICES TO VOLUME I.

APPENDIX A.

(See ch. II, note [39])

THE BATTLE OF THE EAGLE AND THE SERPENT.

Homer, Iliad, lib. xii, 200:

> [Greek:
> Oi rh' eti mermaerizon ephestaotes para taphroi.
> Ornis gar sphin epaelthe peraesemenai memaosin,
> Aietos upsipetaes ep' aristera laon eergon,
> Phoinaeenta drakonta pheron onuchessi peloron,
> Zoon et aspaironta kai oupo laetheto charmaes.
> Kopse gar auton echonta kata staethos para deiraen,
> Idnotheis opiso ho d'apo ethen aeke chamaze,
> Algaesas odunaesi, mesoi d' eni kabbal' omilo
> Autos de klagxas peteto pnoaeis anemoio.]

Pope's translation of the passage, book xii, 231:

> "A signal omen stopp'd the passing host,
> The martial fury in their wonder lost.
> Jove's bird on sounding pinions beat the skies;
> A bleeding serpent, of enormous size,
> His talons trussed; alive, and curling round,
> He stung the bird, whose throat received the wound.
> Mad with the smart, he drops the fatal prey,
> In airy circles wings his painful way,
> Floats on the winds, and rends the heav'ns with cries.
> Amid the host the fallen serpent lies.
> They, pale with terror, mark its spires unroll'd,
> And Jove's portent with beating hearts behold."

Lord Derby's Iliad, book xii, 236:

> "For this I read the future, if indeed
> To us, about to cross, this sign from Heaven
> Was sent, to leftward of the astonished crowd:

A soaring eagle, bearing in his claws
A dragon huge of size, of blood-red hue,
Alive; yet dropped him ere he reached his home,
Nor to his nestlings bore the intended prey."

Cicero's telling of the story:

"Hic Jovis altisoni subito pinnata satelles,
Arboris e trunco serpentis saucia morsu,
Ipsa feris subigit transfigens unguibus anguem
Semianimum, et varia graviter cervice micantem.
Quem se intorquentem lanians, rostroque cruentans,
Jam satiata animum, jam duros ulta dolores,
Abjicit efflantem, et laceratum affligit in unda;
Seque obitu a solis nitidos convertit ad ortus."

Voltaire's translation:

"Tel on voit cet oiseau qui porte le tonnerre,
Blessé par un serpent élancé de la terre;
Il s'envole, il entraîne au séjour azuré
L'ennemi tortueux dont il est entouré.
Le sang tombe des airs. Il déchire, il dévore
Le reptile acharné qui le combat encore;
Il le perce, il le tient sous ses ongles vainqueurs;
Par cent coups redoublés il venge ses douleurs.
Le monstre, en expirant, se débat, se replie;
Il exhale en poisons les restes de sa vie;
Et l'aigle, tout sanglant, fier et victorieux,
Le rejette en fureur, et plane au haut des cieux."

Virgil's version, Aeneid, lib. xi., 751:

"Utque volans alte raptum quum fulva draconem
Fert aquila, implicuitque pedes, atque unguibus haesit
Saucius at serpens sinuosa volumina versat,
Arrectisque horret squamis, et sibilat ore,
Arduus insurgens. Illa haud minus urget obunco
Luctantem rostro; simul aethera verberat alis."

Dryden's translation from Virgil's Aeneid, book xi. :

"So stoops the yellow eagle from on high,
And bears a speckled serpent through the sky;
Fastening his crooked talons on the prey,
The prisoner hisses through the liquid way;
Resists the royal hawk, and though opprest,
She fights in volumes, and erects her crest.
Turn'd to her foe, she stiffens every scale,
And shoots her forky tongue, and whisks her threatening tail.
Against the victor all defence is weak.
Th' imperial bird still plies her with his beak:
He tears her bowels, and her breast he gores,
Then claps his pinions, and securely soars."

Pitt's translation, book xi. :

"As when th' imperial eagle soars on high,
And bears some speckled serpent through the sky,
While her sharp talons gripe the bleeding prey,
In many a fold her curling volumes play,
Her starting brazen scales with horror rise,
The sanguine flames flash dreadful from her eyes
She writhes, and hisses at her foe, in vain,
Who wins at ease the wide aerial plain,
With her strong hooky beak the captive plies,
And bears the struggling prey triumphant through the skies."

Shelley's version of the battle, The Revolt of Islam, canto i. :

"For in the air do I behold indeed
An eagle and a serpent wreathed in fight,
And now relaxing its impetuous flight,
Before the aerial rock on which I stood
The eagle, hovering, wheeled to left and right,
And hung with lingering wings over the flood,
And startled with its yells the wide air's solitude

"A shaft of light upon its wings descended,
And every golden feather gleamed therein—
Feather and scale inextricably blended
The serpent's mailed and many-colored skin
Shone through the plumes, its coils were twined within

By many a swollen and knotted fold, and high
And far, the neck receding lithe and thin,
Sustained a crested head, which warily
Shifted and glanced before the eagle's steadfast eye.

"Around, around, in ceaseless circles wheeling,
With clang of wings and scream, the eagle sailed
Incessantly—sometimes on high concealing
Its lessening orbs, sometimes, as if it failed,
Drooped through the air, and still it shrieked and wailed,
And casting back its eager head, with beak
And talon unremittingly assailed
The wreathed serpent, who did ever seek
Upon his enemy's heart a mortal wound to wreak

"What life, what power was kindled, and arose
Within the sphere of that appalling fray!
For, from the encounter of those wond'rous foes,
A vapor like the sea's suspended spray
Hung gathered; in the void air, far away,
Floated the shattered plumes; bright scales did leap,
Where'er the eagle's talons made their way,
Like sparks into the darkness; as they sweep,
Blood stains the snowy foam of the tumultuous deep.

"Swift chances in that combat—many a check,
And many a change—a dark and wild turmoil;
Sometimes the snake around his enemy's neck
Locked in stiff rings his adamantine coil,
Until the eagle, faint with pain and toil,
Remitted his strong flight, and near the sea
Languidly fluttered, hopeless so to foil
His adversary, who then reared on high
His red and burning crest, radiant with victory.

"Then on the white edge of the bursting surge,
Where they had sunk together, would the snake
Relax his suffocating grasp, and scourge
The wind with his wild writhings; for, to break
That chain of torment, the vast bird would shake
The strength of his unconquerable wings
As in despair, and with his sinewy neck
Dissolve in sudden shock those linked rings,

Then soar—as swift as smoke from a volcano springs.

> "Wile baffled wile, and strength encountered strength,
> Thus long, but unprevailing—the event
> Of that portentous fight appeared at length.
> Until the lamp of day was almost spent
> It had endured, when lifeless, stark, and rent,
> Hung high that mighty serpent, and at last
> Fell to the sea, while o'er the continent,
> With clang of wings and scream, the eagle past,
> Heavily borne away on the exhausted blast."

I have repudiated the adverse criticism on Cicero's poetry which has been attributed to Juvenal; but, having done so, am bound in fairness to state that which is to be found elsewhere in any later author of renown as a classic. In the treatise De Oratoribus, attributed to Tacitus, and generally published with his works by him—a treatise commenced, probably, in the last year of Vespasian's reign, and completed only in that of Domitian—Cicero as a poet is spoken of with a severity of censure which the writer presumes to have been his recognized desert. "For Caesar, " he says, "and Brutus made verses, and sent them to the public libraries; not better, indeed, than Cicero, but with less of general misfortune, because only a few people knew that they had done so. " This must be taken for what it is worth. The treatise, let it have been written by whom it might, is full of wit, and is charming in language and feeling. It is a dialogue after the manner of Cicero himself, and is the work of an author well conversant with the subjects in hand. But it is, no doubt, the case that those two unfortunate lines which have been quoted became notorious in Rome when there was a party anxious to put down Cicero.

APPENDIX B.

(See ch. IV, note [84])

FROM THE BRUTUS—CA. XCII., XCIII.

"There were at that time two orators, Cotta and Hortensius, who towered above all others, and incited me to rival them. The first spoke with self-restraint and moderation, clearly and easily, expressing his ideas in appropriate language. The other was magnificent and fierce; not such as you remember him, Brutus, when he was already failing, but full of life both in his words and actions. I then resolved that Hortensius should, of the two, be my model, because I felt myself like to him in his energy, and nearer to him in his age. I observed that when they were in the same causes, those for Canuleius and for our consular Dolabella, though Cotta was the senior counsel, Hortensius took the lead. A large gathering of men and the noise of the Forum require that a speaker shall be quick, on fire, active, and loud. The year after my return from Asia I undertook the charge of causes that were honorable, and in that year I was seeking to be Quaestor, Cotta to be Consul, and Hortensius to be Praetor. Then for a year I served as Quaestor in Sicily. Cotta, after his Consulship, went as governor into Gaul, and then Hortensius was, and was considered to be, first at the bar. When I had been back from Sicily twelve months I began to find that whatever there was within me had come to such perfection as it might attain. I feel that I am speaking too much of myself, but it is done, not that you may be made to own my ability or my eloquence—which is far from my thoughts—but that you may see how great was my toil and my industry. Then, when I had been employed for nearly five years in many cases, and was accounted a leading advocate, I specially concerned myself in conducting the great cause on behalf of Sicily— the trial of Verres—when I and Hortensius were Aedile and Consul designate.

"But as this discussion of ours is intended to produce not a mere catalogue of orators, but some true lessons of oratory, let us see what there was in Hortensius that we must blame. When he was out of his Consulship, seeing that among past Consuls there was no one on a par with him, and thinking but little of those who were below consular rank, he became idle in his work to which from boyhood he had devoted himself, and chose to live in the midst of his wealth, as he thought a happier life—certainly an easier one. The first two or three years took off something from him. As the gradual decay of a picture will be observed by the true critic, though it be not seen by the world at large, so was it with his decay. From day to day he became more and more unlike his old self, failing in all branches of oratory, but specially in the rapidity and continuity of his words. But for myself I never rested, struggling always to increase whatever power there was in me by practice of every kind, especially in writing. Passing over many things in the year after I was Aedile, I will come to that in which I was elected first Praetor, to the great delight of the public generally; for I had gained the good-will of men, partly by my attention to the causes which I undertook, but specially by a certain new strain of eloquence, as excellent as it was uncommon, with which I spoke. " Cicero, when he wrote this of himself, was an old man sixty-two years of age, broken hearted for the loss of his daughter, to whom it was no doubt allowed among his friends to praise himself with the garrulity of years, because it was understood that he had been unequalled in the matter of which he was speaking. It is easy for us to laugh at his boastings; but the account which he gives of his early life, and of the manner in which he attained the excellence for which he had been celebrated, is of value.

APPENDIX C.

(See ch. VII, note [144])

There was still prevailing in Rome at this time a strong feeling that a growing taste for these ornamental luxuries was injurious to the Republic, undermining its simplicity and weakening its stability. We are well aware that its simplicity was a thing of the past, and its stability gone The existence of a Verres is proof that it was so; but still the feeling remained—and did remain long after the time of Cicero—that these beautiful things were a sign of decay. We know how conquering Rome caught the taste for them from conquered Greece. "Graecia capta ferum victorem cepit, et artes intulit agresti Latio". [1] Cicero submitted himself to this new captivity readily, but with apologies, as shown in his pretended abnegation of all knowledge of art. Two years afterward, in a letter to Atticus, giving him instructions as to the purchase of statues, he declares that he is altogether carried away by his longing for such things, but not without a feeling of shame. "Nam in eo genere sic studio efferimur ut abs te adjuvandi, ab aliis propre reprehendi simus"[2]—"Though you will help me, others I know will blame me. " The same feeling is expressed beautifully, but no doubt falsely, by Horace when he declares, as Cicero had done, his own indifference to such delicacies:

"Gems, marbles, ivory, Tuscan statuettes,
Pictures, gold plate, Gaetulian coverlets,
There are who have not. One there is, I trow,
Who cares not greatly if he has or no."[3]

Many years afterward, in the time of Tiberius, Velleius Paterculus says the same when he is telling how ignorant Mummius was of sculpture, who, when he had taken Corinth, threatened those who had to carry away the statues from their places, that if they broke any they should be made to replace them. "You will not doubt, however, " the historian says, "that it would have been better for the Republic to remain ignorant of these Corinthian gems than to understand them as well as it does now.

That rudeness befitted the public honor better than our present taste. "[4] Cicero understood well enough, with one side of his intelligence, that as the longing for these things grew in the minds of rich men, as the leading Romans of the day became devoted to luxury rather than to work, the ground on which the Republic stood must be sapped. A Marcellus or a Scipio had taken glory in ornamenting the city. A Verres or even an Hortensius—even a Cicero—was desirous of beautiful things for his own house. But still, with the other side of his intelligence, he saw that a perfect citizen might appreciate art, and yet do his duty, might appreciate art, and yet save his country. What he did not see was, that the temptations of luxury, though compatible with virtue, are antagonistic to it. The camel may be made to go through the eye of the needle—but it is difficult.

NOTES:

[1] Horace, Epis., lib. ii., 1.

[2] Ad Att., lib. i. 8.

[3] Horace, Epis., lib. ii., 11. The translation is Conington's.

[4] Vell. Pat., lib. i., xiii

APPENDIX D.

(See ch. XI, note [235])

PRO LEGE MANILIA—CA. X., XVI.

"Utinam, Quirites, virorum fortium, atque innocentium copiam tantam haberetis, ut haec vobis deliberatio difficilis esset, quemnam potissimum tantis rebus ac tanto bello praeficiendum putaretis! Nunc vero cum sit unus Cn. Pompeius, qui non modo eorum hominum, qui nunc sunt, gloriam, sed etiam antiquitatis memoriam virtute superarit; quae res est, quae cujusquam animum in hac causa dubium facere posset? Ego enim sic existimo, in summo imperatore quatuor has res inesse oportere, scientiam rei militaris, virtutem, auctoritatem, felicitatem. Quis igitur hoc homine scientior umquam aut fuit, aut esse debuit? qui e ludo, atque pueritiae disciplina, bello maximo atque acerrimis hostibus, ad patris exercitum atque in militiae disciplinam profectus est? qui extrema pueritia miles fuit summi imperatoris? ineunte adolescentia maximi ipse exercitus imperator? qui saepius cum hoste conflixit, quam quisquam cum inimico concertavit? plura bella gessit, quam caeteri legerunt? plures provincias confecit, quam alii concupiverunt? cujus adolescentia ad scientiam rei militaris non alienis praeceptis, sed suis imperiis; non offensionibus belli, sed victoriis; non stipendiis, sed triumphis est erudita? Quod denique genus belli esse potest, in quo illum non exercuerit fortuna reipublicae? Civile; Africanum; Transalpinum; Hispaniense; mistum ex civitatibus atque ex bellicosissimis nationibus servile; navale bellum, varia et diversa genera, et bellorum et hostium, non solum gesta ab hoc uno, sed etiam confecta, nullam rem esse declarant, in usu militari positam, quae hojus viri scientiam fugere posset.

* * * * *

"Quare cum et bellum ita necessarium sit, ut negligi non possit; ita magnum, ut accuratissime sit administrandum; et cum ei imperatorem praeficere possitis, in quo sit eximia belli scientia, singularis virtus, clarissima auctoritas, egregia fortuna; dubitabitis, Quirites, quin hoc tantum boni, quod vobis a diis immortalibus oblatum et datum est, in rempublicam conservandam atque amplificandam conferatis? "

* * * * *

"I could wish, Quirites, that there was open to you so large a choice of men capable at the same time, and honest, that you might find a difficulty in deciding who might best be selected for command in a war so momentous as this. But now when Pompey alone has surpassed in achievements not only those who live, but all of whom we have read in history, what is there to make any one hesitate in the matter? In my opinion there are four qualities to be desired in a general—military knowledge, valor, authority, and fortune. But whoever was or was ever wanted to be more skilled than this man, who, taken fresh from school and from the lessons of his boyhood, was subjected to the discipline of his father's army during one of our severest wars, when our enemies were strong against us? In his earliest youth he served under our greatest general. As years went on he was himself in command over a large army. He has been more frequent in fighting than others in quarrelling. Few have read of so many battles as he has fought.

He has conquered more provinces than others have desired to pillage. He learned the art of war not from written precepts, but by his own practice; not from reverses, but from victories. He does not count his campaigns, but the triumphs which he has won. What nature of warfare is there in which the Republic has not used his services? Think of our Civil war[1]—of our African war[2]—of our war on the other side of the Alps[3]—of our Spanish wars[4]—of our Servile war[5]—which was carried on by the energies of so many mighty people—and this Maritime war. [6] How many enemies had we, how various were our contests! They were all not only carried through by this one man, but brought to an end so gloriously as to show that there is nothing in the practice of warfare which has escaped his knowledge.

* * * * *

"Seeing, therefore, that this war cannot be neglected; that its importance demands the utmost care in its administration; that it requires a general in whom should be found sure military science, manifest valor, conspicuous authority, and pre-eminent good fortune—do you doubt, Quirites, but that you should use the great blessing which the gods have given you for the preservation and glory of the Republic? "

* * * * *

On reading, however, the piece over again, I almost doubt whether there be any passages in it which should be selected as superior to others.

NOTES:

[1] "Civile; " when Sulla, with Pompey under him, was fighting with young Marius and Cinna.

[2] "Africanum; " when he had fought with Domitius, the son-in-law of Cinua, and with Hiarbas.

[3] "Transalpinum; " during his march through Gaul into Spain.

[4] "Hispaniense; " in which he conquered Sertorins.

[5] "Servile; " the war with Spartacus, with the slaves and gladiators.

[6] "Navale Bellum; " the war with the pirates.

APPENDIX E.

LUCAN, LIBER I.

"O male concordes, nimiaque cupidine caeci,
Quid miscere juvat vires orbemque tenere
In medio."

"Temporis angusti mansit concordia discors,
Paxque fuit non sponte ducum. Nam sola futuri
Crassus erat belli medius mora. Qualiter undas
Qui secat, et geminum gracilis mare separat isthmos,
Nec patitur conferre fretum; si terra recedat,
Ionium Aegaeo frangat mare. Sic, ubi saeva
Arma ducum dirimens, miserando funere Crassus
Assyrias latio maculavit sanguine Carras."

"Dividitur ferro regnum; populique potentis,
Quae mare, quae terras, quae totum possidet orbem,
Non cepit fortuna duos."

"Tu nova ne veteres obscurent acta triumphos,
Et victis cedat piratica laurea Gallis,
Magne, times; te jam series, ususque laborum
Erigit, impatiensque loci fortuna secundi.
Nec quemquam jam ferre *potest* Caesarve priorem,
Pompeiusve parem, Quis juspius induit arma,
Seire nefas; magno se judice quisque tuesur,
Victrix causa deis placuit sed victa, Catoni.[1]
Nec coiere pares; alter vergentibus annis
In senium, longoque togae tranquilhor usu
Dedidicit jam paee ducem, famaeque petitor
Multa dar in vulgas, totus popularibus auris
Impelli, plausuque sui gaudere theatri;
Nec reparare novas vires, multumque priori
Credere fortunae, Stat magni nominis umbra."

"Sed non in Caesare tantum
Nomen erat, nec fama ducis, sed nescia virtus
Stare loco; solusque pudor non vincere bello.
Acer et indomitus; quo spes, quoque ira vocasset,
Ferre manum, et nunquam te merando parcere ferro;

Successus urgere suos; instare favori Numinis" —Lucan, lib.i.

Note:

[1] For the full understanding of this oft-quoted line the reader should make himself acquainted with Cato's march across Libya after the death of Pompey, as told by Lucan in his 9th book.

* * * * *

"O men so ill-fitted to agree, O men blind with greed, of what service can it be that you should join your powers, and possess the world between you? "

"For a short time the ill-sorted compact lasted, and there was a peace which each of them abhorred. Crassus alone stood between the others, hindering for a while the coming war—as an isthmus separates two waters and forbids sea to meet sea. If the morsel of land gives way, the Ionian waves and the Aegean dash themselves in foam against each other. So was it with the arms of the two chiefs when Crassus fell, and drenched the Assyrian Carrae with Roman blood. "

"Then the possession of the Empire was put to the arbitration of the sword. The fortunes of a people which possessed sea and earth and the whole world, were not sufficient for two men. "

"You, Magnus, you, Pompeius, fear lest newer deeds than yours should make dull your old triumphs, and the scattering of the pirates should be as nothing to the conquering of Gaul. The practice of many wars has so exalted you, O Caesar, that you cannot put up with a second place. Caesar will endure no superior; but Pompey will have no equal. Whose cause was the better the poet dares not inquire! Each will have his own advocate in history. On the side of the conqueror the gods ranged themselves. Cato has chosen to follow the conquered.

"But surely the men were not equal. The one in declining years, who had already changed his arms for the garb of peace, had unlearned the general in the statesman—had become wont to talk to the people, to devote himself to harangues, and to love the applause of his own theatre. He has not cared to renew his strength, trusting to his old fortune. There remains of him but the shadow of his great name. "

"The name of Caesar does not loom so large; nor is his character as a general so high. But there is a spirt which can content itself with no achievements; there is but one feeling of shame—that of not conquering; a man determined, not to be controlled, taking his arms wherever lust of conquest or anger may call him; a man never sparing the sword, creating all things from his own good-fortune trusting always the favors of the gods. "

END OF VOLUME I.

CPSIA information can be obtained
at www.ICGtesting.com
Printed in the USA
LVHW030242120223
739205LV00007B/24